Elizabeth Gundrey

ENGLAND BY BUS AND COACH

SPHERE BOOKS LIMITED

SPHERE BOOKS LTD

Penguin Books Ltd, 27 Wrights Lane, London W8 5TZ (Publishing and Editorial)
and Harmondsworth, Middlesex, England (Distribution and Warehouse)
Viking Penguin Inc., 40 West 23rd Street, New York, New York 10010, USA
Penguin Books Australia Ltd, Ringwood, Victoria, Australia
Penguin Books Canada Ltd, 2801 John Street, Markham, Ontario, Canada L3R 1B4
Penguin Books (NZ) Ltd, 182–190 Wairau Road, Auckland 10, New Zealand

First published in Great Britain in this revised edition by Sphere Books Ltd 1988

Printed and bound in Great Britain by
Richard Clay Ltd, Bungay, Suffolk
Set in Monophoto Palatino

Contents

Illustration Acknowledgements

We are most grateful to all those organisations who contributed line drawings, including: Bury St Edmunds Tourist Guide; Carlisle Castle; City of Durham Tourist Guide; English Heritage; The Minack Theatre; Perensey Castle; Quebec House; Richmond Castle; Rochester Upon Medway Tourist Information; Round House Crafts Centre; South Pennines Tourist Information; Suffolk Coastline Tourist Information; Thoresby College; City of Winchester Tourist Information; Yarmouth Castle; The Youth Hostels Association. Also, to those organisations who contributed drawings to the previous travel books, some of which are reproduced in this edition. Brighton Pavilion *courtesy of Brighton Resort Services Department*; Palace Street and The Cathedral, Canterbury *courtesy of John Berbiers*; The Promenade, Cheltenham *courtesy of Cheltenham & Gloucester Building Society*; Pilot Street, King's Lynn *courtesy of King's Lynn Preservation Trust Limited*; Lowestoft Highlight and Beccles from the River *courtesy of Waveney District Council*; Severns Building, Nottingham *courtesy of City of Nottingham Public Relations Office*; St Michael's Mount near Penzance *courtesy of Penwith District Council*; Peterborough Cathedral from an old print; The Barbican, Plymouth *courtesy of Chris Robinson, New Street, Barbican*; the *Mary Rose*, Portsmouth, from an old print; Salisbury Cathedral, from an old print; The Abbey, Sherbourne *courtesy of the Tourist Information Centre*; Bear Steps Hall, Shrewsbury *courtesy of Shrewsbury Civic Society*; The Inner Bailey, Taunton Castle *courtesy of Somerset County Museum Service*; Friar Street, Worcester *courtesy of Worcester City Museum Service*; Abbeydale Industrial Hamlet, Sheffield *courtesy of Publicity Department, City of Sheffield*; Jarrow Hall, Newcastle upon Tyne *courtesy of Northumbria Tourist Board*; The Guildhall, Carlisle *courtesy of City of Carlisle*; The City Museum, Lancaster, drawing by David Oldroyd, from *A Walk around Historic Lancaster* by John Champness; Wool Exchange, Bradford *courtesy of Bradford Economic Development Unit*. Drawing of 'The Friars' on p. 290 is by kind permission of *Newcastle upon Tyne City Libraries*.

What's the difference between a bus and a coach? Sometimes it's hard to tell – but in general buses do a local job, travelling at under 20 miles an hour along country lanes to call at little-known villages, while coaches can do at least 60 miles an hour on major roads, hurrying from one major town or city to another. Buses are usually less comfortably furnished but, outside peak hours (when they carry adults to and from work or children to school), are likely to have few passengers. Coaches are often quite full.

On coaches you can, and may be wise to, book a seat in advance at a coach station, through a travel agent, or (quoting Access or Visa credit-card number) by telephoning a major coach station about a week before. Look in the telephone directory under National Express (their Victoria, London, number is 01–730 0202, 8 a.m. to 10 p.m.; or, for credit-card bookings, 01-730 3499).

Introduction

Into the making of this book have gone journeys totalling some 6000 miles.

Very enjoyable journeys, for on a coach or bus one sees far more through the big, high window than from a low car – or from a train which whizzes through the countryside, rarely touching more than the outskirts of towns or villages. There are only a few hundred stations where you can catch a train, compared with tens of thousands of bus and coach stops, some 300 of which are named in this book. And what a relief not to be coping, in a car, with traffic and parking problems (not to mention the cost of petrol now).

I find coaches, and even the humble bus, a more comfortable way to travel than by train – for a variety of reasons. At the start of a journey, there is never any need to cross a bridge over a railway line, nor to heave baggage up: the driver will give a hand and, on coaches, stow it in the capacious boot for you. Special provision can be made for disabled people if their needs are notified in advance.

Once seated, passengers stay seated, whereas on trains there is often a restless to-ing and fro-ing. Coaches seem to me steadier than some swaying trains. There are regular stops for refreshments and toilets (except on the non-stop Rapide coaches, which have these on board, see page 247). Dogs are accepted on most coaches other than Rapides. Smokers are confined to rear seats.

Buses and coaches are more likely to set you down feeling fresh, and exactly where you want to be – close to town-centre shops and sights, for instance – whereas many rail stations are on the dingier edges of towns, which can mean quite a trek to the centre. This offsets the train's main advantage, speed. Some coaches take, in fact, little longer than the equivalent train, though they may not run as frequently.

Almost invariably, the coach is a good deal cheaper. All coach and bus companies offer a variety of economy tickets, too. There are usually discounts for children, over-60's and (on the coaches) students, as well as a range of bus passes that may entitle you to unlimited travel for anything from a day to a month. On most coach journeys (outside peak periods), a return journey costs no more than a single provided you do not travel on a Friday or Sunday. It pays to ask what's available before you set off. Overseas visitors can, at British Tourist Authority offices in their own country, buy an inexpensive Britexpress pass which gives unlimited travel for a period at a big discount, on a very high proportion of the express coaches: this card is also available to members of the Youth Hostels Association, see page xxiii. (There are also discounts for groups of 10 or more.)

Bussing about

For visitors who want to reach the parts of England unknown to those who troop round the overcrowded 'sights', this is a good way of seeing a slice of country life. England has a better local bus service than any country in Europe and perhaps in all the world. In Spain you may be obliged to rise at dawn to catch the only bus of the day, and in Norway you could easily spend £100 on fares within two or three days.

It is extraordinary that buses (ordinarily so familiar a sight) suddenly become invisible when touring for pleasure is the objective. In the information office of a bus station one summer day I heard a couple ask to book for a round-trip excursion. When they learned that no seats were available for a week, they walked out disappointed and vanished. Yet right outside the door an ordinary bus going to the same destination stood waiting, with plenty of empty seats. On an excursion every seat is filled, the coach belts along, stops are few, and one gets off with the crowd and on again when the driver dictates. It is amazing that anyone could prefer that to the airy, easy-going bus! Perhaps it is because city buses are tedious (all stop-start-stop, and queueing at bus stops) that country buses are ignored, but they are a very different species and far pleasanter to use.

Although in some areas more services are available in summer than in winter, most buses keep going throughout the year; so for a short out-of-season break in spring or autumn they are ideal (and warm when the weather turns chilly), particularly if a midweek break is possible. At off-peak times accommodation is often much cheaper, and English scenery can be at its most beautiful when the first blossoms and the fresh greens of spring appear, or when autumn colours glow.

My ideal bus journey involves finding attractive routes (for the journey is the object, not the destination) and linking up a number of different bus services in the course of a day. An hour or so at a time spent relaxing on a bus between pottering in a country town, visiting a rural museum or sitting in the sun on a cliff top or river bank makes a pleasant alternation of activities. There's a lucky-dip element in bussing around, for often one's halts are dictated by the routes and times of the buses – and sometimes this has led me to discover something unexpected. But above all, bussing is to do with enjoying landscapes and countryside.

Not for me the record-beating efforts of, for example, the four schoolboys who covered 280 miles in one day using the £2 day-tickets issued by a Kent bus company. They started before 5 am and it was nearly midnight when they returned home; at about 1½p per mile they certainly proved bus travel can be cheap. But for me the big attraction of the buses is their relaxing, leisurely pace, and I deliberately average only about 70 miles a day with plenty of opportunities to 'stand and stare'. Studying maps and timetables, I avoid built-up areas and busy roads – my chosen routes lead to lanes sometimes so narrow that two vehicles (a rare encounter) cannot easily pass each other, and which arrive at villages 'unknown to grandeur and unknown to fame'.

I like bussing about mainly because I feel both free and relaxed. Free because it's easy and cheap to get away by this means for a day or two: it's so simple to give oneself a few days' holiday, perhaps at the end of a business trip or after a visit to relatives, by hopping on a handy bus. For such brief breaks I can travel light, with no need to lug a suitcase about – just a small nylon holdall weighing only a few ounces. I feel relaxed because of the slow speed (average 15 mph), and at this pace one sees far more than from a car, particularly wildflowers and small architectural details. Whenever there is a choice of bus routes between two towns, the less direct one is almost invariably the better choice as it is more likely to amble through byways and country lanes free of traffic.

On the journeys described in this book the stages of bus-riding lasted between $\frac{1}{2}$ and 1 hour as a rule – not so long that the ride ever became tedious, but long enough to provide a welcome rest between sightseeing in the towns and villages where I changed buses.

Friends have asked whether, with one eye on the clock and my mind on the departure time of the next bus, such sightseeing ever became a frantic dash. Dashing not being my style, the answer is no – though sometimes this meant missing a place of interest because it was on the far side of town. However, since buses nearly always go into town centres, there has invariably been plenty of interest at hand, and it is surprising how much one can see in less than half-an-hour if that is all the time available. The secret of using limited time successfully is threefold: get off at the best stop for one's purpose (ask the driver, conductor or another passenger to advise); pinpoint what's interesting on a street plan so as to waste no time hunting for it; and if you haven't already got such a plan, pop into the nearest estate agent and ask for one. The best idea of all, if there is a Tourist Information Centre at hand, is to ask them to pencil onto a town plan the most interesting streets that can be walked in whatever time you have and to advise you where to catch your next bus onward.

Another thing I enjoy on a bus is the contact with a variety of people. Colonel's lady and Judy O'Grady both go shopping on the same bus and exchange chat: it's a great leveller. And an extra bonus is making small discoveries unknown even to guidebook writers (all car-borne, I fancy). Several times in villages dismissed as 'commonplace' I, from my high vantage point on a bus, have spotted something of interest beyond a wall or hedge.

Gourmets read recipe books in their armchairs, gardeners while away the winter deep in seed catalogues, and I now browse through bus timetables and route maps with a connoisseur's eye – journeying in imagination to fells and waterfalls, over bridges and alongside village greens, through lanes, down valleys and beside the sea – planning in winter where next spring may take me.

It all began one autumn when I decided to journey the length of England by this means – taking days over a trip one might do in hours by express coach or train. I was warned it would be impossible. Friends painted a gloomy picture of three-day holdups for buses that run only twice a week, and of hours spent standing in the rain at a bus-stop in some industrial slum while wind blew the fish-and-chip wrappers round my ankles. But Confucius he say, 'Journey of 300 miles begins with one step.' There was only one way to find out whether these prophets of doom were right. I packed a small bag and set off.

I certainly do not want to suggest that readers should follow slavishly the routes I travelled. Much of the fun is in working out one's own journeys. I purposely do not quote bus service numbers or schedule times for this reason and because they are inevitably altered from time to time.

How that journey turned out is described later in this book. But it was just a beginning.

What coach travel is like

Most coaches seat people in rather more comfort than on aircraft, for example. Being a six-footer, I make for the seats behind the driver or next to the emergency door because these have most leg-room – but the others aren't bad as a rule (though some companies do put in more seats at the expense of leg-room) and I have rarely travelled on a coach where I did not have a double seat to myself, although this is less likely at weekends. The driver's side is also the one to make for when travelling north if you don't want to be exposed to the afternoon sun. But the other side is the one with traffic-free views.

Seats are comfortable, with headrests, overhead lights and adjustable ventilators; and coaches are clean. (At least, most coaches are like this – some operators have lower standards.) A few coaches have tinted windows or else blinds to use when the sun streams in; and in some the seat-back angle is adjustable.

On longer journeys, refreshment stops of ¼ to ¾ hour are allowed for in the timetable – a welcome break for eating, W.C., nappy-changing or just a stroll to stretch one's legs and one's dog's (though if several coaches halt simultaneously, there can be queues for services). No dogs on Rapide coaches, however. Coaches can be more flexible than trains – for instance, in an emergency, one waited while I made a phone call.

Whereas on trains you have to pay extra to reserve a seat, this is not the case on coaches. Should a National Express coach be full, every effort is made to provide alternative transport. If you have not booked a ticket, you may still be able to get on – provided that there are seats to spare.

Timing your journey

An autumn journey is full of pleasure, and the warm bus protects one from bad weather. Spring, too, is a good time to go, particularly in the West Country, when flower festivals are held – but avoid the May bank holiday weekends if you can.

Summer, yes – buses are so little used by the typical tourist, who thinks only in terms of excursions and coach tours or a car, that even in summer they are not crowded. However, the towns and 'sights' are apt to be thronged in July and August, the school holiday period. Winter is not a good time to travel because, what with condensation inside and mud splashes outside, bus windows in the country are often impossible to see through, and darkness falls very early, especially after the last Saturday in October when the clocks are changed over to winter time until late March. In spring and autumn towns are mercifully free of tourist crowds, though most of the stately homes are open (the majority close in winter). One sometimes finds more buses running during school term times, on market days, or on the days when Women's Institutes have their regular meetings.

Sunday travel may be best avoided because services are fewer then, particularly in the mornings, and information offices are closed. Do not set off early on weekdays, unless you want to be part of the rush hour to work. Market days can be fun.

A note to overseas visitors

If you visit none but the famous (and crowded) sights you will not see the 'real' England and you may hear more foreign languages than regional English accents. However, a number of the one-, two- or three-day tours in this book can be tacked onto more conventional sightseeing – starting out from such famous tourist spots as Stratford-upon-Avon, Windsor, Oxford, Salisbury, York or London itself. Others are conveniently placed in relation to the ports or airports at which overseas visitors arrive or depart.

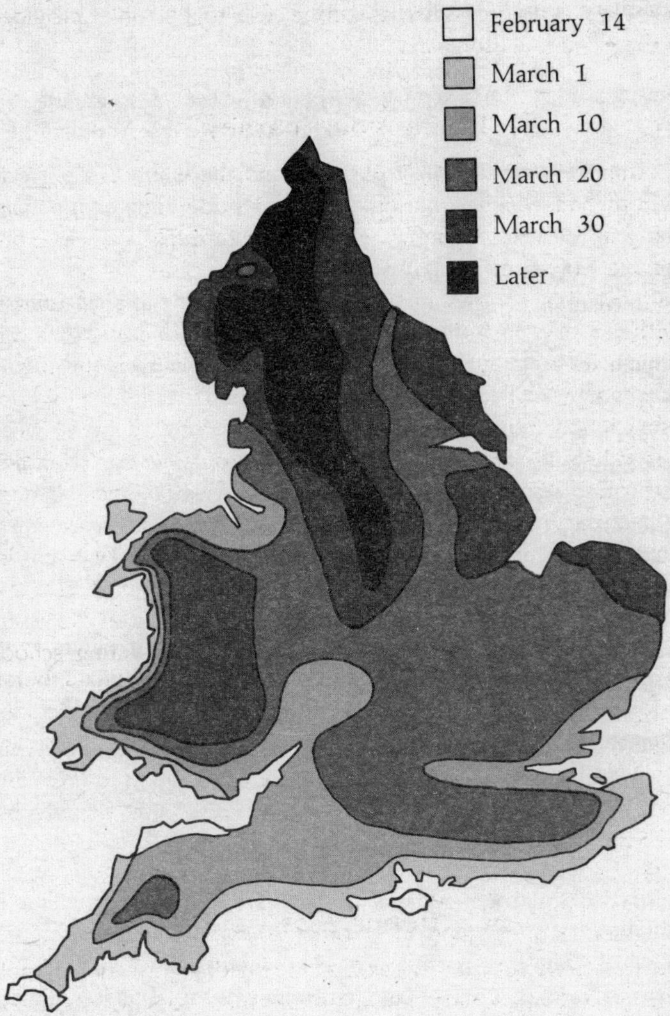

When to go where?

This map shows where spring starts earliest – the tip of Cornwall is where plants start growing as early as February; when a mean daily temperature of at least 43°F can be relied on, as a rule. In March it starts spreading round the south and west coasts. Not until April do hilly areas warm up.

Here are some suggestions:

PORT	BUS TOUR
Newcastle	Roman Wall to London route; *or* to Carlisle
Hull	Roman Wall (from Doncaster); *or* Yorkshire Dales
Harwich	East Anglia *or* Lowestoft
Tilbury	London's Countryside
Sheerness	Dickens *or* Apple Blossom Trail
Dover, Folkestone	Cinque Ports route
Southampton	Isle of Wight tour, Salisbury Plain *or* New Forest
Plymouth	South Hams, Cornwall *or* Scillies
Liverpool	Lake District
AIRPORT	
Heathrow	London's Countryside (starting at Windsor); *or* to Cheltenham *or* Portsmouth
Gatwick	Norman Conquest route, *or* to Brighton
Birmingham	Shakespeare's England *or* Northern Tour
Manchester	Yorkshire Dales

Before setting off from your own country you can obtain more information from any overseas office of the British Tourist Authority. Remember that, on the whole, in the south of England spring comes earlier than in the north, and that the east tends to be less rainy than the west.

Distances and bus-stops

Britain is in a metric muddle at present. Though some maps are in kilometres, signposts and most other sources of information still use miles – one mile is equal to 1.6 kilometres.

Both overseas visitors and Britons new to London always underestimate its vast size. It takes at least an hour to cover the distance from the centre to one of the edges – a boring hour through mean streets and industrial areas in most cases, and often involving traffic jams. It is better *not* to stay in this expensive city while making day-trips out but to move around it as described in Chapter 5.

Concerning bus-stops, usually a metal post is placed wherever buses will draw up if hailed; it may or may not state the service number of the bus concerned, and where different services run in the same place this occasionally gives rise to confusion if they stop at different posts. In the country there may be no posts because the locals are familiar with the buses' habits. The only solution to these problems is to ask someone. Incidentally, just to confuse you still further, the signs occasionally bear a number which is *not* the bus number but the number of the stop.

But timetables often name an inn as the stopping place. Sometimes the bus does not actually stop outside it but on the opposite side of the road, or even a few yards further along. Beware!

Incidentally, I have almost always found buses very punctual. The only exceptions are those within and near big cities where traffic and larger numbers of passengers often play havoc with schedules.

Coach/bus stations

A bus station is the terminus of most routes and is usually (unlike some railway stations) right in the centre of a town, which is handy. Sometimes, depending upon what you want to visit, it may be better to get off before the bus station is reached: the conductor or driver is a good source of advice on this, or look at the town street plans that are often included in timetable books. Some bus stations are just bare yards, others are a huge complex of buildings. Facilities vary a lot: the WCs at some involve a few minutes' walk and often no soap or towel is provided. It's worth noting on arrival just where they are, in case you are short of time on turning up for your next bus. There may be a café, a large street plan of the town and (at the biggest ones) a left-luggage office, useful only if you intend returning to the bus station and only if it will still be open then (some close early). Information offices, where they exist, have a tiresome habit of being closed or equipped only with information about their own services and not neighbouring ones – another reason for arming yourself with your own set of timetables before you set out. Bus conductors, who carry timetables, are sometimes more knowledgeable, but don't depend upon it.

Tourist information

Many towns have Tourist Information Centres now, but they are often some distance from the bus station. A number will book accommodation for travellers (some charge for this service). They vary in their opening hours and may be closed when you arrive in the evening or before you depart in the morning, so it may be worth the effort to write to them beforehand asking for their free leaflets, mini-guides to their towns, street plans and so on: with only limited time it really is worth equipping oneself with this kind of information rather than waste half-an-hour wandering in wrong directions. Some Centres confine their information to their own town, others range over a much wider area. Most have lists of places that have connections with colonial history, such as the birthplaces of George Washington and Captain Cook, which may be of particular interest to overseas visitors; booklets in various languages; information for disabled people; and so on. (More about these Centres on page xvii.)

Guidebooks can greatly increase the interest of a bus journey: many can be borrowed from a library. Once again, don't rely on finding what you want on arrival – get it before you start. One exception to this rule is a street plan, which is best bought, or picked up from an estate agent, locally.

For information about the entire region, much of it free, write to the relevant Tourist Board (see page 305) *before* you finalize your plans. This will help you work out interesting routes to follow.

Finally, buy local papers as you go along and listen to local radio before breakfast to get an idea of the real-life preoccupations of the people around you. There is no quicker way of picking up the genuine flavour of a community that is new to you; even the classified advertisements differ from place to place. In addition, local radio stations sometimes announce changes to bus services that you may need to know about.

Travelling light

One big advantage the car tourist can undeniably claim over the bus passenger is that the former can pack everything including the kitchen sink without much trouble. Buses have room for baggage but few of us want to carry much weight about. A nylon shoulder-bag weighs least. Forget about sponge-bags and suchlike – use thin plastic bags for everything, with plentiful rubber bands to keep them secure, clothes rolled up compactly, timetables bundled together and so on. The thinnest of showercoats (with hood), pencil and paper for route-planning each day, and a 100-watt light bulb are desirable without being too heavy. Why the light bulb? Because so many hotel bedroom lights are dim, and so many timetables are poorly printed. A magnifier helps.

Where (and when) to travel

Buses. Finding out when and where the buses go is difficult because there are so many different bus companies, some of them very small. The best thing is to enquire at local Tourist Information Centres (600 towns have one), and anyone intending to do much travelling in England really needs to get a list of these – free from the English Tourist Board, Thames Tower, Blacks Road, London W6 9EL (tel. 01–846 9000). The Information Centres have bus timetables, and can tell you the addresses of local bus companies from which to buy copies yourself if you wish. Local bus stations are another source (to locate these, look in the telephone directory – often under National Express). A third source of information is the public transport officers of county councils, who can be located through the County Hall of the area in which you are interested – normally in the county town (see list at end of book). And finally there is the Bus and Coach Council to which some 2,000 bus and coach companies belong (52 Lincolns Inn Fields, London WC2A 3LZ; tel. 01–831 7564): they publish a free booklet showing which companies operate in each county, with addresses and phone numbers.

I like to have timetables to study before setting out. Sending stamps to the value of about 50p when ordering a timetable book will probably suffice, and the bus company can tell you if a few pence more are needed. Some bus timetables are better than others, not only for the clarity of their presentation but for the amount of extra information they give. Most will tell you when market days and early-closing days occur in each town, a few list sights worth visiting, and usually town street plans are included which show the location of important places in relation to the bus station and bus-stops. Libraries often have timetables as well as guidebooks; some county councils also issue timetables and can answer questions on the phone (ask for the public transport officer). New editions usually come out each spring.

Some people find timetables difficult to understand, so at the end of this chapter is a page on how to read them: taken slowly there's nothing difficult about them. However, it does take some time to work out a route with their help so that you can time your arrival at the town or village you want to explore and be sure of getting on another bus going where you want to go. You can always phone the bus companies for advice.

Some rural areas have small red vehicles that are both mail vans and carriers of passengers. They usually start from a town post office and call at small village sub-offices, often going to places that have no other bus – really off-the-beaten-track rides. Stamp collectors in particular seek them out because they often use postage stamps on tickets, with a special mark of cancellation, and special pictorial postcards. There are, at the time of writing, about two or three in each of the following: Cumbria, Lincolnshire, Northumberland, Kent, Surrey, Sussex, Berkshire, Hampshire (including Isle of Wight) and Oxfordshire. Their timetables can be had from post offices.

Coaches. With coaches, getting information is easier. The majority are run by National Express who publish a twice-yearly book of timetables and maps for £3.90 (1988 price), obtainable from coach stations or from the headquarters of National Express, 4 Vicarage Road, Birmingham, B15 3ES (tel. 021–456 1132). This is supplemented by a quarterly Local Express Guide, £1.50, covering a number of other coach services associated with National Express.

As to other coach companies, these are the major ones, with the counties (in italics) where they mainly operate:

Wallace Arnold, 52 Grosvenor Gardens, London SW1W 0AW; tel. 01–730 8235. *Serves Yorkshire and other counties.*

Grey–Green, 53 Stamford Hill, London N16 5TD; tel. 01–800 8010. *Serves most of East Anglia: Norfolk, Suffolk, etc.*

Harris, Manor Road, West Thurrock, *Essex*, RM16 1EH; tel. 0708 864911.

Percival, Lamarsh Road, *Oxford*, OX2 0LE; tel. 0865 246509.

Premier, King Hedges Road, *Cambridge*, CB4 4PQ; tel. 022023 7262.

Tellyn, Harcog Motor Centre, Witham, *Essex*, CM8 1HN; tel. 0376 521331.

Tourmaster, Tavistock Street, Dunstable, *Bedfordshire*, LU6 1NE; tel. 0582 64331.

Whittle, 105 Coventry Street, Kidderminster, *Worcestershire*, DY10 2BH; tel. 0562 2966.

Yelloway, Weir Street, Rochdale, *Lancashire*, OL16 1HG; tel. 0706 47561.

How to read timetables

Some people seem to go into a deep coma at the sight of a timetable – all those figures look too much like tortured hours in maths lessons. But in fact they are quite simple to follow if you set about it in the right order.

Nearly every timetable book includes a *map* showing where the bus services run. Unless you already know what's what, study this in conjunction with a guidebook (or the brochures that tourist offices hand out) in order to pinpoint which places will be interesting to visit.

Then turn to the *index* in the timetable book and look up the towns and villages that have taken your fancy. The names are at the front of the book in alphabetical order, and this index will give you the numbers of the service(s) that go to it.

Turn to the page dealing with a particular service, giving its *timetable*: the services are in numerical order. Here you will find not only the times at which the buses reach a town but also what other towns or villages they call at (and when). In the case of large towns, the list will note where its main stops are. Here is an example from a bus timetable:

PENZANCE (Bus Station)	0905	1010	1110	1210	1410	1615	1810	2010
Penzance (Promenade)	0910	1015	1115	1215	1415	1620	1815	2015
Newlyn Bridge	0913	1018	1118	1218	1418	1623	1818	2018
Buryas Bridge	0917	1022	1122	1222	1422	1627	1822	2022
Drift Cross Roads	0921	1026	1126	1226	1426	1631	1826	2026
Tregonabria	0925	1030	1130	1230	1430	1635	1830	2030
Crows-an-Wra Cross Roads	0930	1035	1135	1235	1435	1640	1835	2035
Friend's Burial Ground	0935	1040	1140	1240	1440	1645	1840	2040
Sennen Cove	0943	1048	1148	1248	1448	1653	1848	2048
Sennen (First and Last Hotel)	0952	1057	1157	1257	1457	1702	1857	2057
LAND'S END (Hotel)	0956	1101	1201	1301	1501	1706	1901	2101

From this it is easy to see what choice of buses there is from, say, Penzance to Sennen Cove (three during the morning, five after midday) and how long the journey takes (roughly 40 minutes).

At this point, check whether the service runs every day *and* all round the year: look at the top of the page and at the footnotes, too. This is vital! Some run only once a week, for example. (The word weekday means Monday through to Saturday.)

Timetables are always printed in the continental manner – 1 pm is written as 1300 hours, 2 pm is 1400, 3 pm is 1500, and so on. Sometimes a name has a symbol against it to indicate that it has a rail station, a ferry, etc. These could be useful links between one bus service and another.

Alongside or below each timetable appears its twin for the return journey – it's no good arriving late and hoping for an hour's stop if the only return service leaves in a few minutes. Study this, too, before setting out.

What exactly do you want from your journey if it is not a simple there-and-back trip? If you intend to get off for a short break at, say, Sennen Cove (in the above example) and then continue on to Land's End, you may find that the next bus does not depart until two hours later, which might or might not suit your plans. Alternatively, you might want to go on to somewhere not on this bus route at all – Mousehole, let's say. A quick look again at the map and index and you will discover that if, on your return journey from Sennen Cove that afternoon, you get off at Newlyn Bridge, you can easily pick up another bus there to get to Mousehole. Turn to its timetable and you will find a choice of sixteen before nightfall and that the journey takes only eight minutes.

PENZANCE (Bus Station)	1445	1500	1515	1545	1600	1615	1645	1700
Penzance (Promenade)	......	1505	......	......	1605	......	......	1705
Alverton Estate	1452	......	1522	1552	......	1622	1652	......
Newlyn Bridge	1456	1508	1526	1556	1608	1626	1656	1708
Newlyn (Red Lion)	1500	1512	1530	1600	1612	1630	1700	1712
MOUSEHOLE	1508	1520	1538	1608	1620	1638	1708	1720

PENZANCE (Bus Station)	1715	1745	1800	1845	1900	2000	2115	2215
Penzance (Promenade)	......	......	1805	......	1905	2005	......	......
Alverton Estate	1722	1752	......	1852	......	......	2122	2222
Newlyn Bridge	1726	1756	1808	1856	1908	2008	2126	2226
Newlyn (Red Lion)	1730	1800	1812	1900	1912	2012	2130	2230
MOUSEHOLE	1738	1808	1820	1908	1920	2020	2138	2238

When doing circular tours starting and ending at the same town but not coming back exactly the same way I went out, I found I made use of three to six buses to accomplish the day's circuit – working out the routes was part of the fun, but it took quite a bit of time each evening.

Where to Stay

To use as a travelling companion, buy a current copy of Elizabeth Gundrey's "Staying Off the Beaten Track", her annual illustrated guide to moderately-priced inns, farms, small hotels and country guest houses of character – chosen for their attractive ambience, comfort and good food. Many are on or near the routes described in "England by Bus and Coach" or have hosts willing to pick you up from the nearest stop. Each one is described in detail: quite a lot give discounts to readers (the book contains £15-worth of vouchers usable against the cost of certain accommodation); and caring hosts are often very willing to cater for individual needs – such as clothes-washing facilities, special diets, children or dogs.

The book is on sale in the shops. It can alternatively be ordered by using the coupon overleaf.

The Family Holiday Association

The royalties from this edition of "England by Bus and Coach" are going to a charity which provides short holidays for people in very great need. These are families which are not only below the poverty line but particularly needing a holiday: those with severely handicapped children, mothers coping on their own, living in very bad housing, or with other grave problems. Experience has shown that even a short break can make all the difference between a family being able to go on coping or breaking down under the unrelieved stress of such lives.

On top of the cost of the holiday, there is of course also the cost of coach travel. To get one Midlands mother to the seaside and back costs about £12; a child, about £8. If you are willing to help with such fares, do please use the coupon overleaf to send a donation to this very worthwhile cause.

"Staying Off the Beaten Track" appears annually. To obtain the current edition – or, if you order late in the year, the next one as soon as it appears in January – send this coupon with a sterling cheque or P.O. made out to Explore Britain for £5.50 (post inclusive) to:

EXPLORE BRITAIN, Alston, Cumbria, CA9 35L

NAME (capitals) ______________________________

ADDRESS (UK only) ______________________________

____

____

____

To make a donation, please send your cheque to:

FAMILY HOLIDAYS ASSOCIATION
Hertford Lodge, East End Road, London N3 3QE

If you would like a receipt and a leaflet about the Association, please give your address here:

NAME (capitals) ______________________________

ADDRESS ______________________________

____

____

____

Youth Hostelling

So-called Youth Hostels (even some 80-year-olds use them!) are not what they used to be. The buildings are the same, in great variety: they range from converted castles to former shepherds' huts to purpose-built modern buildings. But in many the spartan atmosphere which prevailed decades ago is long gone.

Attractively decorated inside, with extra touches like pictures and books (sometimes, with handsome antiques too, and plenty of flowers), the average hostel will probably have good carpets, comfortable armchairs, possibly a crackling fire as well as central heating, and, in my experience, really excellent meals from fresh produce (unless you choose to self-cater – ingredients are sold by hostel shops). Hefty breakfasts and packed lunches are provided; but rarely alcoholic drinks. You may find television, indoor or outdoor games and attractive gardens: every hostel differs in what it offers.

Where bedrooms are concerned, in addition to larger one-sex dormitories there are now, in nearly 200 of the hostels, rooms with 4–6 beds suitable for families; and about 30 also have self-contained family accommodation, most with their own kitchen, living-room and bathroom. In these, you can come and go as you please at any time of the day. (They are not subject to normal opening times – which vary from hostel to hostel.)

There are 260 hostels in England and Wales (which are listed, at the back of this book, towns which have a Youth Hostel are indicated – with their telephone numbers). The majority are accessible to travellers by bus or coach. To stay at any of them, you pay a small fee to become a member of the Youth Hostels Association and receive a directory of all the hostels, a quarterly magazine, discounts on certain tourist sights and on travel insurance, invitations to YHA events and to local group meetings near your home. Then you pay for each night's accommodation (plus hire of bed-linen) and meals. Membership entitles you to buy a Britexpress coach pass (see page viii).

Costs Adults can join for £6.50 a year. Children under 16, free if their parents are members; 12–16, travelling without parents, £1.50; 16–20, £3.50. Accommodation costs per night vary according to the standard of the building (hostels are graded); for adults, from about £2.50 to £4.80 for a bed; £1.70 for breakfast; about £2.15 for evening meal. Hire of sheets or sleeping-bag liner, 60p. Self-contained holiday annexes adjoining some hostels are available too.

To join, call at any hostel or post the form below to:
YHA, Trevelyan House, St Albans, AL1 2DY. (Tel. 0727 55215)

YOUR NAME (capitals) ______________________________

ADDRESS ______________________________

______________________________ POSTCODE ______________

DATE OF BIRTH ______________________________

I ENCLOSE £

FOR _____ ADULT OR _____ CHILD (12–16) MEMBERSHIPS.

SIGNATURE ______________________________ DATE ______________

English Heritage Membership

If you appreciate England's historic monuments, it's worth joining a special 'club' by becoming a member of English Heritage.

A membership card entitles you to visit English Heritage properties without payment – Hampton Court and the Tower of London, too; half-price admission to many buildings in Wales and Scotland; a beautifully produced quarterly magazine, with articles by experts, colour photographs, details of forthcoming events in English Heritage properties ranging from concerts to mediaeval jousts, book reviews, and even a children's page (children are enrolled in the junior section, Keep, with its own events, badges, etc.); an illustrated handbook describing all the sites, worth £2; a map of England showing where they all are; guided tours and talks exclusive to members, particularly where local branches flourish; and the offer of books and souvenirs by post, at special prices.

To join, either call at an English Heritage property or post this coupon to English Heritage, Box 43, Ruislip HA4 0XW. If applying for more than one person, send lists of names (IN CAPITALS) with childrens' birth dates.

England by Bus and Coach describes dozens of English Heritage properties accessible by bus or coach.

☐ **Individual:** £10 a year

☐ **Family groups:** £20 for two parents and all children under 16, who will be enrolled in KEEP. Each receives a card.

☐ **Senior Citizen:** £6 for people qualifying for the state pension.

£________ is enclosed*/may be debited to the credit card shown below.

*Cheques should be made payable to ENGLISH HERITAGE.

Access/Amex/
Barclaycard No ☐☐☐☐☐☐☐☐☐☐☐☐☐☐☐☐☐☐☐☐☐☐☐☐☐☐

Mr/Mrs/Ms Initials:__________ Surname (capitals):______________

Address:____

______________________________ Postcode:________________

EEB

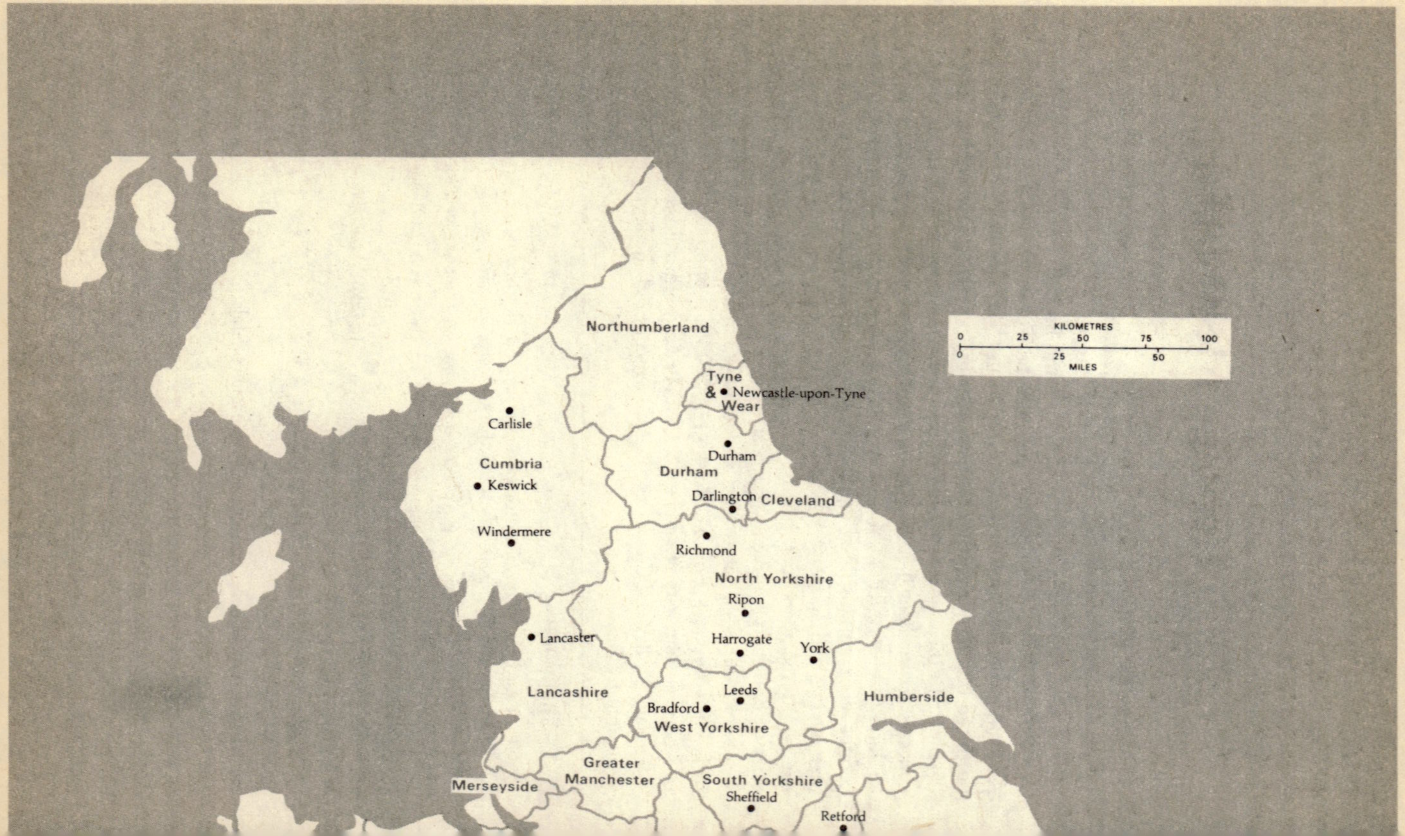

KILOMETRES
0
25
50
75
100
0
25
50
MILES
Northumberland
Tyne & Wear
Newcastle-upon-Tyne
Carlisle
Cumbria
Keswick
Windermere
Durham
Durham
Darlington
Cleveland
Richmond
North Yorkshire
Ripon
Lancaster
Harrogate
York
Lancashire
Leeds
Bradford
West Yorkshire
Humberside
Greater Manchester
Merseyside
South Yorkshire
Sheffield
Retford

Map showing principal towns described in the text.
Each has a Tourist Information Office.

Part One

BUS JOURNEYS

1

From the Roman Wall to London

Hexham – Durham – Darlington – Bedale – Ripon – Harrogate – Leeds – Doncaster – Retford – Tuxford – Newark – Grantham – Stamford – Corby – Kettering – Bedford – London

This, my very first long-distance bus journey, was taken in late autumn, one of the driest for 200 years, from the Roman Wall to London (strictly, from Hexham, the nearest bus centre to the middle of the Wall). Except after 4 pm when school children flock on to the buses, I rarely found more than half-a-dozen other travellers though they seat 40 or more, and sometimes I was the only passenger. What other form of transport offers the luxury of so much space to oneself? Yet for housewives and pensioners in isolated areas, the country buses are vital. Even if they run only once a week, they fill the essential need for travel to shopping centre, dentist, cinema or clinic – and they are a kind of social club, too, whose drivers become unofficial community officers or sometimes even social workers.

My route started in the high Pennines, passed through the great Vale of York and the eastern plains and by the Chilterns to London. I wanted to explore the in-between places – not the most famous cities or beauty-spots but those towns and villages the main roads do not reach. The bus routes determined where exactly I went, which gave the journey a surprise element. I chose to go when few others would be travelling for pleasure, setting out on the last day of October. The area east of the Pennines is less prone to rain than the west.

Though there was no rain on the hills, the hunchbacked, twisted trees spoke of fierce and frequent winds, and so did the thick coats of the cattle and shaggy fleeces of the sheep. The women wore knitted wool hats like tea-cosies, pulled firmly down to defeat the weather.

Hexham

A young soldier, little more than a boy when he enlisted, was sent to keep the peace on an unruly frontier far from home. There he died – killed by one of the guerillas he was under orders to control. There is nothing unusual about this in a world accustomed to such warfare. But this soldier's tombstone commemorates the death of a Roman legionary, and it stands in a Christian church.

The Latin inscription, translated, reads:

> To the gods, the shades, Flavinus of the Cavalry Regiment of Petriana, a standard-bearer of the White Troop, aged 25, and of seven years' service, is here buried.

The stone tells more of the story than these words reveal. A carving shows vividly not only Flavinus the cavalryman on his rearing horse but, crouching in the undergrowth below, an ancient Northumbrian with his dagger thrust upwards to hamstring the horse before killing its rider.

The stone, dug up in the abbey precincts nearly a century ago, now stands in Hexham Abbey – itself built in 674 from stones brought from the nearby Roman fort at Corbridge (where Flavinus' regiment was stationed), part of the Emperor Hadrian's immense fortifications stretching across the north of England from Newcastle to Carlisle. Over a million cubic yards of stone went into the making of Hadrian's Wall and its associated forts, many of which still stand in place. The rest began to be used for the building of farms and churches when the Romans, heavily beset elsewhere, withdrew from their distant outposts in Britain, in 407AD, after some 300 years of occupation. Some of the legionaries must have been glad to move back to warmer latitudes.

When Hexham Abbey was built (by St Wilfred) it had no equal for size and magnificence outside Italy, and it is still impressive – starting with an exceptional Saxon crypt, though when I arrived this was occupied by archaeologists investigating discoveries made in the course of recent maintenance work. Among the arches one can find a Roman altar and other Roman relics.

The font incorporates part of a Roman pillar, and elsewhere a Roman god passes a comfortable retirement within a Christian recess. How ecumenical can you get?

The abbey's dominant feature is the great 'night stair' descending into the south transept. Down this vast flight of steps would come, every midnight, all the clergy of the abbey for the candle-lit service of matins. Their dormitory at the top of the staircase, unheated even in the northern winter, no longer exists, but the well-worn steps are still used by choirboys who descend in procession before services at more conventional hours. The abbey was attacked in 1296 by raiding Scots who set fire to it, and traces of molten lead from the roof still cling to some of these ancient steps.

On the landing is a small room where refugees could take sanctuary (the dispute would later be settled in an ecclesiastical court). Severe penalties were imposed for seizing anyone fleeing to sanctuary, rising in magnitude according to the spot where the interception took place: from £16 if on Hexham's outskirts to £144 if within the church itself, coupled with penances for sacrilege. But the worst penalty of all was reserved for anyone who violated the sanctuary of Bishop Wilfred's stone seat itself, know as the Frid or Frith stool and still standing after 1,200 years, behind the altar. For such a one, there was no pardon. The concept of church sanctuary was not completely abolished until 1727.

The hard and violent times the abbey silently recalls are a sharp contrast to the scene just outside it on a Tuesday, market day, when the square is filled with stalls selling curly Cumberland sausage, strong boots, crabs and home-made preserves. Many of the voices have a Scots accent, and Scottish mutton pies are in most bakers' shops (a good portable lunch for bus travellers).

Nearby is the 14th-century Moot Hall, which houses changing exhibitions, and just behind it the Manor Office of the same period, now used as a Tourist Information Centre but still showing relics of the days when it was used as a gaol (until 1824). Worth a detour are Hexham's award-winning swimming pool, ingeniously created only a few years ago in a disused wool warehouse, and, near the bus station, the Midland Bank's circular building with its terracotta frieze of cherubs with early Victorian pennies, shillings and sovereigns.

From Hexham to Durham

With a grinding of gears my first bus (of 20) swung out of the bus station and into roads hemmed with ancient yew and holly hedges, larch and rowan, past peat-diggings and flocks of horned and black-faced Swaledale sheep. There was a clamour of busy rooks above and a vista of serpentine rises and descents leading ahead.

'Is your mum all right? I've not seen her on the bus lately,' the driver asks a girl. Everyone knows the driver, and he knows every-one. The local bus provides more than passenger transport – it's also a channel of communication and a parcel service. Shopping trailers and baby buggies are heaved on and off, old gentlemen with crutches are pushed up or handed down, news is passed on and congratulations or commiserations are exchanged. 'Can you manage, pet?' the driver enquires of a 70-year-old lady who finds the high step difficult. 'Where do you want off, pet?' (Further south 'pet' becomes 'love' and, further south still, 'love' becomes 'dearie'.)

On we go between ploughed fields and cottage gardens still cheerful with nasturtiums, Michaelmas daisies and marigolds. The prevailing sandstone, aptly called millstone grit, is dark and coarse. A pair of tethered goats nibble a grass verge. Logs are piled high ready for winter hearths. The bracken is turning brown and the birch and oak leaves gold, but a plantation of conifers spreads a patch of dark green like a baize cloth.

On the rare occasion when there is a visitor to the old people in a nearby geriatric hospital, the driver may make a strictly unofficial detour to the hospital if it is raining. But on this day the weather was as he put it, 'very canny': in fact, it was a good year altogether for the farmers.

Open-cast coal mining further along the road had made a great gash in the green hills. But the driver said only people with week-end cottages object to the sight. For the locals it means more jobs, and for the farmer who owns the land several thousand pounds a year in compensation until the fields are restored. A grass hillock which we pass, topped by a chapel and an ornate mausoleum, was once the spoil heap from open-cast mining.

The route to Durham involved changing at Consett, once a steel town whose tall chimneys dominated the high horizon: now all gone. (One of its few claims to fame is that it produced the first Salvation Army Band, in 1879.) It was once a place of gaunt, satanic shapes, the churches' blackened towers eccentrically angular by contrast with the rounded cooling towers and the pillars of smoke. Now all is cleaner and brighter, but it is a fairly characterless place – except for a lively covered 'flea market' where one may pick up bargains among the old china and other bric-a-brac. The stone of the walls here is reddish from iron in the ground, by contrast with Hexham's grey; at Lanchester, a little further on, the stone is yellower and there are some good stone period houses built around a village green.

Durham

Durham deserves a book to itself and at least a day of any traveller's time. But all I had was half an hour or I would miss my connection. My disappointment was tempered by knowing the cathedral already – and by making a small new discovery in the backstreets of Durham.

The city's jewels, its cathedral and castle, stand high up on what is almost an island of rock within a loop of the River Wear. You see them suddenly and spectacularly framed in an arch of the railway viaduct as the bus enters the city.

The cathedral's massive splendour dates from early Norman times and its vastness alone is impressive. It is the noblest Norman cathedral in England, perhaps in the world. Once it had red-and-black painted decorations, but now its interest lies in the variety of unusual local stones used in its construction, some (called Frosterly marble) thick with fossils, and in the elaborate carving of later centuries, particularly in the Chapel of the Nine Altars. An old account vividly describes some of the original details: 'From pillar to pillar was set up a border very artificially wrought in stone with marvellous fine colours, very curiously and excellently, finely gilt with branches and flowers.' But during the Reformation much was deliberately removed on the orders of Henry VIII, and more damage was done when Cromwell used the cathedral to hold 4,000 prisoners-of-war.

Even so, it is a cathedral of exceptional beauty and so are its surroundings – the deanery, the canons' houses round a green, Prebends Bridge, the mills by the weir and the narrow streets of the old city. Next to an ancient bridge is a shopping centre that recently received an award as one of the five best new buildings in

Europe. Its shops and car parks are well concealed under a higgledy-piggledy roofscape that blends with the look of the medieval city.

My own discovery during my brief stop was a hilly cobbled road near the bus station: South Street. So steep is the climb that a handrail is provided, but the effort is worth it for the view of the cathedral's west end, seen across treetops and in a silence broken

Durham Cathedral

only by the shallow murmur of water slipping over the weir below. South Street itself is a gem – a backwater of Regency houses, brick and stucco, with curving sash windows or wooden bay windows projecting over the street at first floor level with decorative plasterwork, fanlights over the doors and handsome brass knockers. Jane Austen might have felt at home here. At the foot of the hill a sensitive modern development fully does justice to its setting: a terrace of small homes which, while thoroughly of today and very original in concept, uses local materials and takes up the motif of projecting windows in such a way that new is in complete harmony with old. That half-hour was well spent.

Durham to Darlington

As I ate my pie alone on the top deck I watched the flocks of gulls that had flown far inland to find *their* meal – whatever pickings a plough was turning up from the soil. They have to move fast because a diesel-drawn plough doing seven furrows at once may cover three acres in an hour – work that would once have taken more than a day. Many fields were black where farmers had burned the stubble in order to get rid of weeds and improve the fertility of the soil for next year's crop. The bridge over the River Wear at Croxdale is parallel with another (medieval?) no longer able to take today's traffic, its sharp stone cutwaters still cleaving the current. Beyond the hedges one sees from time to time the disused tracks of local railways lately closed in the interests of economic management and now vanishing under tangled weeds and waving grasses.

The bus made a detour to scoop up passengers in Newton Aycliffe, a recently sprouted garden city with trading and industrial estates on its outskirts. Though the houses are undistinguished the corporation has at least planted road verges, filled rosebeds liberally, and put in groves of young trees that promise to hide factories from view in years to come. Then a brief ride through a landscape of rolling fields, now pale with mist creeping from hedge to hedge, and Darlington comes into view.

Darlington

This is a town that was made famous by steam, so railway buffs immediately make for the museum at North Road Station where

George Stephenson's famous engine 'Locomotion' is housed, along with other historic locomotives and a model railway. The Stockton-Darlington railway was the first public line in the world (begun in 1825), used mainly for transporting coal. Stephenson, who worked in a colliery, used whatever money he could save to buy himself an education in engineering at evening classes. The success of his Stockton-Darlington line brought him the job of designing the Manchester-Liverpool line and the famous 'Rocket' locomotive, which drew a train at an alarming 15 mph.

However, Darlington's history goes back much further than George Stephenson. The 'lady of the north', its medieval church, occupied my brief stay in the town. St Cuthbert's austere beauty makes it one of the most noble parish churches in the country, and its 200-foot tower can be seen for miles across the low-lying district around it. The Saxons had a settlement here that included a church, but the present one was started around 1180 by Bishop Puiset of Chartres, a nephew of that great patron of church builders, Henry II, England's first Plantagenet king.

Some arches in the nave lean very noticeably because of the great weight thrusting down from the huge tower – its spire alone weighs about 150 tons. The graceful spire-like cover to the font, made in the time of Charles II, is also one of the tallest of its kind. Fonts needed covers because people used to steal the sanctified water for magic or medicine.

Darlington to Bedale

Daylight was fading as I left. The next stretch of the journey was through a flat landscape. White-and-brown sheep grazed, ducks dabbled among reeds strangling a village pond, and a covey of partridges was busy in stubbled fields. The region had a well-to-do look, with Dutch barns crammed with hay, apples heavy on the trees and spacious Georgian houses near the fine bridge over the Tees at Croft (which also boasts a spa hotel). Lewis Carroll (Charles Dodgson) grew up there, in the Old Rectory. By the time the bus reaches North Cowton and Brompton, villages built around greens, the architecture has changed and stone houses are outnumbered by brick ones. The day was drooping, the soaking branches dripped and the bustling rooks had put themselves to bed in disconsolate rows along the electricity cables by the time we got to Bedale.

Bedale

What is lost in clarity is certainly made up for in atmosphere if you find yourself visiting an old church at twilight, particularly in the company of a recumbent Yorkshireman and his wife, once lord and lady of the manor, who have been lying there in stone for some four or five hundred years. One may feel more at ease in the open churchyard outside, particularly at Bedale which has a large sloping lawn with yews from which to watch darkness drop its curtain over the fields beneath. The churchyard has a number of elegant table tombs – horizontal slabs supported by six pilasters or urns – and a very ornate memorial to Nancy Day, though its red sandstone has been much weathered by three centuries of wind and rain. The church tower at Bedale, so built that it could provide a defensive post in times of trouble, has many gargoyles, which make convenient perches for the roosting pigeons whose cooing was a pleasanter sound than the rusty rasping of a brood of pheasants not far away. Through the gargoyles' throats rainwater is conveyed well away from the church walls, sometimes in a gargling rush that gives them their name.

Bedale itself, once noted for horse breeding, consists of late-Georgian houses and shops flanking a broad cobbled street where a market is held on Tuesdays. Already the shops, here as elsewhere, were beginning to put their Christmas goods on display, and their bright lights twinkled invitingly through the slight rain as twilight slipped into darkness. Wensleydale cheese, made locally, was much in evidence. As no café remained open after 5 pm, I was glad to take cover in the Old Black Swan (pubs are open round the clock on market days) until my next bus arrived. The publican collects hats which hang from every beam in the ceiling – military and naval ones, straw, felt and tweed, a fez, a beret, a Dolly-Varden, a kepi, a Tyrolean one and even a bowler – and on the walls are various bits of blacksmith's gear. Some pubs almost double as mini-museums.

Bedale to Ripon

No moon, no stars. It was a mistake to continue travelling after darkness deepened because I saw nothing of the view except pale windows lighting up in scattered farms. I was too late in the year for October's 'hunter's moon' which, like the 'harvest moon' of September, hangs low, large and reddish as a lantern to illuminate the way.

For part of the time we were on the old Roman road known as Deor or Deer Street, now the A1, passing through Melmerby. The sole passenger, I chatted to the driver about life on the buses. The pay isn't too much but there's plenty of overtime, he said, though no one may drive for more than 7½ hours in one day.

On his recommendation, when we reached Ripon I made for the Unicorn to find a bed for the night. This is a 400-year-old coaching inn with creaking stairs, named after the Unicorn coach that used to turn in under its big arch to deposit travellers breaking their north-south journey as I was doing. The hotel is said to be haunted by an 18th-century bootboy called Crudd (his picture, in which he holds a coin between his jutting nose and chin, hangs in the hall), but no bootboy came for my shoes that dark, dank night even though it was Hallowe'en. (I returned again to Ripon, after my Dales journeys described later in this book, and had a more luxurious stay at the spacious Ripon Spa Hotel – excellent food, and a beautiful garden, surprising for a hotel virtually in a city centre.)

Ripon

'Except ye Lord keep ye cittie, ye Wakeman waketh in vain'. This cryptic message greets you in huge lettering as you enter Ripon's market square. It is carved along the top of the imposing Georgian town hall by Wyatt that faces the equally imposing obelisk in the middle of the square. What this is all about becomes apparent at 9 pm every night of the year. But first, the events which led up to the Wakeman's existence.

About 655AD a little monastery was built at the village of 'Rhypum' by Wilfred. The crypt remains – one of the few Saxon buildings that can still be seen in England – beneath the present cathedral. The church he built was destroyed by the Danish Vikings in one of their innumerable raids two centuries later, and for a time Christianity was blotted out in Yorkshire.

It was because of the incessant Danish raids that Ripon acquired its Wakeman. Alfred the Great, who alone offered effective resistance to the invaders, gave Ripon a horn and a charter in 886AD and appointed the first Wakeman with the job of keeping a lookout all through the night ('wake' used to mean an all-night vigil before a saint's feast day, though now in the north it refers rather to traditional days off work). Every night on taking up his post he would sound his horn as an assurance to the citizens that he was on duty.

Gradually the Wakeman became an official of considerable power in the city, a kind of mayor. The night-long patrol ceased centuries ago, but the tradition of the 9 pm horn-blowing continues – one long-drawn mournful note at each of the four corners of the obelisk. The modern incumbent whom I encountered, paid £1 a night for his services, was a young sales representative with a rubicund face, good lungs and exactly the kind of Toby-jug presence one might hope for in such a prestigious blower of horns. The current horn, dating from 1865, is from a buffalo and is resplendent with gold mounts. The horn-blower wears a buff frockcoat and a cocked hat, white gloves and a silver arm badge. It was worth going to Ripon just to see him – but a bit of an anticlimax when he drove off in his little Fiat with the horn in the boot.

By lamplight on Hallowe'en I explored some of the 'gates' of Ripon ('gate' means a way or road, in this context): High Skellgate, Water Skellgate (where a millrace once flowed), Blossomgate, Bondgate and so on, with passages leading to picturesque courtyards behind. Ripon, now a centre of the paint industry, was once a spa and the municipal baths have a grand portico as befits spa baths, with handsome spa gardens adjoining. In this direction are many of the antique dealers, craft shops and the town's old pie shop. The Wakeman's timbered house, built around 1250, still survives and is used now as a Tourist Information Centre.

One good modern building stands among the old façades of the market square itself. It has an arcade in which are preserved ancient beams from a house that once adjoined it, premises which until the Reform Act of 1832 gave the occupant (usually the mayor) the sole right to nominate Ripon's MP. Some of the front doors of buildings in the square were deliberately set back a few inches to avoid a one-time tax of two pence on all houses with doors opening on to the square.

The cathedral is floodlit at night, and I was there on an evening when bell-ringing practice pealed out joyfully over the town. At the back of the cathedral are a house where James I stayed in 1617 (now rather spoilt by a white pebbledash finish), almshouses and the ruins of a tiny 15th-century chapel. A steep flight of steps, with flagstones and cobbles, leads up to the south door of the cathedral.

It is a most magnificent building despite the eccentricities such as columns of unequal height and a round arch in the lofty nave that cuts across the pointed one beyond. After the 12th-century tower collapsed in 1450 the design was changed, for fundraising was unequal to the cost of rebuilding in the original style.

Among the cathedral's monuments is a painted figure of 1637, the very essence of civic pomp, which (it is no surprise to discover) is that of the last Wakeman, who became Ripon's first mayor. The big ruff fans out around self-satisfied cheeks made fat by so much puffing on that horn (and so much good living, no doubt).

There is much else to see, like the 36 fine choir stalls with oak canopies delicately carved by a Ripon craftsman, whose work became so famous that he was employed in other cathedrals, too, and his surname was changed from Bromflet to Carver (he, too, served as Wakeman, in 1511). The misericords, folding seats against which the priests could lean while standing during long services, bear on their undersides carvings of griffins, serpents, angels, a mermaid, Jonah in the whale and such homely subjects as a fox stealing a goose and pigs dancing to bagpipes. The roof of the choir is jewelled with bosses decoratively carved in stone and gilded. In the north aisle, a heraldic window tracing a family's ancestry back to Edward II incorporates the arms of the Washington family, the stars and stripes of which ultimately went into the design of 'Old Glory', America's national flag. (Washington Old Hall, the home of George Washington's ancestors, is to the north near Sunderland.)

Ripon to Harrogate

The main road runs quickly through handsome countryside. Chestnut trees were in full autumn magnificence at the edges of rolling fields with well-kept hedges. The fields themselves were a patchwork of rich green grassland, brown earth and golden stubble. Ripley, one of Yorkshire's oldest and least spoilt villages, comes and goes too quickly, a beautiful place of pink-brown stone, pointed

Gothic windows framed in white, dripstones as shapely as in the Cotswolds, and abundant flowers. There is an old market cross and stocks. Against its church walls Cromwell shot some of the Cavaliers captured after Marston Moor, the battle in which the Roundheads finally broke the Royalist hold on Yorkshire.

The women on the Yorkshire buses have a decided 'no nonsense' set to their mouths. Good sensible shoes and felt hats replace the head-scarves of County Durham or the woolly caps of Northumberland. One supposes those bulging shopping bags to be full of parkins and gingerbread men, brandy snaps, fruity 'cut-and-come-again' cakes and practical woollen underwear.

As we neared the end of the journey, a perfect example of *homo sapiens Harrogatensis* got on – a well-matured gentleman in tweeds, deerstalker and shoes polished till they shone like horse chestnuts. He was accompanied by (what else?) a Yorkshire terrier.

Harrogate

In 1571 a certain William Slingsby accidentally discovered a spring of health-giving water when his horse stumbled over it – and from this there grew up (but not until the 18th century, when such things became fashionable) one of Britain's most famous spas. Nearly 90 such springs are now known in the district, their origin being some ancient upheaval in the earth's crust which crumpled and split layers of rock like so much paper, impregnating the water underground with sulphur and other minerals.

So it is appropriate as well as convenient to start any walk around Harrogate at the Royal Pump Room where, in a cellar museum, one such spring still bubbles up. Taste the water and you will understand why it was nicknamed 'the Stinking Spaw'. Defoe said, 'Those who drink from it are obliged to hold their noses.' The Tourist Information Centre nearby (in the Royal Baths) has a useful leaflet for anyone with half an hour or so to spare, giving the route for a walk that takes in Farrah's (still making the toffee in blue-and-silver boxes which has brought them fame since 1840), the graceful dell known as the Valley Gardens and the Sun Colonnade, a glass-covered walk 600 feet long. Montpelier Parade is a wide boulevard that recaptures the flavour of Harrogate in its Victorian heyday.

The town is full of Regency terraces, monumental houses clad in the scarlet of Virginia creeper, and spacious streets where shops shelter behind glass canopies with white iron lacework. You may buy good tweeds, furs, jewellery or antiques – or a skipping-rope, walking-stick, flute or mint humbugs. It's a town of real leather handbags and brogues, sheepskin coats and Burberries.

Harrogate has teashops the way lesser towns have pubs, and in the Pump Room the teacups clattered discreetly to the accompaniment of a real live pianist just as they may have done when the ill-fated family of the last Russian Tsar stayed here. Then the streets were thronged not with buses and cars but landaus and broughams. The street names, such as Raglan and Albert, recall the heroes of the time. A statue of Victoria at her golden jubilee, looking down from a perch uncommonly like a small version of the Albert Memorial in London, seemed distinctly unamused at the temerity of a solitary skateboarder in these surroundings.

Harrogate to Leeds

My intention had been to go to Tadcaster, a market town where the so-called Ark (a half-timbered house with two carvings known as Noah and his wife) houses a brewing museum that is open on midweek afternoons. But for buses out of Tadcaster neither I nor the Harrogate bus station had a timetable, and the general opinion (wrong, as it later turned out) was that I would be stuck there until the next day. So reluctantly I headed for Leeds, pausing briefly at Wetherby on the way.

Wetherby is a village of odd angles and many archways. Traffic goes round a small town hall in the middle, at the shady back of which is a stone-pillared arcade called the Shambles, where butchers tried to keep their meat cool in the days before refrigeration. Now the small shops are boutiques. Its other touch of individuality is a shop called 'The Shoe Tree', with a sprouting golden boot hanging out as a sign.

A wholefood shop provided me with excellent home-made pie to eat as the bus swung out of the town and across the River Wharfe. A memorial angel on the bridge pointed a reproving finger at the naughtily bubbling weir below. Bridges in this part of the world are often lofty because even crawling streams may suddenly run high and furious when rain falls heavily on the distant hills from which they flow.

Leeds

There is nothing traditional about the northern outskirts of Leeds. Its suburban semis, all pebbledash and coloured paint, could be put down anywhere in England. They are succeeded by Edwardian stone mansions set on high banks with shrubberies and steep flights of steps. Then come the slum terraces, interspersed with patches of derelict land, and with these the first West Indian faces of my journey so far. Used-car lots succeed one another and are then succeeded by new-car showrooms. Old red-brick warehouses give way to new concrete skyscrapers, huge car parks, underpasses and flyovers. Nothing pleased the eye except Alf Cooke's Packaging Works, a fine piece of industrial Victoriana with Italianate red-and-white brick arches to the long row of first-floor windows and Corinthian pillars all the way along the top storey.

Leeds has a notable art gallery near its wedding-cake of a city hall (in The Headrow, not far from the Vicars Lane bus station). It is celebrated for its sculptures by Henry Moore, Jacob Epstein and Barbara Hepworth, an outstanding Rembrandt, many other fine oil paintings (mostly English) and a huge collection of watercolours. Thomas Girtin's landscapes of Yorkshire are excellent. The glass-roofed shopping arcades off Briggate are worth exploring, too. In Thornton's Arcade a pair of jack-o'-the-clocks, mechanical figures, strike the hours below a large clock. Cast-iron curlicues, carved stone balconies and multi-coloured mosaics make a palace out of County Arcade. The mosaics spell out a Victorian morality lesson: figures of liberty, art, peace and justice are on an equal footing with commerce and labour. No miners or mill-hands would have recognized themselves in the well-scrubbed figures languidly reclining with mine lamp or spindle held in a graceful hand. But when these arcades were built no miner or mill-hand could have had the means to go shopping there.

In the shops below these fantasies, commerce is a reality. Mr Addyman, the butcher, had a window full of black puddings, brawn, 'stand' pies (more familiar to most of us as raised pies), tripe and savoury ducks – delicacies mainly unknown to the supermarket shopper. Next door to him were electronic organs. I bought a traditional 'fairing' to take home to my family, gingerbread men, and one of those solid Yorkshire cakes made with 'Old Pekulier' (*sic*) ale. Too solid for my liking, as it added another 1½ lb to my bag.

Also within easy walking distance are Kirkgate Market (flanked with rows of plump cherubs) and a Jacobean church in New Briggate that still survives in the middle of 'the great town's harsh heart-wearying roar'. (That was Matthew Arnold's phrase a century ago – what would he think of today's din?) 'Briggate' means the road to the bridge – a bridge so wide that in the Middle Ages a cloth market was held on it.

Leeds to Doncaster

The bus pulls out through a depressing area of housing estates set against a landscape of cooling towers, pylons, gantries and blank, windowless warehouses, sooty land and grey sky. Even in the 18th century the area round Leeds was described (by Defoe) as 'a waste of black, ill-looking, desolate moors'. The word 'slum' comes from 'slump' (which meant a marshy place), because the first factories were often sited by a river or canal with workers' houses around them – damp, ill-drained and jerry-built.

The road went through Pontefract (in the castle of which Richard II was murdered) and then at last we reached some broad sweeps of countryside again, peewits (lapwings) grazing in the sombre fields and a burst of red poppies – a reminder that Remembrance Day was near – catching the last light of the afternoon.

The rural view soon passes. Castleford has a mining college and, on the horizon, tips and pithead wheels make it plain that coal is king in the country ahead. The old miners' songs are still sung in these parts – ballads like this, once sung by a miner to his pit pony:

> I shall be glad when this shift is done.
> Then I'll be up there, out in the sun.
> Thou'll be dahn 'ere, boy, in this dark 'ole,
> Still gruntin' and groanin', pullin' this coal.

Doncaster to Retford

To get from one bus station to another involves a roundabout drive on a minibus. This gives glimpses of some fine Regency buildings in South Parade and, in a shopping centre, an interesting new library looking rather like a branch of Sainsbury's (which, after all, may be more inviting to the young). A water-bus provides trips on the River Don. But for the most part, except during the racing season, Doncaster has a very workaday face, as befits a town which owes its living to coal and the building of locomotives.

A pearly-pink sunset provided the backdrop to the trees of the Bawtry Forest as we passed into Nottinghamshire. The bus started off full of schoolchildren but many had alighted by the time Bawtry was reached. There several wide-arched coaching inns surround the market place. Soon afterwards we left the A1 – the Great North Road of coaching days – to get to Retford and the well-named River Idle just before nightfall, and I booked into the last room left at the White Hart.

Retford

A large cannon in front of the church points directly at the White Hart, but it is a long time since it fired a shot in anger. Retford has had other troubles, though. In 1528 it had a great fire when the whole town was burnt, including the church. In 1651 a storm blew down the church tower. Later, plague repeatedly hit Retford, and the parish register contains a recipe (early 18th-century) for its cure: a pennyworth of dragon water, a pennyworth of olive oil, some methrodate and treacle. The patient is then to scrape out the middle of an onion and fill it with pepper, roast it, add it to the previous mixture and drink it. The recipe further advises sweating and putting soap and bay salt on one's feet at night. 'With God's Blessing', it concludes, 'you shall recover' (though whether from the plague or from the remedy, who shall say).

The fine Perpendicular church is dedicated to St Swithin, of whom a quaint little Portuguese statue stands above the south door. I was very lucky to find the church floodlit after nightfall, and the bell-ringers were hard at practice on the ten very melodious bells. This change-ringing (the peals being rung in varied permutations, quite different from playing tunes) is something peculiar to England.

Though Norfolk is the county whose churches are famed for their carved oak angels in the roofs, I found them in Retford, too, and in other churches from here to Bedford – plain, painted, gilded, soaring, kneeling or playing music. The superstitious believed real angels hovered invisible in the roof of every church. When the Cromwellians destroyed other images lower down in the churches, the angels escaped because they were too high to reach.

Early morning saw stall-holders already setting out their goods under colourful striped awnings in the market square. The sun was bright and the air breezy. Once, all goods sold in markets were subject to taxes that went to king, lord or, later, to the township. Now stall-holders pay rents instead. The cross which some markets have in the centre was often called a butter cross, because it was there that farm women sat to sell their butter and eggs. In the 16th century, market halls were sometimes built to shelter them in a pillared area, with a room above used for meetings of the town council and similar purposes.

One of Retford's more attractive parts is Grove Street, off the square, which has attractive 18th-century doorways with fluted pilasters, bow windows and good ironwork. The local council has dealt kindly with this road, planting laburnums and well-designed wood seats. Instead of a kerb, a wide new gutter of purplish-red bricks seems to give the little street greater width.

Retford to Tuxford

In this part of the world sugar beet is one of the important crops. Harvesting it that year was heavy work, for the rust-red soil was dry and hard to break – so hard, said the bus driver, that the annual ploughing contest had had to be abandoned. The fine weather meant prolonged summer in the cottage gardens, still full of flowers, and Askham, a village on the brow of a slight hill in this otherwise flat region, was looking particularly pretty. The bus follows lanes that wind among the villages and crosses the old Chesterfield canal, where a traditionally painted narrow-boat was moored (70 feet long but only 7 feet wide, so as to pass through the narrowest canals). In 1830 William Cobbett described quite well-to-do Yorkshire families, of farmers or skilled artisans, crossing England by canal to Liverpool in one of the first waves of emigration to America, as 'fugitives from the fangs of taxation'. Many of the cottages have red pantiles in place of the slate roofs which are universal further north.

Tuxford

How did such a small place as this come to have such a fine grammar school? No longer a school, alas, but the handsome Jacobean building houses a library (in marked contrast to that supermarket library at Doncaster). One of the windows is now a fake. Long ago bricked in to avoid the window tax that was imposed between 1695 and 1851, a *trompe l'oeil* window has been painted in its place. (Householders paid double if they had more than ten windows and double again for over 20, so it could sometimes save a lot to brick up just one.)

Across the way is the medieval parish church. Never was any church more damp and chilly, but it is worth a visit all the same for the sake of its fine Perpendicular woodwork – the screen in particular. Though the church is dedicated to St Nicholas, it has two memorials to St Lawrence (martyred by being grilled on a kind of toasting-rack): a 15th-century stained-glass window and a carved stone of the same period showing the saint and his gridiron. There are some alabaster tombs from the time of James I and a fine roof with carved bosses and painted angels. Alabaster, mined in the Midlands, was popular for effigies because it was easy to carve.

This is hunting and shooting country (the hunting season began that day), and Tuxford houses both a gunsmith and a maker of pigeon traps. There are few other tradespeople in the village, yet between them the shops can sell you anything from pigs' trotters to coal tongs, catapult elastic to shoehorns, things hard to find in city shops. Facing the big coaching inn, the Newcastle Arms (named for one of the greatest dukes in the Dukeries), is a signpost that could claim to be the prettiest in Britain. All curly iron with a lamp on top, it was erected in 1886 and restored about ten years ago. The village was once known disparagingly as Tuxford-in-the-Clays, but that is at least a little better than another unambiguously called Foul Mire. 'Good land, bad travelling' says an old country proverb of these clays which were spread over the East Midlands when the glaciers of the Ice Age melted.

Tuxford to Newark

Flat though most of this route is, it goes through some especially pretty villages – Normanton and Sutton in particular – with half-timbered houses, black and white like the local magpies. All that is left of a windmill is the brick stump, looking sadly amputated. Such brick windmills came in during the 18th century (the earlier ones being made entirely of wood) when building in brick first became popular. There were blackberries in the hedgerows still, at least where the mechanical hedge-rippers had not yet been busy, tearing and mutilating as they go. Dozens of brown-and-yellow buntings take wing as we pass.

The stone houses of the north have petered out. Walls here are mostly whitewashed or bricks are used in a chequered pattern. The grass seems particularly green and lush, the broom yellow as butter. The small roads used by the local buses give one a distinctly superior feeling whenever they spring over the tops of motorways beneath – there are all those poor folk pounding along at 70 mph and seeing so little of England as they go.

Newark's lofty church spire comes in sight above the trees and then its castle ruins on the banks of the River Trent, that long river which, rising in the west, used once to bring 4,000 tons of Cheshire cheese a year right across England for consumption here in the east.

Newark

Newark's 12th-century castle, where King John died after his flight across the Wash, was largely destroyed by the Royalist armies in 1646. The town, held by the Cromwellians, had been under siege for three years. Even in Saxon times it had been regarded as the key to the north because of its commanding position where main roads and river meet. Some relics of that siege remain in the town museum, including square coins specially minted inside the beleaguered town and a hoard of nearly 500 silver coins buried in a panic and never dug up again by their unknown owner, who may have died in battle.

The museum (in Appleton Gate, only a few minutes from the bus station) has an extraordinary collection of bygones which bring alive the details of daily life the way it used to be: tinder boxes and sulphur matches needing a flintlock to ignite them; a man-trap to catch poachers; a spiked collar put on dogs used in bear-baiting (legal until 1835); sharp cock-fighting spurs; clumsy, rusty dentistry tools. From an old chemist's shop came a large wooden panel listing sixpenny 'cures' on sale: 'Nerve and digestive tablets', 'Back drops' and 'Pink pills', described as being 'for pale people'. The formulae are given, too – a cure-all simply called 'Family Doctor' consisted of nitric acid and mint in water.

Not many yards away is Chain Lane, leading to the Market Square and the old shop of a modern chemist – but, thank goodness, not so modern as to have thrown out the great glass flagons of coloured water and the rows of old pharmacy jars, still half full, with labels like 'Ol. origami' and 'Tinc. camphor'. The excellent Mr Cherrington was still selling some of the things that have vanished from the shelves of the chain chemists, such as real sponges from the seabed, those spouted china cups for feeding invalids with beef tea, and 'Dr Nelson's improved inhaler'.

Newark's vast Market Square is undoubtedly the richest I encountered on my journey. Its town hall is everything that a town hall should be – portico above steps, arches above portico, balcony above arches, columns above balcony, and pediment over all – with Justice teetering on top, scales crooked, sword bent, but still loyally supported by a mangy lion and unicorn. Down the next side of the square are a stone colonnade and two former posting inns from the time of Edward III, one with rows of carved angels on its façade. I bought pasties at the Olde Pie Shop for a picnic by the town weir below the church. Beyond the shop an arcade leads to Stodman Street and the house where Prince Rupert, the Royalist leader, stayed in 1645 after his defeat at Marston Moor.

The shops were selling seasonable muffins, chestnuts and cobs, and fireworks (only three days to Guy Fawkes Day). I was sorry I had not turned up on a Wednesday, when there is not only a food market but a cattle market, too, and an auction on Beast Market Hill. However, the quaint backstreets of the town are entertainment enough for so brief a visit.

And, of course, I took a quick walk round the magnificent church, started in 1160. More roof angels (painted and with wide-spread wings gilded), medieval stained glass, a huge brass to a 14th-century merchant, and throughout a feeling of loftiness and light. There is a colourful and poetic monument to John Johnson, twice mayor of the 'loyal and unanimous' corporation of Newark, who died in 1659. It begins:

> Noe gawdy tryumph nor a flattring verse
> Can gild his fame or add unto his herse . . .

and then goes on with a considerable length of 'flattering verse' surrounded by much gilding. Where medieval epitaphs pray for the soul of the departed in the next world, later ones vaunt his or her achievements in this one.

The church has a chantry chapel endowed by a wealthy parishoner in order that masses might be said for his soul in perpetuity. Thomas Mering bequeathed for this purpose 'all my clipped wole and all my floke of shepe'. Another memorial, to Anne Markham (1661), shows the lady with all her seven children in miniature. Like many churches in the area, this one suffered from Cromwell's campaigns. Newark's spire, 240 feet of it, is said to have been built high in an attempt to outdo Grantham's, but in this it fails, for the Grantham spire is taller by over 30 feet.

Newark to Grantham

The countryside continues to be rather flat with heavy clay soil. Warm red brick predominates in the villages, well set off by white-framed windows with leaded panes and porches of white trellis, like a red dress with snowy collar and cuffs. The names of some houses, recently refurbished, show how village communities are shifting and the old order changing – names like 'The Old Vicarage', 'The Old Smithy', 'The Old Schoolhouse' and even 'The Old Post Office'. One fine manorial-looking house has decorative gables in the Dutch style, a reminder of the many links between the Netherlands and Lincolnshire, the southern part of which was once called 'Holland'. Of two alternative routes, the more interesting is the one involving a change at Long Bennington – an attractive village, named for the unusual length of its main street.

This part of England has always been celebrated for its geese (the first fowl ever to be domesticated), a flock of which grazed oblivious to the fact that this is the time of year when roast goose appears on the table and goose fairs used to be held – the Nottingham and Stamford ones were famous. The weather around Martinmas (11 November) is often fine, and this year was no exception. Called in Germany 'old wives' summer' and in England 'goose summer', this is the time when one may sometimes see gossamer (from 'goose summer') in the fields. It comes from a species of small spider which spins threads that may fly through the air and then fall to ground, where dew can condense on them.

Innumerable old sayings foretell that a fine autumn like this one, with many berries and leaves still on most trees, will bring a hard winter. (And it did!)

Grantham

The bus rides in along a road lined with Georgian houses raised up on a bank, as so many are in Bath. It passes 'the oldest hostelry in Britain' (the limestone 13th-century Angel, with a weatherbeaten angel carved in a doorpost). Originally a hostel of the Knights Templar, it was visited by Edward III, housed King John's court for a while, and was the place where Richard III first learned that his friend the Duke of Buckingham was leading a revolt against him and then signed an order for the execution of 'him that had most cause to be true, the most untrue creature living'.

Grantham may pre-date the Romans, but little is known of its far past. It was the scene of Cromwell's first notable victory in the Civil Wars when in 1643, although outnumbered, he defeated 24 troops of the king's force, doing much damage to the town and the church. Sir Isaac Newton attended the grammar school which still stands beside the church. With the coming of the railway age Grantham lost its previous importance as a coaching centre, and now even the motorway bypasses it, which makes it a pleasant town to visit.

Close by the bus station and hidden away above the public library is the town's museum – small but excellent, for it has been well designed and lighted. Its exhibits are mainly of local life from the earliest time onwards. The night watchman's rattle and the town crier's bell share a case with one of the splendidly decorated truncheons issued during the General Strike of 1926 to special constables enrolled to help the police keep order. There is an interesting set of bronze weights (trons) with the town arms on them, used by the tronator – an official who checked the weight of wool brought to market. Cutters for making quill pens, candle snuffers, silk winders, goffering mangles for ruffs, pocket pistols and irons heated by the insertion of a glowing coal – these 'unconsidered trifles' together build up a picture of home life long ago. The case devoted to Newton starts with a sundial which he cut in stone at the age of nine, and ends with a model of an Apollo Saturn V rocket and a commentary relating the conquest of space to Newton's theories.

One of Grantham's famous pubs is not a spacious coaching inn, but a modest little place called the Beehive; its sole claim to fame is its sign, an actual beehive in a tree outside. A verse reads:

> Stop, traveller, this wond'rous sign explore.
> And say, when thou hast viewed it o'er and o'er,
> Grantham, now two rarities are thine.
> A lofty steeple and a living sign.

The road where it stands leads on to 14th-century Grantham House, now a well-furnished National Trust property only occasionally open to the public (but the garden deserves a glimpse at any time), and to the church. If the verger can be found to open it, its ancient library of chained books is worth exploring. It dates back to Tudor times when books were too valuable to be left accessible to thieves. Building of the church began in the reign of Henry II, and probably its magnificence is due to the fact that the masons who built Salisbury Cathedral worked here too. It was not completed for nearly 300 years, and St Wulfram's is now a mixture of Norman, Perpendicular and Decorated styles of architecture. It is one of the most richly ornate churches in this area.

This is a church of angels: up in the roof of the choir (blue and gold), on the reredos behind the altar, on the organ, and on the cusps of tomb arches – but these last have had their heads hacked off by Cromwell's men. There is some fine modern stained glass in this church and a marvellous font cover with a carved spire that reaches almost to the roof of the church. By the font lies an unusual register of baptisms – every page has a country flower hand-painted on the vellum, with old-fashioned names like fumitory, enchanter's nightshade or codlins-and-cream. Curious and sometimes grotesque little stone heads peer at you from every corbel.

There is much more to Grantham – the George Inn where Dickens had Nicholas Nickleby stay on his way to Dotheboys Hall, the ancient market cross, the town conduit built in Elizabeth I's reign and still providing fresh spring water, and many quaint backstreets. Margaret Thatcher's birthplace, a grocer's shop, is now a restaurant. A pleasant spot to end a visit is Catlins – a grocery that smells as few do now of freshly roasted coffee, cheese and ham, with a panelled tea-room above in which hot buttered toast or a featherlight cream cake and a pot of tea will still leave you change from 50p. A Cromwellian sword was found under a floor there during recent renovations.

Grantham to Stamford

'Coming with me, luv?' enquired the driver as he saw me hovering uncertainly at the bus station. The bus on this stretch of the journey was an express (virtually a coach), luxuriously comfortable by comparison with the local buses, and dearer.

The trees were almost bare on this windswept road, silhouetted against a mother-of-pearl sunset. There were only four of us in the warm cocoon of the bus, and chat sped the journey along until I left the bus to search for a bed for my third and last night on the road.

Stamford

'Here you die young if you die before 80, it's so sleepy,' said Miss Mason as she served my dinner at the White Heather café later that evening. She was a fount of enthusiastic information about this unique town. Sleepy it may be, but its attractions were lively enough to keep me walking until well after dark, and I was up early next day to explore it further. Stamford really needs a whole day to itself.

It is an ancient town of stone on the River Welland (Stamford derives its name from 'stone ford'), a town of alleyways, arches, steep steps and many spires, crypts and cellars. Much of its creamy limestone came from the nearby Ketton quarry. Like so many other towns in the east of England, it has seen war after war. Boadicea pursued the fleeing Ninth Legion of the Romans across the ford in 61AD, the marauding Scots attacked it in Saxon times, and the Vikings from Denmark ravaged it in the 9th century as they did so many towns on that side of England. In 1460 the Lancastrians stormed it during the Wars of the Roses, and it knew the upheavals of the Civil Wars. But later it was spared an even more disruptive effect than war – a proposed railway junction – and so one can still see this town very much as it must have been in medieval and Tudor times, particularly now that the A1 bypasses it.

The stone town owes its character to the fact that it is surrounded by quarries in the belt of limestone that stretches diagonally across England from south Yorkshire to the Cotswolds. Once its square mile was enclosed by defensive walls (one bastion still remains, in West Street), within which flourished a dozen monasteries or friaries and 14 churches, six of which are still there (but mostly kept locked up). Over 600 houses, ranging from one to four hundred years old, are officially listed as being of historic importance. Stamford has always been a prosperous town and was famous for its cloth (prominent at Henry VIII's meeting with Francis I on the Field of the Cloth of Gold in 1520). Even after the blow of Henry's dissolution of the wealthy monasteries, the town recovered and grew rich again on the wool trade. Much of this money went to pay the Tudor masons and wood carvers whose work still makes Stamford so beautiful.

The houses tucked away on Barn Hill (off Red Lion Square) are mainly of a later period, however: fine examples of Queen Anne and Georgian architecture. I walked up it at dusk and by lamplight read a plaque describing how in 1646 Charles I spent one of his last free nights in hiding there, fleeing next morning disguised as a servant. Two days later he was betrayed and taken into the captivity that was to end with his beheading. The lane winds round to Scotgate, on the opposite side of which almshouses are hidden away around a peaceful courtyard. Further along is a disused brewery in which an interesting museum has been set up (morning tours around it end with a beer tasting).

At the other corner of Red Lion Square the High Street, now a pedestrian way, is full of buildings with character and side passages over which upper storeys almost touch, virtually shutting out any glimpse of the sky. A left turn leads to Broad Street, wide as its name suggests, and lined with houses that have the handsome porches and fine bay windows typical of Georgian times. Behind their dignified fronts are now conducted the mysteries of Chinese take-aways and hairdressers, surveyors and solicitors.

Brown's Hospital, comprising 15th-century almshouses and a chapel with exceptional stained glass, carried on its door a 'Visitors welcome – please ring' notice, but as no one answered my ring I wandered in the gloaming through cloisters where the scent of roses drifted heavily on the humid evening air.

Next morning, in bright sunshine, the shops in St Mary's Street were opening up: Kelham's, a bow-fronted grocery selling green gunpowder tea, ham on the bone and Spring's Lincolnshire mincemeat; Battels, for pottery and dolls made from the disused wooden bobbins of an old woollen mill; Lamb the ironmonger, whose shop front is adorned by five gold cherubs with garlands which were sadly in need of a lick of the paint he sells. Many of the women with empty shopping baskets were heading further along, however, to join the queue at the early Georgian Assembly Rooms (now an arts centre with a chandeliered ballroom) where the Women's Institute opens its doors at 9 am for its weekly market of home-made cakes and jam, home-grown herbs and fruit.

Next door, carpenters were at work in the old theatre, which was about to throw off a century of silence and dust. This little gem is one of England's oldest provincial theatres, built for £800 in 1768 so that touring actors should no longer have to perform in inns or stables. Macready, Kean, Kemble and Mrs Siddons all played there – and so did acrobats and can-can dancers. Sometimes charity performances were staged: one was to benefit soldiers disabled at the battle of Waterloo, another was for cotton-mill workers made unemployed when the American Civil War cut off supplies of cotton in 1863. After 1871 the theatre fell on hard times, its fittings were stripped and it was eventually reduced to taking in dog shows, bazaars and a disco. By the time the Duchess of Gloucester reopened the 170-seat theatre, much of its original elegance had been restored – and perhaps its reputed ghost will tread the boards once more.

South of the river, in the district of St Martins, stands the famous George coaching inn with its gallows sign – a beam stretching right across the Georgian High Street (at one time this was a common device, but few are left). The George is a place of ingle-nooks and underground passages. At the back is a cobbled garden, bright with hanging baskets of geraniums and fuchsias, that is lamp-lit at night. Once pilgrims walked there, for it is on the site of the 'House of the Holy Sepulchre', a Norman hostel for those on their way to the Holy Land. The sunken lawn was once a carp pool providing Friday fish. The present building goes back to Tudor times. In its heyday as a posting inn, 40 coaches would daily come and go through its courtyard on their way to York or London. Highwaymen, kings, Sir Walter Scott and the Duke of Cumberland, fresh from his victory at Culloden in 1746, were among its visitors.

A portrait of another famous customer, Daniel Lambert, hangs in the hall: he weighed 52 stone when he died in 1809. You can still eat well at the George.

St Johns Lane is a mere crack between houses. It leads down to the riverside, where there were pretty paved gardens behind the Olde Barn restaurant, and the little 'gothick' Bath House (now someone's home). Further along stands what was once a watermill owned by the Crown, now imaginatively restored as a day school for mentally handicapped children. Sacks of flour can still be seen in Kings Mill Lane and, through an open door, I saw a baker hard at work.

Stamford to Corby

The two-decker bus climbs up High Street St Martins, turns a corner and suddenly one is in the countryside and the next county without any suburban or industrial sprawl. Gentle hills, stone farms, ancient oaks and a crocketted church tower – the view must be the same as in coaching days. Then, as we passed through a succession of pretty limestone villages, the 20th century showed itself again in a mobile shop, from which a woman was choosing her weekend joint, and a plane landing at the RAF base at Wittering.

The branches of oak trees lashed the roof with a quick, sharp crack and the road switchbacked up and down all the way. The winter sun, low in the sky, emphasized the textures of hay, thatch and stone walls. Thatched roofs become more common as one nears the reedy Fen country, some having decorative scallops along the ridge of the roof and all wearing wire hairnets these days to keep out birds (or beasts: rats, too, appreciate a cosy bit of thatch). Reeds are also sometimes brought from Scotland, or the straw from wheat is used. Thatch over 15 inches thick not only keeps homes warm but should last nearly a century (it needs to, since re-thatching can cost thousands of pounds). Thatching was a dying craft until newcomers who could afford to pay for it began buying up derelict country cottages.

In these parts, hay is now mechanically gathered up in the shape of a giant toilet roll rather than in brick-like bales. Sheep, cows and pigs lay dozing in the fields, and swans idled amongst the reeds.

The soil in this region is chocolate brown, sometimes almost black. Right across a newly-sown field a farmer had stretched wires between trees and strung up multi-coloured plastic sacks as a latter-day 'scarecrow' that gave the field a circus gaiety. Outside one village near Corby a real circus was setting up. Travelling entertainers were once part of the great fairs held on certain saints' days, when goods were brought from far afield and, even in fairly recent times, labourers would line up hoping to be chosen for hire by local farmers.

Many of the cottages have decoratively fretted bargeboards under the eaves or at their porches. Their demure lattice windows and the neat rows of leeks and cabbages in their gardens give them a storybook air – this could be Hansel-and-Gretel country (even the bricks are marzipan colour, and the white paint is like icing). But before long a view of factory chimneys announces the presence of Weldon. Its main street has a terrace of mean Edwardian houses, whose builder's sole effort to give them individuality was the casting in concrete of such hopelessly inappropriate names as 'Myrtle Cottage', 'Woodbine Cottage', 'Hawthorn Cottage' and the like (memorial slabs to the wildflowers which once were there, perhaps). At Weldon, stone has been quarried for centuries.

But, Weldon apart, the longish ride from Stamford was one of the prettiest on my route, and I shared the feeling of the stout woman who heaved herself off at Corby saying to the driver, 'Thank you for a beautiful ride! I enjoyed that – it were *luvly*.'

Corby to Kettering

'The manufactures I take to be as well worth a traveller's notice,' said Defoe, 'as the most curious thing he can meet.' Up to 1980, no traveller could fail to notice Corby's main manufacture, for the steelworks outside it stretched for miles and the air smelt of sulphur. In fact, even in Roman times Corby had iron works, which were later mentioned in Domesday Book. Now all gone, and in the place of steel are electronics and packaging firms, toolmaking and food factories. But Corby itself is a shiny new town of concrete, Snowcem and Marley tiles. Its shopping centre has escalators, and its houses are like those ideal homes you see in television commercials. It is bright and breezy with lots of open space and municipal lawns mown smooth as billiard cloth.

North has now imperceptibly changed to south, or nearly so – along the main street comes a London-type taxi with its 'for hire' light on. It's only a short way to Kettering, past the interesting new children's centre at Rockingham Dene. Roca's *ing* (family) had their *ham* (village) here in Saxon times. Next to this is the boot trade's research association, for this is Northamptonshire, the shoe industry's prosperous stronghold. You won't see many down-at-heel feet getting on and off the buses here.

Kettering

On this visit Kettering let me down. The art gallery was closed for repairs. The Tourist Centre was closed for the season. The library had no information to hand out about the town. The ancient church had an impressive exterior, but was stark inside. Its high tower houses an outstanding peal of bells (a full ten of them, which is rare, the earliest dating from Charles I's reign), but they were silent on the day I turned up. One of the bells had recently cracked, and until over £5,000 could be raised for recasting it the full peal would stay silent.

I looked among the market stalls for some local produce to take as a picnic among the pansies in the art gallery gardens, but found only Leicestershire cheese and prawns from Thailand. Feather cornice-brushes, mugs with the Muppets on them, plastic ones with names of football clubs: these are the kind of trivia which have replaced the cheap ribbons and laces that first gave us the word 'tawdry' from 'St Audrey', on whose feast days were held fairs with cheap trifles for sale.

Kettering to Bedford

A rattlebones of a bus trundled me through an area of marshes and trickling brooks. Gipsies (or more likely, just ordinary 'totters' and not the true Romanies of Indian origin) were camping in deluxe motor caravans by the wayside – all white paint and chromium without, frilly curtains and plastic knick-knacks within. Higham Ferrers has a pleasant square and a long street of stone houses, but there is little else of interest until Rushden.

There I broke my journey to look at the unique strainer arch in the church that stands high above the rooftops. The lacy carving of this unusual arch across the nave looks too delicate to be anything but ornamental, yet on its strength depends the entire structure. Without it, the 600-year-old spire and all the church would crash in ruins. It was inserted in 1370 when the pillars in the nave started to give way.

The church has much else of interest, too: an angel roof, a rare Wyclif pulpit, a newly restored and repainted Elizabethan monument, medieval glass and ancient heads carved in stone both inside and outside the church. The most elegant lettering I have seen was on two 18th-century memorial tablets outside the eastern wall of the church, the words and decorations delicately incised in the slate by a mason who was as much artist as craftsman. They are so obscurely placed that few but the chirruping sparrows are likely to see them.

Though the land from here on is so flat that any small mound seems like a hill, the bus twists and turns along lanes where trees meet overhead in a mingling of green, gold and russet. Sharnbrook is a village of whitewash and thatch but there was little else to see until, gathering speed on the main road and with the wind whistling by us, we approached Bedford.

Bedford

This is John Bunyan's town – remember Kipling's poem 'A tinker out of Bedford . . .'? Plaques mark where he was baptized (in a stream), tried, imprisoned for 12 years and where 300 years ago he wrote *Pilgrim's Progress.* Sculptures of scenes from that book are on the walls of the library and the base of his statue. But most interesting of all are the Bunyan church and museum. The latter contains, among much else, editions of *Pilgrim's Progress* in 200 languages, the portable anvil he carried everywhere, a violin he made in metal and a flute made from the leg of a stool in his prison. The church doors are particularly fine with scenes from the book cast in bronze. Usually nonconformist chapels are plain, even ugly, but not this one.

Having visited the Bunyan museum and church earlier in the year, I decided to concentrate on other things this time. Behind shops near the bus station is the new Harpur Centre, built on the site of an old school. The splendid 1804 'gothick' façade has been carefully retained on one of its sides. The core of this new shopping centre (designed by Frederick Gibberd) is a brick walk spiralling gently down from one level to another – not only an imaginative architectural feature, but kinder to toddlers and the elderly than a staircase would have been. Leaving by the Harpur Street exit (still flanked by splendid scarlet, gold and black Victorian lamp posts) one soon comes to the church and, on Wednesdays, a ploughman's lunch in the vestry if you are so inclined. Here is another magnificent angel roof, carved screen and misericords dating from the time of Agincourt; an unusual brass showing a knight wearing both armour and mayoral robes; and a very early stone pulpit from which Wesley once preached. Brasses came in between the 13th and 15th centuries to replace the great tombs with stone effigies that took up so much space. Britain has some 4,000 brasses, ten times more than the rest of Europe. Inconspicuously lodged in the south porch is a sad little gravestone of someone of no importance: Patience, the wife of a publican, who died aged only 37 when George I was king. During her brief life she bore 25 children, and the last childbirth killed her.

The church and path lead towards the river, its embankment gracefully balustraded with stone pillars where once there were wharves for the shipping of corn to Holland. The River Ouse is always busy with swans and in the distance a white iron footbridge springs in a delicate arch across the water. Along the embankment is the local museum (a hotchpotch of toys, horse-drawn fire engine, pots, an Egyptian mummy and old prams), but it is best to keep as much time as possible for Bedford's least publicized treasure-house – the Cecil Higgins Art Gallery, a few yards further along, near the fountain and scented garden for the blind.

Mr Higgins, a local brewer, was a man of taste as well as wealth. At his death in 1949 he bequeathed to Bedford his exceptional collections – of watercolours and prints, glass, porcelain, lace and *art nouveau* furniture. Not only are the contents superb but so is their setting, a purpose-built gallery, which is itself a delight to the eye and with perfect lighting. Downstairs are pictures by Constable, Blake, Fuseli, Turner, Rouault, Cézanne, Dégas and Renoir – how many other provincial towns can muster such an artistic roll as this? Upstairs are the glass and china with, at the far end, the surprise of a lily-pool over which a life-sized Chelsea swan seemingly floats, together with Meissen ducks, on a rosewood raft. Mr Higgins used to serve his guests soup from this virtually priceless swan tureen, and it must have reminded him of the herd of swans on the Ouse which are such an inseparable part of the Bedford scene. Swans, once valued for their meat, used to be under royal control, and special swan courts dealt with anybody who kept or killed one without a licence. Beaks were marked to indicate ownership. (The Crown still exercises such rights on the River Thames.)

And so to London

The sky was like clotting cream as I boarded my last bus. We were soon through Bedford's industrial outskirts where the tall chimneys of the brickfields loom over claypits drowned in stagnant grey. The few trees were already bare of leaves.

This part of the world was one of the earliest brick-making areas in England, partly because the technique was learnt from Holland and partly because clay for brick-making was here in abundance. In Tudor times bricks were used only for important buildings, but the demand for fire-resistant homes grew after the Great Fire of London (1666) and accelerated as supplies of timber began to run out in the 18th century. When the railways came, bricks began to be distributed even to the parts of Britain that had formerly used stone. Their widespread use in lieu of timber and stone was deplored then just as we now deplore the ousting of bricks by concrete.

I had been impressed by the skill of the drivers in Bedford's big bus station on a Friday at rush hour, each slotting his big craft into the right bay at exactly the right angle while a dozen others were coming or going at the same time. The company liveries varied – green, white or red – and some of the buses were double-deckers, some singles. There are clean buses and dirty buses, smooth ones and boneshakers, some with well-upholstered seats and others with utilitarian plastic-and-metal. Drivers come silent or chatty, spruce or grubby, young or old, but I had not encountered a single sour one (unlike some in London, where traffic conditions make bus driving an ulcer-ridden occupation).

Despite the hour, even this bus to London had only a handful of passengers – as always, mostly women shoppers. The darker the haze outside, the cosier the bus seemed. A long string of tiny streetlights defined a distant horizon as passengers got on at Houghton, well-muffled up against an English November night.

At Ampthill we were held up by the only traffic jam of my entire journey (and we were late arriving, also for the first time). The bus had to mount a kerb in a narrow street in order to get through what was once a tranquil centre of lace-making and millinery. The engine panted and hummed. Vast lorries laden with bricks strained their way through. How Ampthill's little Georgian houses must be shaken (and their occupants' nerves, too).

Night blanked out the rest of the journey until London, when it was at last time to alight: *four days (17 hours on the road), 300 miles covered in 22 buses, 17 towns visited and 11 counties, and 13 rivers crossed since I left the lonely spaces of Hadrian's Roman Wall.*

Looking back

A journey like this – cutting one lean slice down the length of England – brings home the tremendous variety the English scene can offer within a single trip, even though my journey was down one side of the country only and through the less spectacular lowlands. But it is a part of England particularly rich in villages, old spires, markets, coaching inns, limestone buildings and traces of historic events from the Romans to the Industrial Revolution.

In the north there is stone everywhere, for bridges as well as houses. In the south, where rocky moorlands give way to woodlands, timber is more in evidence and black-and-white timbered houses begin to predominate.

The roads themselves are full of diversity. The coach routes, often going over lengths of Roman roads, contrast with those twisting lanes which – apart from the Celtic ridgeways across the hills, going from one Iron Age hill fort to another – are probably among the oldest roads, made by the Saxons. Zigzags often indicate that once the lane turned and turned again in order to go round the edge of an old bog or outsize oak long departed, or round some field that was hedged in a thousand years ago. Exceptionally narrow lanes usually pre-date wagons or coaches and so may go back before Tudor times when goods were normally carried by packhorse (low parapets on small bridges also date from those days, to accommodate the packs that bulged over on either side of the horse). Straighter, wider roads between village and village, with broad grass verges, are likely to have been laid out in the 18th century as part of the general reorganization when the common lands were enclosed. Now some of the scenery has changed yet again as farming, building and road-making methods have changed. There are many losses, but they are few when measured against the whole beauty of England, still to be found not far off the beaten track, where the little buses go.

Note: As mentioned, I deliberately avoid most big cities. However, it is possible to do this journey slightly differently in order to take in famous historic centres. There is a leaflet called 'East of England Heritage Route' which details a six-cathedral trail (Durham – York – Lincoln – Peterborough – Ely – Norwich), available from the East Midlands Tourist Board (see page xx).

2

Scenic Splendour

Worcester – Kidderminster – Bridgnorth – Much Wenlock – Shrewsbury

It took a bit of slow huffing and puffing one midsummer day, for the bus to edge through the brick-and-privet suburbs of Worcester, past Barbourne Park and out to where fields of vegetables stretched towards a horizon of sharp-peaked hills. There were occasional black-and-white farmhouses in the middle distance, ponds green with weed, and 'pick your own' fields where stout, pink-faced ladies bent double to gather their strawberries. The road curved its way through the hills, sometimes hemmed in by tall hedges that brushed the bus windows, or powdered with a shower of blossom falling from tall trees. Here and there the earth showed reddish – almost the colour of carrot soup.

Kidderminster is not a town that aims to please: its outskirts are a squalid jostle of carpet factories and car parks, with no attempt at orderly layout or screening from view. There are canyon-like streets between grimy brick factories of Victorian vintage, and gasometers. (A firm of estate agents is named Doolittle and Dalley: now *there's* honesty in advertising!)

The scenery improved after that – marguerites crowding the verges, bright green bracken spreading up the hillsides. Sometimes the view was shut off as we went through deep cuttings in the hills, and then suddenly a vast panorama would spring into sight. The summer grass was so tall that lambs lay half-hidden in it, little black heads raised in curiosity to watch us speed by. Black hens scratched in a dusty farmyard, cows sought the shade under spreading oaks. A number of inns round here are called the Royal Oak, for this is Civil War country where the story of Charles' hiding-place in an oak tree is still retold.

Our road twisted and turned, swaying the passengers in the

coach. The remaining stretch of the journey has some of the most beautiful scenery of any routes described in this book, and with great variety. We passed a lake in a valley, Dudmaston (a National Trust property), a pine forest, the calm and shining River Severn, red sandstone cliffs by the road and then the old town of Bridgnorth.

This is one of England's two-level towns – the upper half is perched on a clifftop, with a cliff-side railway to lower foot-passengers to the part below. We entered Bridgnorth through the low town. It was a squeeze to get in past the terraced cottages, lopsided little black-and-white houses, small antique shops and medieval inns, all crammed together – with inn signs and hanging flower baskets adding colourful touches to the scene. We crossed the river, where boys were fishing from grassy banks, in order to make our way to the upper (Georgian) town along a road of serpentine bends. In the red cliffs were doors where cellars had been gouged out. Colourful vetch and clover sprawled by the wayside, garden roses and mock orange blossom scented the warm air as we reached the top.

Out among the fields, a light breeze riffled through the wheat, giving it the appearance of shot silk; and the far hills, half lost in a haze of heat, seemed like a pile of soft blue pillows. There were villages of sandstone houses, occasional magnificent gateways or glimpses of stately homes, and always, beyond the lush grass or the fields of grain, a vast unspoilt landscape spreading over hundreds of acres – a succession of views of incomparable beauty, for mile after mile.

We were high up, among big fields already turning to a ripe gold, bordered by beech hedges or others where briar roses rambled at will. In one field, hundreds of poppies spread in a great scarlet swathe through a field of wheat. In another, two farm labourers – mahogany faces shining with sweat – heaved bales of hay into a stack. At Much Wenlock, there were half-timbered houses and dry-stone walls.

Shrewsbury announced itself with a dramatic exclamation mark: a 130-foot column (to the memory of Lord Hill, Wellington's second-in-command at Waterloo), which stands high above the town centre. The bus sped swiftly down from here, passing what is left of the abbey (red stone walls contrasting with green grass) and then across one of the ten bridges that give access to the old town, which stands on what is virtually an island – for Shrewsbury was built within a horseshoe bend of the River Severn, which encircles it almost like a moat.

We swept round the south-east perimeter – following the line of the old town walls. Unlike car drivers, we could see over the top and look down to the lawns and gardens below, and over rooftops. To the right stands a most unusual church, St Chad's: a classical building with a round nave. And then we had arrived – drawing up right in the centre of the town and beside one of its treasures, the huge Tudor mansion, now a museum of local history, known as Rowley's House.

Medieval Market Town

The old town of half-timbered houses and inns is compact, confined to the top of the mound around which the River Severn forms a natural moat (except for the north side, where a Norman castle, largely rebuilt by Edward I, guards the landward approach). This makes it ideal to explore on foot all the alleys, byways and old houses galore which are what, collectively, give Shrewsbury so much character. No grand vistas or towering cathedral here: instead, the town has an intimate character. Its oddly angled streets (with such names as Dogpole, Wyle Cop, Coffeehouse Passage, Shoplatch and Water Lane) still follow the medieval plan – or lack of plan. A street map is essential.

Right in the centre is The Square, a good starting point and, like other Shrewsbury streets, full of hanging flower baskets during summer. The open-pillared Old Market Hall, built in the reign of Elizabeth I and embellished with carved figures, is sometimes still used for its original purpose: when I was there, a 'flea market' was doing a busy trade, well protected from the rain that suddenly poured down. The square is a medley of architectural styles: for example, an early Victorian music hall now houses the Tourist Information Centre, Woolley's House dates from Queen Anne's reign and the Plough Inn is largely Tudor. Banks and shops occupy what were once wool merchants' houses, their half-timbered façades ornate with carved mouldings, warriors and suchlike.

I left the square to make my way up the steep and narrow slit of Grope Lane, the leaden sky scarcely visible between the overhanging upper storeys (no need to explain why this alley got its name). At the top are Bear Steps, with a 14th-century hall now

Bear Steps Hall, Shrewsbury

restored to its former glory, along with an arcade of little shops adjoining it. The Civic Society often have interesting exhibitions here, and there is a café. This was a quiet spot, adjoining the churchyard of St Alkmund, where the loudest sound was the chirping of sparrows and the splash of rain.

Another narrow alley led past Prince Rupert's Hotel (it, too, started life as the mansion of a Tudor cloth merchant) to St Mary's Church, a red sandstone building standing on a green. Its interior is particularly colourful – the rugged stone walls mottled in pale or pinkish colours (the overall effect is pearly) and light entering through the rich and rare Jesse window, as detailed as a tapestry, with over four dozen biblical personages depicted in rows – 14th-century work. The roof is full of carved flowers and fruit. Eight heraldic angels spread their wings wide. Even the tiled floor is colourful. An electric polisher hummed and there was a smell of Brasso in the air as pinafored ladies busied themselves among all this glory. This noble church stands in the district where most of the Tudor cloth merchants lived, and just outside is their Drapers' Hall, a fine example of timber framing in Shrewsbury style – quatrefoils in the main timbers, and cable-like carving.

I walked round the back of the church and past the huge Greek portico of the Royal Salop Infirmary which, founded in 1747, was one of the first public hospitals in Britain, but is now full of luxury flats. From here, Dogpole led downhill, past more black-and-white buildings, the classical Guildhall – cheerful with fuchsias and geraniums, an Italianate tabernacle (now a 'pot shop' which attracts bargain-hunters), the Olde House of herringbone brickwork between timber framing, and many big arches for coaches with views beyond. Dogpole Court was particularly attractive – brick paving, baskets of flowers and shining brass doorknockers.

The narrow alleys which in Plymouth are called 'opes' in Shrewsbury are called 'shuts': now what may *that* suggest about the psychological outlook of their respective inhabitants, I wondered, as I turned up the winding thoroughfare of Wyle Cop (Welsh for hilltop) to look for St Julian's.

This disused church is now a crafts centre, with booths for leatherworkers, jewellers, knitters, enamellers and so on – making and selling their wares in the odour of sanctity. The marble pulpit wore a rakish signboard, 'To the restaurant'.

I had loitered my time away, and had seen only a little of what Shrewsbury has to offer. There was time only to go (via the house where Clive of India lived as Shrewsbury's MP, 1761–74, now a museum with a good china collection) for a stroll in the Quarry Gardens, between the town walls and the river. Percy Thrower used to be in charge here and it was he who, in 1946, designed the colourful flower gardens of The Dingle. Beyond these I found the Shoemakers' Arbour, half hidden by the flowers of a climbing hydrangea, and beyond this some rather charming godwottery of rusticwork. The arbour is the only one to survive out of dozens erected by the various trade guilds of the town.

There was a great deal more that I had barely glimpsed: the Georgian quarter, for instance, as well as many other medieval streets, no fewer than five military museums and the arts centre. But there was only time to slip into the covered market for a punnet of strawberries before running to catch my homeward-bound bus.

3

Shakespeare's England

Oxford – Woodstock – Stratford-upon-Avon – Banbury – Oxford

In summer all the world pounds through Stratford-upon-Avon, and the multi-storey *coach* park is full. But there is nowhere better for a quiet winter or spring break (though even then the accents of America, Japan and Australia can be heard in inglenooks and alleys, and it is wise to book well in advance if you want a seat at the Royal Shakespeare Theatre). In this part of the world they really do know about log fires and hot punch before a roast beef dinner, with deep armchairs to follow.

Oxford

Of my starting point, Oxford, whole books have been written and it is impossible to compress here an account of all that can be seen. If time is limited it is best to make for Carfax in the centre and the nearby Tourist Information Centre to get their free map, which has a two-hour walk marked on it. This includes over a dozen colleges and also one of my favourite places (even in winter), the 17th-century Botanic Gardens by the river.

Shakespeare must have known Oxford and its inns well. The 13th-century tower in Carfax is a relic of the church where he stood godfather to the child of an innkeeper (the inn is now hidden behind an 18th-century frontage at 3 Cornmarket).

The bus to Woodstock goes out past the Ashmolean Museum, classically elegant with urns and wreaths, cornices and Ionic columns, in a combination of cream and white stones; along wide St Giles; past the Radcliffe Infirmary, sedate Victorian houses and immaculate cricket fields; and so out into the countryside.

Woodstock

Woodstock is often overlooked by motorists, for its interesting buildings and cobbled ways lie off the main road. It is a small town of very old houses that were 'modernized' with new façades in early Georgian times. Bay windows, shops, porches with lanterns, white shutters and iron-studded front doors are characteristic of the place. So are the roof tiles of local stone, their sizes skilfully graduated down each roof from small to large. Once off that main road, the quiet is very noticeable. Woodstock is memorable, too, for its stocks with *five* (!) leg holes; and for glovemaking. I sought out the glove-maker's premises off Chaucers Lane (Chaucer's son lived in the house on the corner), down which there are glimpses of a walled garden and a flight of old stone steps. I chose a pair of hand-made kid gloves at 'half the price of London shops, my love', as I was credibly assured.

The Bear is an old coaching inn where bear-baiting used to take place. There has been an inn on the site since at least 1232, but 'inn' is now a misnomer for a hotel that is world famous. Stone, tapestries and pewter give the restaurant its special character; such traditional food as roast sucking-pig and jugged hare are served. Woodstock is full of historic buildings offering good food (and the local beer of Hook Norton); there is also the Terrace Restaurant of Blenheim Palace itself, close to the famous fountains. Woodstock has a particularly good museum of rural life in a house which is itself a museum-piece (and which has a coffee lounge). Sometimes there are craft demonstrations.

Woodstock is overshadowed by its most famous home, Blenheim Palace, a showy masterpiece designed by Vanbrugh and enriched with painted ceilings, carved woodwork and other embellishments that took 70 years to complete. It was started as a gift from the nation to the Duke of Marlborough after his victory over Louis XIV at Blenheim in 1704. Winston Churchill was born in one of its rooms (and is buried in the nearby village of Bladon). The palace is surrounded by a park designed by Capability Brown – he dammed a river to create its lake (everything about Blenheim is on a grandiose scale).

I prefer the grounds to the palace, with all its pomp and glory. One first sees the swirling shape of the lake in its valley, blue as the sky above, with a view over the trees of the 120-foot column bearing a statue of Marlborough. On the other side of the palace is a formal French garden smelling of box hedges, with a fountain splashing. There is a traditional knot garden, huge gilded dolphins in a pool (the sunlight reflected onto them by the water was dazzling), topiary birds and beasts, sweeping lawns, and shrubberies where the only sound is the plop of a fir cone or the scuffle of a pheasant in the undergrowth. The park was deserted when I was there, with not a duke in sight.

The same bus service continues through autumn scenery that glows with the metallic colours of copper beeches and oak leaves turning gold, on the edge of the Cotswolds. Chipping Norton, where tweeds are still woven, has an old Guildhall, 18th-century houses and earlier almshouses. 'Chipping' means market, and the market place is in the heart of the town (now full of antique shops, too). The road is dotted with charming villages built from local stone, many on the banks of the winding River Stour. Along the ridge between Shipston ('sheep's town') and Chipping Norton are flocks of grazing sheep which make it obvious why this is rich wool country. Gradually they give way to cattle and mixed farming.

Stratford-upon-Avon

Out of season, Stratford-upon-Avon can really be appreciated. It shows itself to be beautiful and spacious – a market town that is the essence of what the whole world regards as 'typically English'. That so many superb timbered houses have survived for four centuries is due in part to a timely decline in Stratford's fortunes when other places were busy tearing down and rebuilding themselves. Stratford had to make do with what it already had, and thus many buildings are still as Shakespeare knew them. They have survived not merely the passing of time but, in many cases, the tramp of a quarter of a million pairs of feet a year (and the vibration of traffic to match). At Shakespeare's birthplace a section of wall has been exposed to show its simple wattle-and-daub construction between the great timbers. Will modern materials last as long?

Shakespeare's father was a merchant and alderman, and the house where he was born was naturally a fine one. So were his own house, New Place (which he bought in 1597, dying there in 1616), and his daughter's home, Hall Croft (she married a Dr Hall). This last is one of the most interesting yet least visited of the Shakespeare properties. All are open to the public in winter (not all of them on Sundays), though little is left of New Place. Their gardens are beautiful, even in winter. The birthplace garden has been planted with flowers and trees mentioned in Shakespeare's works, and quinces hung like yellow lanterns on the wintry branches (see *Romeo and Juliet*!).

Stratford Youth Hostel

Even if Shakespeare had never lived there, Stratford would attract visitors to its lovely streets, the banks of the Avon, Clopton Bridge (with its 14 arches built in the 15th century), the lanes of little shops and its ancient inns full of dark beams, inlaid or carved panelling and log fires. In the comfortable lounge of the Black Swan a big wall painting has been uncovered telling the story of Tobias and the Angel.

Traditionally painted with castles and roses, the canal boats waited for next season in the waters by the Shakespeare memorial garden, where ducks and swans gather; further along the river, past the famous theatre, is Holy Trinity Church with Shakespeare's grave. At that time of year, with the sun low in the sky, long shadows were cast by the leaning tombstones and the tall yews.

It is impossible to describe all that makes one day in Stratford far too brief a visit. And when the town has been explored, there are still the nearby villages to which buses go – particularly Shottery, with the picturesque thatched farmhouse where Shakespeare's wife, Anne Hathaway, grew up, and other lovely houses further along the road.

IMPROVING BUS SERVICES

How you can help: see page 215

4

Buses for Bookworms

The Cotswolds

Cheltenham – Painswick – Stroud – Cirencester – Chedworth – Northleach – Burford

Some people's idea of a good day out is to spend it browsing in one bookshop after another – the kind of place where bookish dust has not been too vigorously brushed away and there is a faint aroma of old paper and even older leather. The books are usually crammed from ceiling to floor or even stacked on the ground, and the owner may live like a mole in the dim rear of the shop, half-hidden behind precarious piles of volumes. No one seems to mind too much if after an hour's gentle grazing in literary pastures you spend a pound or less – possibly getting, for a fraction of its original cost, a well-illustrated and well-bound book printed on good paper with wide margins.

This harmless activity can be pursued in many parts of England and, as pleasant bookshops and pleasant surroundings often go together, it is an easy matter to combine book-hunting with bus

riding for pleasure. Planning a route is helped by lists obtainable from the Antiquarian Booksellers Association (26 Charing Cross Road, London WC2; 01–379 3041) and the Provincial Booksellers' Fairs Association (Box 66, Cambridge; 0223 240921). Say which county interests you and they will send a leaflet listing a few dozen bookshops within it, giving their addresses, opening hours and what kind of books they stock. The latter also issues a calendar of book fairs. After that it is a fairly simple matter to look on the map of bus routes to see which ones you can reach in a day's ride. One warning, however. I have found that booksellers are wayward and don't always open at the hours printed in these leaflets.

I chose the Cotswolds for a bus tour covering six towns with very pleasant rides in between. I started by staying for one night at Cheltenham, then moving on to Cirencester, with a 'budget' weekend in Burford. The rolling hills, houses of honey-coloured stone, sparkling rivers and churches of immense grandeur make the whole region a place of outstanding beauty no matter what the season.

Cheltenham

Cheltenham was built for pleasure in the 18th century. A spa where Handel and Dr Samuel Johnson once 'took the waters', its climate is mild and it is a centre for festivals and racing. Above all else, its parks and parades provide a marvellous temptation to while away the time doing nothing in particular. Among the many shops of quality are several booksellers conveniently near one another: Alan Hancox at 101 Montpellier Street, Barrie's at 4 Montpellier Walk and Basement Books at 15 Montpellier Walk. At the other end (49 Clarence Street) is Mr Heynes' shop where there are bargains to be had for as little as one penny, and in between lie shops with new books such as the Promenade Bookshop at 22 The Promenade. If any time is left after this bookish orgy, one can visit the art gallery for its Dutch paintings or (further out, near lovely Pittsville Park) the Gustav Holst museum in the house where the composer was born.

Cheltenham's spine is its great Promenade, running from north to south. I arrived at the coach station near the north end and made my way first to the nearby church and Clarence Street (with museum, art gallery and Heynes' bookshop) before strolling slowly to the south end (with the fascinating Montpellier quarter, more bookshops and Suffolk Square, where I would spend the night). A whole day in Cheltenham is little enough, there is so much to enjoy.

The church, tucked away, has a spectacular rose window 700 years old and interesting memorials, including one to Captain Skillicorne, whose discovery of a mineral spring in 1738 was the beginning of Cheltenham's fame as a spa. The Skillicorne family was still supplying the town with mayors into this century. The peaceful churchyard is famous for its elegant tombstones and quaint epitaphs – especially this one, of 1825:

Here lies John Higgs
A famous man for killing pigs.
For killing pigs was his delight
Both morning, afternoon and night,
Both heats and cold he could endure,
Which no physician could e'er cure;
His knife is laid, his work is done,
I hope to heaven his soul is gone.

The local museum is a good one, with everything attractively displayed and well explained. For instance, a glass case exhibited pots dating from the 15th to 17th century on one side and others by modern craftsmen on the other, showing how the latter are continuing old traditions of shape, decoration or glaze. Upstairs, the ways in which local rocks were formed was clearly demonstrated, with jars of different local soils to compare and an explanation of how these determine the variations in vegetation.

One room is devoted to pieces made by Gimson, a Gloucestershire furniture-maker of renown in the 'thirties. His style was a return to earlier simplicity but with decorative detailing of legs, drawer handles and the like. Another room is full of mementos of Dr Wilson, who died tragically with Scott in the Antarctic. Cheltenham was his home town and his statue (by Scott's widow) stands in the Promenade. It seems to me badly sited – Wilson stares right into a chestnut tree and only the birds can stare back at him.

One could spend a day in Cheltenham simply looking at all the different capitals on its innumerable columns or at the endlessly varied patterns of the wrought-iron balconies. Even the Post Office and the local newspaper's premises look like Greek temples. There are plenty of seats on the wide pavements from which to watch the world go by, and plenty of cafés; the *boulevardiers* give the town a rather continental air. In summer the flowerbeds are bright with begonias and Canterbury bells; around Christmas the great chestnut trees sparkle with lights (their switching on in November is the occasion for a festive procession of choirs, dancers and bands). And the shops! All the temptations of Vanity Fair are displayed there. Cheltenham is the place for antiques and hand-made shoes, oriental rugs and china dolls with straw bonnets, and in the tea-rooms you may order jasmine tea or a cup of hot chocolate with marshmallows.

Yet this is no longer primarily a town of colonels and memsahibs retired from running the empire (the empire is long dead, and most of its colonels, too). In fact there are lots of young people around, for Cheltenham has more than the ordinary quota of colleges.

Nevertheless, change comes slowly and the town still has a distinctive character. Even though such retailers as Habitat, Wallis and Jaeger have forced their own house styles into the Regency Promenade, plenty of mahogany and gilt survives. Such idiosyncratic characters as Mr Sales of the Spa Pharmacy have not allowed modern packages to take over the windows completely. Among the spouted beef-tea cups and old pharmacy jars he displayed some 1880 advertisements for quack remedies, and two staring pairs of glass eyes. Down a backstreet (every Cheltenham backstreet has its surprises) a grocer claiming to specialize in bacon had his wall decorated with a realistic mural of a flitch of bacon: the old chap himself was still busy at the great slicer when I passed by late in the evening ('. . . for killing pigs was his delight; both morning, afternoon and night').

Just off the Promenade is the grand town hall, inside which are great blue pottery urns from which you can help yourself to spa water. It is not chalybeate, as in other English spas, but very alkaline, and it tastes salty.

On the other side of the Promenade Neptune presides over a fountain that draws its water from a river flowing under the road, surrounded by willows grown from cuttings of those that shaded Napoleon's tomb in St Helena.

At the far end of the Promenade I came to Montpellier Walk, famous for its dozens of caryatids – larger than life-size, scantily draped ladies supporting the shops' upper storeys on their heads.

This and the surrounding streets are full of curio shops. After exploring them I sat under a cedar in the gardens opposite to enjoy the scene. The mansard roofs of grey slate slope down to balustrades of creamy stone above façades with large sash windows. This upper storey is hemmed, as it were, with a white band of decorative moulding to separate it from the shop fronts and caryatids at ground level.

The shops were closing. I walked on to find my guest house, passing on the way the Rotunda, now a bank (with dome and anxious-looking lion) and an unusual statue of Edward VII, 'the Peacemaker' – as a plaque at the back calls him – in plus-fours and holding the hand of a barefoot child. Although the Willoughby modestly calls itself a guest-house, its façade – with 30-foot Corinthian columns and a great portico – would not disgrace a 'grand hotel' in lesser towns than Cheltenham.

Next day the bus out of Cheltenham took me through other fine streets such as Bayshill Road (flanked by Cheltenham Ladies College), Montpellier Terrace (pretty little villas) and Bath Road (the impressive buildings of Cheltenham College). Once into the country, the route lay through fields with the Cotswold hills in the distance. Gradually the road wound its way upward, swishing this way and that, the countryside growing lovelier as we went and the views stretching ever further into the distance. We looked down into treetops through which stone chimneys and rooftops occasionally peeped.

The Benedictine abbey of Prinknash lies along this route to Stroud. The monks make pottery for sale, the medieval fishponds have been restocked with trout, and there is a bird park with pheasants, swans and geese.

Painswick

I stopped at Painswick, one of England's loveliest stone villages (its bookshop is in a former inn, the Golden Fleece), with a celebrated churchyard containing 99 skilfully clipped yews standing in ranks, some twinned to form great green arches and all at least 200 years old. Though it is for the yews that this church is most famous, it has a very lovely interior. If one is lucky, the Ancient Society of Painswick Youths may be heard in action. 'Youths' may be a misnomer, but 'Ancient' is true enough: they are the bellringers and their team dates back to 1686 (so do some of the twelve bells, gifts of local cloth merchants whom Cotswold wool made rich). Their record-breaking peal was of 13,001 changes in under nine hours (1920). I imagine that afterwards they headed for the nearby Falcon Inn.

So did I, and I wandered with a glass of local ale to look at the bowling green (laid down in Tudor times), a pretty place with flowerbeds, thatched arbour and old stone walls around it. A coaching inn and one-time centre for cock-fighting, the Falcon also once served as a courthouse.

Painswick is a cobweb of little lanes – Tibbiwell, the Cross, Friday Street – lined with picturesque stone cottages. Its main street has houses of great dignity in the same stone but smoothly dressed, punctuated with well-spaced sash windows and topped with colonnaded parapets. Down by the stream are three mill houses (one was still in use for making hairpins).

The best way to explore Painswick is with the little leaflet with an annotated walk produced by the local Women's Institute. I got a bird's eye view from the top floor of Fiery Beacon, an art gallery whose owner welcomed sightseers.

Stroud

The bus to nearby Stroud continues through the hills to where five valleys meet. The town's narrow streets climb steeply up and down, crowded and bustling. Wool made the town in the beginning, and woollens are still woven there. Alan and Joan Tucker have two shops for new books by the station and five rooms of secondhand ones (in particular they stock modern literature, the arts and wildlife). There is little else of interest in the town: the church is Victorian, the museum very poor, and the old buildings few. But from there it does not take long to get to Cirencester, a busy market town and once the second greatest city of Roman Britain.

The bus passes through the so-called Golden Valley where the old woollen mills still stand, though some are used now for very different purposes from electronics to making corn dollies. In amongst the hills that follow are pretty Cotswold villages such as Sapperton and Daglingworth – the former with a lattice-windowed village school and (unusually) a Queen Anne church, where Stafford Cripps is buried, and the latter with an old circular dovecote of which one gets a glimpse (on the right). This was a journey of great variety and memorable beauty.

Cirencester

The streets of Cirencester have some wool-merchants' tall houses of the 15th century, a weavers' hall and a magnificent church built with the proceeds of the wool trade. It is near this church that Paul Wellar has his shop in Dollar Street, with 70,000 books, new and old, and so do Smallwood & Randall.

The bus enters the town through some of the most interesting of the old streets and draws up by the church – almost like a cathedral in its grandeur. To the original church the great tower was added in 1415 (it houses the oldest peal of bells in the world). A lifetime later the enormous porch went up, and it did duty as a town hall with meeting room above and a cellar below; its lovely fan-vaulting is well lit, and the multitude of odd creatures carved on the exterior are easy to see. Soon after, the nave was rebuilt with Perpendicular arches soaring high on slender pillars, a breathtaking achievement. The colourful windows, the carvings in the roof, the 'wine glass' pulpit (named for its shape) and the wall paintings are just some of the enrichments within. And without is a peaceful old graveyard, reached through a slit of an alleyway with some plant troughs and copper wall lamps.

Before exploring the town it is a good idea to visit the museum (which has won a number of awards for excellence), because it explains Cirencester's past so vividly in a series of spacious and lively displays. For instance, there are not only superbly restored Roman mosaics but recreations of a Roman sitting room and a kitchen, neither wildly dissimilar from home comforts of today. Models of Iron Age barrows make plain what archaeological remains often do not. The techniques of processing wool in the Middle Ages are shown.

Many streets in Cirencester were interesting, but some I remember in particular. Cicely Hill, for instance, is a serene and beautiful street of stone houses leading up to a splendid tree-flanked vista through the great Park. The wide curve of the Market Place, in which honey-coloured stone alternates with stucco in blue, soft pink or cream, was made even more gay on market day by the striped awnings of stalls. The Old Brewery is now converted to provide workshops for craftsmen ranging from a painter of clock faces to a traditional baker (there was also a basketmaker who had even turned his skill to the making of a double bed in wicker).

In the market a farmer from Dymock was selling his own cheeses. After buying from him some real Gloucester cheese, but with a variation (it had nettles in it), I awaited my next bus outside the church, with time to take in all the detail of the Market Place buildings. At sky level there was an infinite variety of cornices, dormers, pediments, gables, mouldings and cupolas with chimneys round or square, made of stone, terracotta or brick.

The bus left town through where a Roman gate had once stood in the city wall, and ahead the Roman road stretched up and down, straight as far as the eye could see. But after a bit the bus left it for winding lanes to little villages.

A signpost pointed to Chedworth Roman villa but we pressed on to the picturesque Chedworth villages (upper and lower). Not only are the old cottages very pretty, but so is the new village hall, where a couple of other passengers helped to heave an old lady off the bus. She stood to wave goodbye as we rattled off once more. Another, white-haired, was short of change for her fare: 'I'm not going to worry about it,' said the driver, 'so don't *you* go grey about it!'

This was one of the best bus routes I'd found, through unspoilt countryside and with views for miles, the road winding down and up all the way and at each turn bringing a new rural scene into view. There were Jersey cows standing in a stream to drink, white geese grazing, a waterside farmhouse with old millstones leaning against the wall, and worn steps up through a little garden to a cottage door. At Yarnworth there is a very tiny church actually in a farmyard. The bus goes to Northleach, a small country town with a 'wool' church almost as fine as Cirencester's (and with outstanding brasses). This was a busy place in coaching days. Here I discovered that long-distance coaches can be useful for short hops too, such as Northleach to Burford.

Burford

The coach sped through rolling country, typically Cotswold landscape, to Burford. This is inevitably my favourite place in the Cotswolds, having spent my honeymoon at the Bay Tree Hotel, a great place for complete comfort, good food, graceful antique furniture and, in winter, four log fires in its various sitting rooms. The original owner, a Tudor magnate, has his resplendent tomb in the lovely church on the banks of the River Windrush. Burford has plenty of other good hotels (the Lamb in Sheep Street, for instance) and almost as many bookshops, of which my favourites are Cotswold Books and Jubilee Books – the latter well-stocked, carpeted and spacious. But there are many other distractions, too, such as craft and antique shops, cobbled courtyards and old inns.

Sunday was spent (with plenty to read!) in a deep chair by one of those crackling log fires.

Note: This area is served partly by very small private bus companies and many services run only once or twice a week (often only on market days, or in summer only).

5

London's Border Country

Gravesend – Wrotham – Ightham – Sevenoaks – Westerham – Reigate – Dorking – Leatherhead (or Guildford) – Windsor – Amersham – Hemel Hempstead – St Albans – Epping – Waltham – Tilbury

Every year millions of Londoners go streaking off far away for a holiday – racing through (or flying over) interesting places without a second glance. One year I decided to take a few days' holiday touring through seven counties yet never finding myself much more than an hour away from Piccadilly Circus. My route formed a circle round London through the Downs to the south and the Chilterns to the north. I crossed the Thames upriver where it is the boundary between Surrey and Berkshire and downriver where it separates Essex from Kent. The journey through hills and valleys was full of contrast, and as the scenery changed with the geology, so did the architecture – weather-boarding, stone, brick or white-wash-and-thatch came and went as county succeeded county.

One could start from any of the towns listed; some are even on the Underground. Others can be reached by train, fast coaches or express buses. 'See London's Town and Countryside' is a useful guide and map; it is free from London Country Buses, Lesbourne Road, Reigate (tel. 07372 42411).

Gravesend

Most guidebooks do not even mention Gravesend, yet once it was a fashionable resort for Londoners who flocked on to steamers for day-trips to its pleasure gardens. And, although its heart has now been ripped out, it still has a lot going for it. Right in the middle is stranded a pretty little Georgian church and beside it a lively statue (presented by Americans) of the American Indian princess, Pocahontas. She married John Rolfe, pioneer of the Virginian tobacco plantations, after saving the life of another Englishman from hostile Indians. Her husband brought her to the court of James I but, as they began the voyage home again, she fell ill and died on board ship as it was passing Gravesend; here therefore she was laid to rest. A memorial window inside the church shows her in Jacobean high fashion, but her statue is as Rolfe might have first seen her in Virginia. Milton Chantry is a lepers' chapel now often used for arts and crafts exhibitions.

Gravesend has a covered market (it was chartered – licensed – in the Middle Ages) in a vast, classically pillared hall; and a weatherboarded smugglers' inn, the Three Daws (jackdaws), by the waterfront from which to watch the ships go by – including, with any luck, one of the old sailing-barges with huge red sails set. Across the river you can see Tilbury, where there is an old fort and very often a Russian liner moored outside its port. A few yards downriver is a tiny church, once a mission to seamen but now an arts centre: and near the Clarendon Hotel some archaeological excavations were in progress when I visited.

The Gordon Promenade (with an old fort) is named for General Gordon, who was responsible for planning fortifications here to repel any French invaders who might have come up the Thames during one of many invasion scares. Further on, yachts are moored in the old canal basin. Once this canal joined the Thames to the Medway, passing through a long tunnel in the chalk hills but, as delays caused by tides made it less than a short cut, much of it was filled in and a railway now runs through its tunnel.

If there is time, take a bus to reach Windmill Hill, not only for the fine view of the Thames and its multitude of craft – from great tankers and container-ships to the small boats carrying the river pilots who navigate the big ships through the tricky estuary – but also because the twisting lanes on the hill still have many of the villas and rustic cottages dating from Gravesend's heyday.

Once out of Gravesend, my first bus soon passed suburban gardens colourful with forsythia and flowering currants and drew up by Meopham's huge triangular cricket green, overlooked by the beautiful smock windmill that has stood there since 1801.

Walls made of flints dug out of the chalk are a characteristic feature along this ride; so is decorative brickwork: grey and red bricks make chequered or diapered patterns on house walls. There are huge timber barns, weatherboarded houses (both very Kentish, deriving from the times when wood was plentiful in the Wealden forests) and lovely stretches of road from here onwards. The trees bear a great weight of ivy and there are tremendous views from the top of the hilly road.

Wrotham

Wrotham is a dozy place now, yet once it was busy with comings and goings at the archbishop's palace next to the old Bull Inn (what is left of the palace is now a private house, the rest of the stones having been removed in 1349 to build a new palace in Maidstone). On a wall nearby, a stone commemorates the assassination in 1799 of an officer who was shot by a deserter here. Roughly opposite is a handsome medieval house, Wrotham Place, from which it is said (but of other places too!) Henry VIII watched for the signal that Anne Boleyn's head had fallen at the executioner's block in the Tower of London.

St George's church has a number of unusual features such as an arcade cut through its tower to allow religious processions to pass under it. This was necessary because the tower abuts on the road, leaving no room for processions to go round it without leaving holy ground. The attractive statue of St George above the door is by a modern sculptor, Willi Soukop, and replaces an older one that was stolen. There are a lot of medieval brasses inside, and, if one peers high up, tiny windows can be seen in a gallery concealed in the stonework dividing nave from chancel. Here nuns could watch the services while remaining hidden from the public eye. The higgledy-piggledy old houses in the High Street are popular with sparrows, which noisily build nests under their generous eaves.

We went on to Borough Green (a characterless place) to change buses for Ightham, which is soon reached after a drive between leafy hedges and buildings of Kentish ragstone (a name well describing its rough appearance).

Ightham

Ightham deserves an hour's break in one's journey. It is a village of half-timbered houses, an old inn (the Green Dragon, with flavoursome real Kent ale called Tusker, from Fremlin's Faversham brewery) and a tiny stream chattering its way among the houses.

The church, a little uphill from the village, is full of interest, beginning with the steps up to a mounting-block by the lychgate, from the days when worshippers arrived on horseback. It was at its best when I was there – the yellow and white flower arrangements from Easter Day still decorated every sill, the pulpit and the font. There are carved Jacobean box pews, a life-size effigy of a knight of 1374 in chain and plate armour (very similar to that of the Black Prince in Canterbury Cathedral) and a memorial of 1641 to Dame Dorothy Selby, a redoubtable dame to judge by her portrait bust sculpted by Charles I's master mason.

The leaflet about the church is well worth reading before looking around, otherwise one might miss details like the carved heads up among the 15th-century roof timbers; the elegant brass (under a mat) of a lady in the sugarloaf hat and ruff that were fashionable in 1626; and the simple memorial of 1921 to a local grocer who became an archaeologist of international renown.

Much of the church's interest lies outside, in the tombstones. Typically Kentish are the ones shaped like head and shoulders (double ones, for husband and wife, look uncommonly similar to bedheads) with a skull incised crudely in the 'head'. Others have cherubs, and one (behind the church) is covered in coats of arms – the work of a famous Victorian architect, William Burgess. An anvil decorates a blacksmith's tombstone, an anchor a sailor's. The most moving of all was small, simple and hard to find among the weeds and ivy: that of General and Mrs Luard, 1908. A few weeks previously my husband had bought for 50p an old volume entitled *Great Stories of Real Life*, from Rasputin to the Marie Celeste, among which the Luard mystery was related. Mrs Luard, a wholly respectable lady and much liked, was shot while walking not far from Ightham, and neither the murderer nor any motive was ever determined. Her stricken husband received a number of anonymous letters accusing him, and he later committed suicide by throwing himself under a train. What the book does not reveal is an earlier Luard tragedy, which a neighbouring tombstone chronicles – the death in action of their son only a few years before. The onward journey goes past the estate (Frankfield) where the murder took place.

The hawthorns in bloom spread their white lace in the hedges, and the banks below were bright with starry yellow celandines. The conical roofs of oast-houses are a conspicuous feature on the way. There are woods of beech, birch and pine along here that are ideal for picnicking, beyond banks of golden, prickly gorse. Beside the sunlit road winding down to Seal, striped with the shadows of slender tree trunks, were tile-hung, half-timbered and weather-boarded houses.

Sevenoaks

Sevenoaks was built strategically in a gap in the North Downs. Its greatest jewel is one of the largest private houses in the country – Knole, built in the 15th and 16th centuries. Filled with valuable paintings and furniture and surrounded by a great deer park, Knole is a small palace – the stone buildings alone occupy four acres – with a mass of turrets, gables, ornate chimneys, battlements and towers outside; inside are galleries, carved panelling, elaborately plastered ceilings and state apartments still with their original furnishings. It is worth staying overnight in Sevenoaks in order to have plenty of time for Knole.

As to Sevenoaks itself, the most interesting part of the High Street is at the far end from the bus depot (and in the lanes which run between it and London Road to the west). I strolled among the little shops and old houses, and down Six Bells Lane (a quaint byway of cottages, cobblestones and small courts) to the church. Next to this stands old Chantry House, its name indicating its connection with the chantry chapel inside the church. The medieval well-to-do would pay for prayers to be chanted for their souls, in perpetuity, in a chapel (chantry) endowed for that purpose. To provide the money, land would be given to the church, and Chantry House stands on such land. At the end of the street is Sevenoaks School, an impressive yet simple building with a few marble statues in niches contrasting rather oddly with the homespun look of the ragstone walls.

Sevenoaks is a good spot at which to stay in order to go bussing about into the countryside (a digression from my 'round London' circuit). Buses go to such beauty spots as Ide Hill and the Darenth Valley, and on Sundays in summer the local bus company runs special 'Rambler' buses.

The next bus on my 'round-London' circuit moved out to

Westerham with views, as it went up and down, of the chalk cliffs quarried in the hills. Much of the beautiful woodland along this route is preserved by the National Trust. The road is fairly busy (though not as bad as it used to be before the new motorway siphoned off traffic), but with plenty of interest. There is a great variety of house-building styles, old inns, dignified houses surrounding the green that gives Bessells Green its name, and willows, bright of bud, beside a stream at Sundridge. Near Brasted sheep grazed in a noble park. Brasted itself is a picturesque village with a green, old stone walls and a lot of tile-hung houses with fine doorways and fanlights; some have grotesque figures carved in their timbers. As in many places on this route, antique shops are numerous.

The road winds on, the tops of the surrounding downs vanishing into mist. Bare boughs were hung with rain like chandelier drops and the wet moss on the beach trunks shone bright green. A smell of wood smoke drifted in when the door of the bus opened.

Westerham

Westerham church came into sight, squatting low on a hilltop, and then the bus drew up beside this little town's steeply sloping green. Here sits Winston Churchill, slumped in an armchair, looking as

Quebec House, Westerham

settled as the church itself. The statue is on a great rugged plinth of Yugoslav stone presented by Marshal Tito and could hardly differ more in style from the other statue on Westerham Green – General Wolfe, elegantly poised, almost as graceful as a dancer, on an urn-shaped plinth. These are Westerham's two famous sons, whose houses can both be visited. Wolfe was born there and Churchill spent many of his later years there.

The National Trust owns Quebec House, the childhood home of General Wolfe, a Tudor mansion of mellowed red brick. Not far off is Squerryes Court with more Wolfe mementoes. Churchill's home, Chartwell, and its lovely gardens are a magnet for sightseers. Though Victorian, the house is a place of space and light, with marvellous views. Its rooms are filled with his things, as if he were just about to play a game of bezique, finish a painting at his easel or continue writing at the desk in his study. (Getting to Chartwell involves a two-mile detour on another bus.) Jane Austen's novel *Pride and Prejudice*, incidentally, is set near Westerham.

The church is worth visiting not just for its interesting interior but because the hillside churchyard with its old tombstones, adorned by well-weathered cherubs and skulls, looks down over the town's old roofs and the valley below.

After lunch I wandered down Water Lane, which leads off the green and goes by streams and stiles to green fields and a pleasant walk below the town, ending up at the far end of the main street.

The bus onward into Surrey was a double-decker with good views from the top. There are rustic bridges over a stream meandering through the outskirts of Westerham, followed by groves of silver birches, pastures, old barns, roadside gorse in golden bloom and attractive houses – some modest, some of consequence. The stretch of road is high and gives long-distance views. The bus detoured through Limpsfield with its terraces of picturesque cottages (the composer Frederick Delius is buried there) and then to Oxted where more substantial homes lie behind high hedges of copper beech. We climbed the steep street of Old Oxted, its ancient houses and inns crammed together as if fighting one another for a grip on the precipitous hill. The almost empty bus swooped and swayed up and down the hilly road through this prosperous part of Surrey.

Downhill the bus goes into Godstone, where the reddish buds

on a tree tapped the bus window as we drew up by the huge green with its round pond and its fringe of well-mannered houses. The cricket field, sodden with rain, waited forlornly for better days.

Beyond Bletchingley, a village of white- and pink-painted houses in a wide street, the road descends and there were views of the Downs' crests before we whisked over the top of the motorway that snaked through the landscape below us. At Nutfield children played in the yard of a traditional old village school. There is a castellated priory looking as if it might be haunted by something grisly out of a Hammer film. Finally we went through Redhill's unlovely suburban sprawl and down into Reigate.

Reigate

Reigate is an attractive town at the foot of the North Downs. Under the remains of the castle on the hill is a tunnel built to save the Prince Regent the bother of going round the hill. The tomb of Lord Howard of Effingham (hero of the Armada defeat) is in the old church, which lies away from the town centre. There are a number of interesting old buildings in the streets, including the Market House in the middle of the main road. Just by this and alongside Lloyds Bank a narrow cobbled slit leads upwards to the gardens that are where the castle used to stand. It is a pretty spot above the hum of the traffic and with views of the roofscape below – a medley of cupolas, chimneys, clocks and weathercocks. Below, the lovely Priory Gardens have a lake, limes, mansion and garden with clipped yews.

The next bus moved out through a street of sedate houses and past more village greens, a classical bridge over the River Mole and flashes of bright scarlet from pyracanthus berries still thick against cottage walls.

Dorking

Dorking's origins are Saxon and its main street was first laid down by the Romans. Dickens stayed at the White Horse coaching inn (in Tudor times it was the vicarage, and before that a pilgrim's hostel), which is where the bus stops. With such a history behind it Dorking is a fascinating place, and down every alley is something interesting. One, for instance, led me to 'Equations of Time', a workshop where two young cabinet-makers were creating grandfather and wall clocks to the highest standards of traditional design – future heirlooms – or restoring old ones. The smell of pine from an old coachyard (where a crafts market is sometimes held) led to another workshop where pine furniture is made. Part of the pavement is on a bank raised above the level of the road, presumably to protect pedestrians from mud and other hazards of coaching days. Some of the shops have bow-fronted windows, an ironmonger's front is elegant with Corinthian pillars and what was once a small inn is now an aromatic Culpeper herb shop. There are gunsmiths in Dorking, leather goods, and – particularly in West Street – craft and antique shops galore, with more along North Street (which leads to the bus station and has many good restaurants to choose from).

North Street also has, facing a group of *cottages ornées* with rustic or Chinese-looking porches, the premises of a little printing company of so unusual an appearance that I knocked on the door to ask their origins. They told me that the ecclesiastical look of the place, with three stained-glass windows and inscriptions carved in the stonework, was conceived by the founder of the firm over a century ago. A one-time architect, he acquired stained glass and other fittings from churches being busily 'improved' with Victorian zeal and re-used them here.

At this point I had to make a decision about which of several routes to follow in order to get to Windsor.

The most appealing alternative was to go via Guildford, an attractive town, and Bracknell. The road from Dorking to Guildford is very lovely indeed, passing through some of the most picturesque villages of the North Downs, with marvellous scenery. Between Bracknell and Windsor, too, are attractive views – I could have gone through Windsor Great Park or taken the Sunningdale-Egham road, which runs by woods, the lovely lake of Virginia Water and Wentworth golf course. However, I took the most convenient route (via Leatherhead) and rather regretted it – though the first and last parts were enjoyable.

The bus turned north, passing white houses set well back behind tall pine trees and cedars and almost vertical chalk hills with trees clinging to them by the merest toe-hold. This was once the main coach route to London. On the right is the Burford Bridge Hotel, a traditional hotel set, long and low, in particularly fine gardens at the foot of steep Box Hill. Nelson, Keats and Robert Louis Stevenson all stayed there for a while. There are no box trees left on the hill because they were all cut down in the 18th century, when their fine-grained wood was in demand for making the blocks used by picture-engravers. The river flowing under the bridge is the Mole again.

Box Hill

There the bus left the main road to clamber up Juniper Hill, a lane that winds and climbs between black-and-white houses and flint walls characteristic of chalk regions, and by a flint church with old stone heads. The red brick houses have decorative red tiling and lozenge-paned windows.

Leatherhead

Leatherhead has several bridges over its rushing river; beyond it Bookham Common is a place of tangled woodland followed by a narrow lane and little bridges across which the bus squeezes with difficulty. After prosperous suburban comforts came the village green of Cobham and flooded fields. Road and river (the Mole still) run together for a while, weirs frothing white. Much of this part of the journey is suburban. However, occasional stretches of larch trees, rhododendron groves, old farm buildings and a pool glimpsed over a wall (hiding it from sight of motorists) made for some relief. The sky was then a pearly salmon colour as daylight began to fade, reflected in the river where pleasure craft waited by a pretty iron bridge. Outside the Georgian houses round Chertsey's cricket green (a bus change needed here) the pyracanthus berries were still thick and red.

Some years ago the acres of gravel-pit pools beside the road from Chertsey to Staines were landscaped and turned into Thorpe Park. This now has a hundred acres of lakes and land with displays illustrating maritime history, a Celtic farm, a Roman port, a Viking longship and much else including water sports.

Buses from Staines to Windsor run beside the Thames for most of the way, crossing Runnymede (where King John put his seal on Magna Carta) and past the memorial to President Kennedy, with views of locks, weirs, islands and boat-houses along the way. Finally Windsor Castle rose into sight above its Home Park.

Windsor

Berkshire's royal town provides plenty of good reasons to stay the night, not only because there is so much to see but because the Old House Hotel (once Wren's home, beside the Thames) is irresistible for teas on the riverside terrace (indoors, rooms are furnished with antiques, several lined with carved panelling).

For the purpose of a flying visit, the first priority is obviously the great castle begun by William the Conqueror and improved by almost every monarch since. At 13 acres, it is the biggest inhabited castle in the world.

Windsor's most interesting shopping street curves downhill in the shadow of the castle walls until reaching the old bridge (now reserved for pedestrians only), with Eton on the other side. There is a promenade by the river, usually gay with pleasure boats and swans. Church Street and nearby Market Street are places to linger in for their Tudor houses and little speciality shops; and Wren's columned Guildhall is nearby. Elegant Park Street, lined with Georgian houses, leads to Windsor Park and its magnificent vistas of the castle to the left and the Long Walk to the right, stretching in a straight line to George III's statue three miles away. One of Windsor's best-kept secrets is that the royal mausoleum in the park, normally closed to the public, can in fact be viewed on a few dates each May. It is incredibly beautiful: a little jewel in early Italian style, housing the great tombs of Victoria and Albert side by side, and surrounded by a stream and garden. Behind it lie the very simple graves of members of the royal family who have died in recent times, including the Duke and Duchess of Windsor.

Eton, immediately across the bridge, also deserves unhurried exploration. The 15th-century part of the college can be visited together with its superb Gothic chapel, containing carvings and wall paintings. In the High Street leading to the college, every second building seems to be an antique shop at which you may buy anything from a clay pipe to a chandelier; most of the rest are old inns or restaurants. Yards built for coaches now hold large tubs of flowers.

I intended an early start on the next day, but first I walked along the river. Canada geese grazed on the banks undisturbed at that quiet hour except when a group of ducks flew in. I walked past a bowling green, dormant at that season, and by beds of daffodils braving the unseasonable chill, until I came to a backstreet leading to a narrow stairway which, rising this way then that and around a Tudor house, emerged into Curfew Yard and the High Street. It was still only 8.30 am and the town was almost deserted. I could see and enjoy as never before the fine Georgian sash windows, the skyline of gables and pediments, shop fronts pillared or arcaded, old red brick contrasting with the smooth stucco of upper storeys in blue, yellow, apricot or dove-grey and the swinging shop signs.

And so to the bus. One is, fortunately, in and out of Slough in a matter of minutes. Beyond, flanked by flat meadows, the Thames is particularly beautiful. Blue and white pleasure craft, freshly painted, were moored in a creek ready for summer to bring tourists, and gulls rested in ploughed fields that were waiting for the spring sowing.

The journey onwards to Berkhamsted in Hertfordshire is a long one. It can be broken at, say, Amersham (Bucks) or to visit Stoke Poges, just off the bus route. The road goes up and down as pussy willows, holly (still bright with berries) and oaks give way to pleasant suburban houses set well back in gardens. In the leafless trees last year's nests were exposed to view, and already noisy rooks were beginning to make repairs for the new season, flying in with new twigs to add to old nests. Pines and rhododendrons were succeeded by silver birch and gorse on the commons, suburbs by fields where crows grazed at the verge of a stream. At Chalfont St Giles a flying glimpse was possible of the pond beyond which John Milton's cottage lies. On through low hills and pastures, past one old inn after another, and soon we reached Amersham.

Amersham

Here I stopped, because it is a very pleasing old town with quaint almshouses and 17th-century market hall in its spacious main street, sheltered by the surrounding hills. Of its many fascinating old inns the Mill Stream (passed on the way in) is the most unusual, for the stream actually flows through it. Wandering among cobbled courts and alleys, I found thatched cottages tucked out of sight.

But the first thing I noticed, opposite the bus depot, was a warning on a cottage wall (dated 1811): 'The Magistrates Acting for this Hundred have given peremptory orders to constables to apprehend all common beggars, ballad-singers and other vagrants so that they may be dealt with according to law.'

Suppressing any urge to burst into song, I wandered along the main street and into the church – like its churchyard, beautifully maintained, a place of light and spaciousness. Amersham and the whole of this area have a history of religious dissent, with Puritan martyrs and Cromwellian associations. There is something Quakerish in the simplicity of even the parish church with its whitewashed walls, a polished pale floor and simple oak chairs. But against these the baroque monuments, carved pulpit (with the four evangelists coloured and gilded) and the royal coat-of-arms stand out even more splendidly. The 'heavenly' chancel ceiling is blue with gold stars.

Behind the pillared market house and its old lead pump lies Market Walk, where ten small speciality shops have tucked themselves into one building. The whole length of the street is worth a lingering walk: brick-and-flint, or timbered houses, wisteria and other creepers, Dutch gables and rippling roofs, print galleries and antique shops – everything is a pleasure to see.

The most direct route to Berkhamsted is semi-suburban. Although there are some attractive views of the pretty River Chess and of beech woods as the bus climbs up and down, the roundabout way via Great Missenden is more picturesque. Throughout this route the Chiltern Hills provide marvellous views, particularly in autumn when the great old beech trees blaze with colour and the ground glows with a carpet of their crisp, fallen leaves. In summer, when the trees are green, they create a pattern of dense shade and flickering sunlight on mossy banks of bluebells. Bricks combined with flints make a characteristic style of architecture for this region.

Berkhamsted is still largely unspoilt despite the busy traffic through it. A little way down Lower King's Road – beyond antique and book shops – lie the Grand Union Canal and the ruins of a Norman castle. The canal, built in the 18th century to bring goods from Northamptonshire to London, today has more pleasure boats and ducks than working barges.

Hemel Hempstead

A short run alongside the canal (and its locks, gaily painted narrowboats and a former watermill) leads to Hemel Hempstead, its new town bright and busy but its 18th-century High Street still surviving in the old part.

It has something of the quality of Amersham but is less self-consciously picturesque. I had a very inexpensive but appetizing lunch in the town hall's gallery, where art students' work and dining tables overlooked the yews of the old churchyard. At the far end of the High Street is an old pump of 1848, now done up in attractive colours, and on the corner of a tiny street called Cherry Bounce was a shop selling every article that can conceivably be made of basketwork – even a pram. As the sun was then shining and the view of the river, lacy white iron bridges and cottages was so attractive, I continued to walk to the village of Piccotts End.

No one ever paused at Piccotts End, except for petrol, until about twenty years ago when first one and then another sensational discovery was made. There are two adjoining 14th-century cottages, whose previous sole claim to fame was that once they were employed as a cottage hospital – in fact, the first ever set up, by the surgeon to George IV. Later they reverted to humble dwellings until, on the death of their solitary 78-year-old occupant, some refurbishing was put in hand by the new owner. What started as a simple job of stripping wallpaper suddenly became a great revelation – no fewer than six layers of paper on one of linen collapsed off the wall in one great mass, uncovering on the plaster beneath a fantastic wall painting that had been preserved in perfect, vivid condition for four centuries. As if that were not enough, a further mural almost as old was revealed in the adjacent cottage some ten years later.

The earlier mural is an enigma. Many of the symbols entwining the conventional representation of the crucifixion and of the Virgin Mary are not just unusual but have associations with heretical beliefs. Was there once in this neighbourhood a group of Cathars, a forbidden sect from the Pyrenees, and is this why their wall painting was kept so carefully hidden from view under a cloth? Both cottages have been lovingly restored and filled with medieval and Tudor furnishings, and they were well worth my stroll from Hemel.

The next part of my ride was suburban at first, until along came fields and farmhouses, and suddenly the great abbey of St Albans appeared on the horizon.

St Albans

I got off before the bus entered the town in order to look at the Roman theatre – unique in Britain. Its small stage and larger central space suggest that it was probably used for religious ceremonials rather than for acting plays. It stood to one side of the Roman city of Verulamium, which extended downhill towards where today's town stands. That town grew up *outside* the Roman walls, possibly where the Romans had their cemetery, and as I walked down Fishpool Street to reach the town I was passing the ghost of the Roman city.

On the way I visited the Roman museum, which has finds ranging from delightful mosaics to the nail-cleaners and ear-picks of 2,000 years ago. A few yards further on, ducks were crossing the road in one direction and swans in the other. Beside their home, the River Ver which gave Verulamium its name, stands a 16th-century watermill restored to order and open to the public.

Fishpool Street winds on and on downhill, lined with Queen Anne, Georgian and Regency houses – some gracious, some quaint, most with individualistic porches and doorknockers. The

16th-century Manor House is now an elegant hotel with five acres of lawns beside the River Ver. The road turned and abruptly I found myself at the foot of the abbey.

The Saxons built the first cathedral (in honour of Alban, a Christian martyred by the Romans), but the present great abbey is largely Norman and 13th-century work. A lot of fine medieval wall paintings have been uncovered inside during the last century or so as the Puritans' whitewash has gradually been cleaned off; once all the walls must have glowed with colourful painted scenes, and its great interior would have been thronged with people. But when I was there, in the twilit gloom there was a stillness until a little procession of two priests and a dozen small choristers (red-robed and white-ruffed) entered to sing evensong for a congregation of two. In the cathedral I bought an excellent paperback, *Cathedral and City*, with first-rate essays on the history of St Albans by various contributors including Robert Runcie, its former bishop, now Archbishop of Canterbury.

I stayed the night at the White Hart, a half-timbered coaching inn right by the abbey, wondering whether my beamed bedroom may have been the one where Lord Lovat stayed in 1746 on his way to the Tower and execution for treason.

The town of St Albans is rich in old inns, historic buildings, byways and (like many other towns on this circuit of London's countryside) antique shops. For a good walking tour round the most interesting parts, start from St Peter's Street (where, ever since Saxon times, a Saturday market has been held), and go along French Row (where French prisoners were housed in the Middle Ages) to the medieval curfew belltower and the gate of the Waxhouse where candles were made.

To get to Waltham I went via Enfield – a dull route, though there are a few interesting buildings surviving among Enfield's bustle. The town of Waltham Cross is notable only for an unusual inn sign of swans on a beam stretching right over the top of a busy road.

Waltham

Waltham Abbey, however, is breathtaking and well worth the journey. Its richness, size and antiquity, and its stormy and emotional history, are all exceptional; and it is also enhanced by the fact that one comes upon it in surroundings that are very undistinguished.

To start with: the legends about it. In 1030 a Somerset carpenter was instructed in a dream to dig in a certain hilltop. Seventy feet down, a black stone crucifix was found. This was taken (again, by mystical direction) to distant Waltham, on the edge of the then vast Epping Forest. There it was housed in a wooden church until – six years before the Battle of Hastings – King Harold built a monastery to house it, to which later monarchs added. The remnant of this Norman church is all one can see, but *what* a remnant! The total structure must have been one of the wonders of the Norman world, for although the Conquest was still to come, the masons (and the stone) were imported from Normandy. When Harold prayed at the foot of the black cross before he went to do battle, it is said that the head of Christ bowed down (an ill omen). Harold's corpse was brought back here for burial after the Battle of Hastings, and his grave can be seen.

Though the present nave seems colossal, the original was three times as long until Henry VIII tore most of it down. But what remains is impressively strong, simple and grand, now enriched by Sir Edward Burne-Jones's stained glass and an elaborately painted ceiling.

In the narrow streets of the town that grew up round the abbey one can still see many ancient timber-framed houses, some leaning at tipsy angles. The walled gardens of the abbey deserve a lingering visit, too.

The onward road climbed among white, weatherboarded cottages through woods of birch and beech (vestiges of Epping Forest) and along an open ridge with far views of distant hills. As the bus splashed through puddles and the driving rain outside lashed the windows, I was dozily lulled by the warmth inside and the rhythmic squeak of the windscreen wipers until Epping and lunchtime arrived conveniently at the same moment.

Epping

Epping has some pleasant Georgian houses at each end of its wide High Street but, fighting with the wind for possession of my umbrella, I was more interested in steak-and-kidney pie at the Thatched House (not, in fact, thatched, but a low-beamed inn).

It is possible to complete the circle around London by going via Ongar, Brentwood and North Ockendon to Tilbury, where there is a passenger ferry to Gravesend. But there is also a tube station at Epping from which one can get back into central London again – the rest of the journey is one of the less interesting stretches. However, I pressed on.

Ongar must once have been picturesque, but it has been badly neglected, and Brentwood seemed to have little to commend it. I was glad to move on to North Ockendon to pick up my last bus. This part of Essex is fairly pretty, though one never goes for long without pylons or distant factory chimneys springing into view. However, there are lots of tree-lined lanes and half-timbered houses. The nearer we got to Kent, the more Kentish did the scene become – a church tower on which flints and ragstone alternated and some weatherboarding, for instance. The scenery is varied by streams and lovely mansions. The bus drew up outside the local museum – easily worth half an hour for its well-designed displays telling the region's history from the Stone Age flint industry to the great docks of the present day. Then, after passing more flat fields with grazing cows against a factory background and yards stacked with timber newly arrived from Sweden, we suddenly arrived at the railway terminus of Tilbury.

Tilbury

The Thames itself is out of sight, hidden behind a high sea-wall and iron floodgates that are ready to slam shut if, one day, the Thames rises to flood levels (a perennial fear). A grey tide was rolling in when I arrived, frothing impatiently. The wiry-necked cranes crowded along the dock sides a little way upstream. I walked downstream along the sea-wall – not just for the fine views of shipping in Gravesend Reach but to visit Tilbury Fort, a 17th-century defence against the Dutch and French with a lavish triumphal gateway. Where the military were once quartered private citizens now have their homes, but the ramparts and guardrooms can still be visited. The World's End, a weatherboarded old inn nearby, has a cosy and interesting interior.

As I waited on the jetty for the ferry to come, I could see Gravesend church spire on the opposite bank (white with a blue-and-gold clock) and the Town Pier. A container-ship laboured slowly past, its twelve great containers looking like children's bricks – green, red, yellow and brown. The ferry soon took us across and I stepped ashore to the cry of gulls and the splash-and-clang sounds so characteristic of the Thames, made by waves on the iron hulls of moored barges called *Dutch Courage* and *Dutch Treat*. My journey had come full circle and once more I was back in Kent.

6
The Cinque Ports

Sandwich – Dover – Hythe – New Romney – Rye – Winchelsea – Hastings

Because the ancient Cinque Ports (now seven, despite their name) are close together along the Kent-Sussex shore, one can reach them all within a few hours, but they are so interesting that a few days' holiday, stopping overnight at two or three, would be a far better way to do them justice. That would also give time to go a little way into the surrounding countryside. The local buses are convenient and frequent. I went early in spring – a spring that seemed reluctant to let winter go. Despite the nip in the air, it was an enjoyable trip – not least because there were few other travellers.

This stretch of coast faces Europe and has always been the part most vulnerable to invasion. Caesar landed here, and later the Romans had to build forts to defend it from the Saxon tribes of Germany. William the Conqueror landed a little further west and in his turn built defensive castles along the shores. Many of Henry VIII's defences against the French can still be viewed, and so can some of the 70 dumpy Martello towers put up when an invasion by Napoleon was feared. Today's invaders, tourists from Europe, are more welcome than their predecessors.

The Cinque Ports gained their unique status in national defence in 1278 when Edward I gave them a charter under which, in return for providing ships and sailors to defend the shore, they were granted valuable privileges of self-government, trading rights and exemption from military service. They thus grew not only powerful but rich, as the remaining medieval houses and noble churches show.

However, the ports' fortunes later declined. When Charles II built up England's navy their services were no longer so vital and, worse still, nature had taken a hand: their harbours were by now silted up (Dover excepted) by the great masses of sand and shingle that are swept in by the Atlantic and deposited along these shores. Because of this Sandwich, New Romney, Rye and Winchelsea are in fact far inland now. Virtually all privileges were eventually withdrawn from the ports.

A Martello tower

This journey is therefore one of great historical interest, through country studded with the massive relics of invasions or invasion scares (from the Romans right up to the Second World War). It runs along a coastline that is still in the making – or unmaking – with scenery as varied as the white cliffs of Dover and the wild, windy marshes around Romney.

Sandwich

My journey started at Sandwich, most senior of the Cinque Ports, but if you prefer to start at the beginning – chronologically speaking – you could make nearby Richborough the first visit, for here stand the massive ruins of the Romans' greatest fortress, built to keep the Saxons out. It is not only the earliest relic of Roman

Britain but arguably the most spectacular. From here started the great Roman road, Watling Street, which ran all the way up to Shropshire.

Sandwich is a delightful town of narrow streets and high-gabled houses jumbled together – medieval, Tudor or later. As well as its riverfront it has a strange artificial stream, the Delf, wandering amongst and under the houses – an early means of water supply. There is a barbican of chequerboard stone, an old Guildhall, and ramparts that are grassy mounds providing a very pleasant stroll around the old town.

One can go direct to Dover, or divert via Deal – not a Cinque Port but interesting for having the best of the Henry VIII castles. It is also where Julius Caesar landed, despite fierce opposition from the Britons, who drove their chariots into the sea against the armoured legionaries as they tried to disembark. A small seaside resort favoured by artists, it is on an attractive bus route that skirts Kent's only coalfield, which in no way spoils the scenery.

The view out to sea is of the notorious Goodwin Sands, their lightships and wrecks, and of the minor shipping busily passing between them and the shore. Here a familiar landmark is the time ball, twin of the one at Greenwich to which it was electrically linked until recently. Its function was to signal the hour by the dropping of the big ball on its spire, so that ships at sea could check their chronometers. (The Tourist Information Centre is here.) The promenade by the long shingle beach leads to Deal Castle but it is worth visiting first the Georgian backstreets which have great charm, relics of the days when Deal was a prosperous and bustling port.

The castle was built to defend the ships that moored at low tide between the Goodwins and the shore. (Though treacherous when high tide barely covers them, the sandbanks at other times form a protection from rough weather in the Channel.) Henry VIII's small castles are built in the shape of a rose, not for any aesthetic reason but because the rounded, petal-like bastions provided for tiers of cannon, each able to fire over a very wide arc. The interior is a maze of passageways.

Walmer, too, has its Henry VIII castle (within walking distance, and near the bus route to Dover) as well as a famous lifeboat, usually to be seen drawn up on the shingle. The castle, altered a lot since it was built, contains exhibits about past Lord Wardens of the Cinque Ports such as the Duke of Wellington (including his boots) and Winston Churchill, and it is surrounded by lovely gardens. The present Lord Warden is the Queen Mother.

Dover

In $\frac{1}{4}$ hour the bus reaches Dover and its castle – a very different fortification, overwhelming in size and site, high up and with spectacular sea views. For thousands of years there has been a fortress here, and still standing within its walls is the 50-foot stump of a Roman lighthouse. When the Normans burned Dover they rebuilt the castle so well that the besieging French found it impregnable in 1216. It is still an important defence and was used in both world wars, and its great central keep is one of the largest in Britain.

The bus down into the town stops in the centre, conveniently near most of Dover's historic sights such as the Roman house which accidentally came to light when a car park was being levelled. It was possibly the house of the admiral in charge of the port. Its painted walls survived because, in erecting a new fort, the Roman army built a great wall right through it, and this was banked up with a mound of clay that preserved the colourful house walls buried inside it. The underfloor heating system also survived intact.

As Dover is not only a port but a garrison town, it is big and bustling. But there are pleasant promenades, cliff-top walks, riverside gardens, a 4,000-foot pier (from the end the view of the castle and the famous white cliffs shows them in all their grandeur), and a honeycomb of underground passages. Dover is also a great place for statues and other memorials.

Tiny St Edmund's chapel is worth seeking out, built by one English saint (St Richard of Chichester) in honour of another, in 1253. Bulldozers were whining and lorries changing gear outside, but inside were sanctified peace and simplicity – whitewashed walls, a floor of cobbles and ancient oak roof-beams fastened to one another with wood pegs. The chapel is near the Town Hall ('Maison Dieu'), which has great coloured windows telling of royal comings and goings through the port: Edward III off to the Hundred Years' War, Henry VIII embarking for the Field of the Cloth of Gold, Charles II's restoration. The floor vibrated to a crescendo from the organ in the great hall, and all the pomp and circumstance were in complete contrast to St Edmund's.

Next door is a typical town museum, a hotch-potch of local bric-à-brac alongside souvenirs donated by intrepid Victorian travellers. On television that night David Attenborough was showing trees in Arizona's petrified forest and that morning I stroked the polished, stony remains of one – in Dover's museum.

Flints from amongst the chalk go into the building of walls hereabouts, and they were much in evidence on the short bus ride to Folkestone. Beyond lie the high hummocks of the North Downs.

Folkestone

There are two Folkestones – low and high, one old and workaday and one leisured and more recent. Decimus Burton laid out the latter in the grand manner early in Victoria's reign. I got off the bus in Tontine Street and walked back a little along The Stade beside the old harbour. I could smell fish before I saw it displayed on stone slabs in the fish market. Out of the Channel mists a ghost ship suddenly loomed – the Sealink ferry from Boulogne.

The long climb up Remembrance Road to the other Folkestone is worth the effort. Along this road thousands of soldiers marched (many to their deaths) to embark for France during the First World War. As well as a conventional memorial at the top, the city fathers planted this road with rosemary ('for remembrance'), bay and pines. These scents now mingle with the tang of the sea below to give an almost Mediterranean aroma to the air.

Folkestone, once described as 'a miserable little fishing town', got a new lease of life when the railway came in 1853. And at the top of Remembrance Road one is suddenly transported into this new world of stately Victorian hotels with names redolent of nobility, saints or statesmen of a century ago. The buildings stand at attention along a wide promenade of neat box hedges and still neater lawns, deserted when I was there except for a worker repainting the curlicues and ships on the wrought-iron street lamps. At the centre of the Leas, as the promenade is called, William Harvey (who discovered the circulation of the blood and was born in Folkestone in 1578) clutches his still, cold heart with fingers of bronze.

Opposite Trinity Church in Sandgate Road I waited by a Victorian pillarbox (hexagonal, with a pie-crust top) for the bus to Hythe. It makes its way between Sandgate's timbered buildings, some with wood balconies or shutters, and beside a shore where surf thrashes the shingle ceaselessly.

Hythe

Not only the Martello towers in this area recall how lively was the fear that Napoleon would invade: the road into Hythe sees the beginning of the Royal Military Canal, built as a defence against the emperor and still found useful in the two world wars. The canal was in effect a 60-foot-wide moat, its inland bank built high, which deliberately followed a zig-zag route so that cannon could be strategically placed at each angle. Now people fish and boat on it, it is flanked by gardens, and a glorious 'Venetian' water carnival is held every other summer.

The little streets of Georgian houses around the church are attractive and the church itself is one of the finest in Kent, built with the once-rich proceeds of herring fishing. Children are fascinated by its more macabre side – a crypt stacked with thousands of skulls and bones, believed to be Roman, but more probably medieval. They also enjoy (and so do adults!) the miniature railway that steams its way for 14 miles across the marshes to Romney as an alternative to getting there by bus. The ten steam locomotives are mostly replicas (one-third size) of main-line expresses of the 1920s. There is a railway exhibition at New Romney station, and near Dungeness are an old lighthouse and lifeboat station to be visited.

A worthwhile detour, 10 minutes by bus, is to Saltwood Castle, where the knights plotted Thomas à Becket's assassination. It is a romantic semi-ruin draped in creepers, but its gatehouse is still occupied.

Hythe is now separated from its peaceful canal by a multi-lane roadway to accommodate the juggernaut lorries from the Continent which used to pound through the narrow High Street. I walked through the colonnade below the town hall (an incised stone says 'All Persons are requefted to unite their Endeavours to keep this Place clean and to prevent BOYS or others from dirting the fame') and thence up a narrow hill leading to the church and to the backwaters of Bartholomew Road, Malthouse Hill and other lanes lined with ancient houses.

At the hill's foot is the old malt house, now an antiques market, within sight of the Red Lion bus-stop. A few yards away, I gave in to the temptation of a generous cream tea at Betty's in what was, from 1892 until 1921, a tram shed (the tramlines can be seen in the cobbles of the forecourt). The trams, nicknamed 'toast-racks' – photographs make the reason plain – were horse-drawn.

The bus shelter stands right by one of these strategic zig-zags in the canal, and from there the bus reaches Dymchurch in a few minutes (unless one breaks off to visit Lympne Castle first).

From Hythe onwards the ground is utterly level – onetime marshes (now drained), flat as a billiard table, stretch out into a misty, never-ending distance. There is little to see, a total contrast to the Downs at the start of the journey. The high sea-wall blots out the view on the other side of the bus.

Dymchurch, once pretty, is very sleazy now. Its vast sandy beaches are an attraction to children, but its only claim to attention is a Martello tower housing a museum of anti-Napoleon defences. The tower was sited here to defend the sluices which control the drainage of the marshes: the land lies many feet below sea-level and if the sluices were destroyed the sea would flood it. This was smuggling country, and Dymchurch is where Russell Thorndike set his series of novels about Dr Syn, the smuggler-parson, whose deeds are now celebrated in a biennial Dr Syn carnival.

The marshes here and beyond New Romney have not always existed. Once the sea covered the area, exposing only muddy saltings at low tide. The Romans built not only the sea-wall but another (the Rhee Wall) alongside the River Rother which, at that time, flowed through the saltings where the Appledore-New Romney road now runs. Thus the Romans turned the saltings into drainable land they could use as pasture. Later Thomas à Becket, among other landowners, drained more saltings on the other side of the Rhee Wall and created Walland Marsh between New Romney and Rye, now some of the richest soil in the world. Its grass is so excellent that the hardy Romney Marsh sheep need no extra feeding (nor any shelter) in winter. Their shepherds, known as 'lookers', lead isolated lives on these windswept marshes. Ask the bus driver where to get off for New Romney: some buses only pause outside it and then whisk off elsewhere.

New Romney

New Romney was new in Saxon times (old Romney having been superseded when its harbour silted up). It used to be an important port before the River Rother left it, suddenly changing its course after the great storm of 1287. The Georgian houses in its wide street were in many cases the homes of 'owlers' (smugglers) who, even during the war with France, carried on illicit bartering of wool for contraband silk, brandy and tobacco. The extent to which the land in these parts changed its level is made vivid at the church, a particularly splendid Norman one, where the ground is now more than half-way up some of the older pillars. The church is often locked against vandals, and I had to content myself with wandering among the tombstones where lichen – gold, green, grey and even crimson – obliterates the inscriptions with its patterns. Down West Street are old priory walls, another reminder of the town's vanished status.

An infrequent bus travels 12 miles across the Walland Marsh with its drainage ditches, isolated farms, very few trees and an occasional old inn. It is a place of vastness and solitude.

Rye

Beautiful Rye seethes with tourists during summer, but in spring only the locals were out and about, and not many of them. I could see the cobbled streets and medieval buildings as never before. It is worth picking up a street plan from the Tourist Information Centre before venturing into the warren of little streets perched on Rye's hill, which was once almost an island surrounded by sea on three sides.

Conduit Hill (up which water was once pumped to a great cistern in the churchyard) leads to the High Street where above the shop fronts are upper storeys of scalloped tiles (known as beavertails) and timbered overhangs leaning at precarious angles. Some shops hang out signs, such as an iron kettle at the ironmonger's and brass pestle-and-mortar at the chemist. For over three hundred years the grammar school has dominated the centre, its red brick slowly mellowing. Now one can rent a holiday flat in it. Down sidestreets one can glimpse cobbled yards and ancient cottages, wreathed in forsythia and clematis, or Brave Bessie, a ship's figurehead of 1820 standing guard outside a crafts shop.

The road continues down the winding slope of the Mint, a street of old houses that have oak doors with carved linenfold panels and worn stone steps. A few have pargetted walls (decorative plasterwork). Past the many potteries (one makes the decorative house-name plaques which are a feature of Rye) lies the Strand, with wooden warehouses converted to restaurants and antique shops along the waterfront.

Ascending back again to the centre, I strolled up one of England's famous streets, now almost deserted – Mermaid Street. It is worth pausing to look back every few yards at changing perspectives of cobbles and window boxes. At the end, to the right, lies the Tudor house where Henry James and then E. F. Benson once lived – its lovely garden alone is worth an unhurried visit – and the marvellously preserved square surrounding the ivied churchyard. Every other house seems to be of outstanding interest architecturally or historically, with evocative names like St Anthony of Padua, Friars of the Sack, or the Old Stone House. Off it is another fascinating byway, Watchbell Street, with glimpses of gardens and courts at each side. At the end is a lookout over the boats and marshes lying far below the town and a view of the distant ruins of Camber Castle, wreathed in mist.

The great church has windows of the most vivid blue and a very unusual, very ancient clock – its enormous pendulum hangs right down into the nave, the steady tick-tock louder than the murmured prayers of the worshippers. Rye's old bells sound a splendid peal over the marshes.

Ypres Tower, nearby, is another lookout point. It is a forbidding grey bastion (now a really interesting museum) which in its time repulsed the French and housed prisoners. The curious oval Water House, on the way back to the town centre, was built in 1732 to provide a supply of water to the top of this hill town; people brought their buckets to the pump outside it. Now the great gauge outside shows it is empty, its function taken over by progress and plumbing.

The log fire, Tudor beams and home-made food of Fletchers (in Lion Street) provided a welcome break. The house is named after the Fletcher of Beaumont and Fletcher, 17th-century dramatists, who lived there. Then I went down East Cliff, through the great stone Land Gate and thus, reluctantly, back to the bus station. Rye is so full of good places at which to stay, eat, shop or just look that one could happily linger for days.

The bus onward circles round the bottom of Rye's hillock and, looking backward, one can see how the town is heaped up above what was formerly sea – the ridge far to the right of the bus route was once a sea cliff. Now the only water is in the narrow river running alongside the road and in the drainage ditches, the haunt of moorhens.

Winchelsea

Winchelsea is another town on a hillock that was once a sea-girt island. The bus climbs into it by a steep road with hairpin bends, passing one of the ancient stone gates that date from the time when this was a defensively walled town.

What a contrast with busy Rye. This sleepy 'town' of 500 people is unique – an example of town planning 13th-century style. There was another Winchelsea once, but the great storm of 1287 swept over it and buried it under sand. Those who survived built a new Winchelsea laid out in 39 squares and with a magnificent church of Normandy stone and Sussex marble. It is fortunate that this was built just when the Decorated style was in its early days, an outstanding period in English architecture. What stands now is only a fragment of the whole, the 70-foot choir, for the French destroyed the rest. Its stone effigies of knights and other worthies are dappled with the light from exceptional modern stained glass (the blues are particularly rich) with intricate designs that deserve unhurried study. It is said that some of the great marble figures were retrieved from the old, inundated Winchelsea.

Many of Sir John Everett Millais' paintings were done at Winchelsea, some in the church. The town flourished when it was a port for wines from Bordeaux (houses built on old foundations have enormous ancient wine cellars), but, as the sea receded, it became a quiet retreat and is mercifully free of traffic still.

The church bookstall provided me with a particularly well-produced 'Town Walk' booklet which took me through one fascinating street after another, and to a former 13th-century wine cellar, now a coffee shop and art gallery.

Perhaps because of its history – apocalyptic storms, four invasions, the Black Death, and finally the catastrophic departure of the sea which ruined its life as a port – there can be few places as calm as Winchelsea now.

A half-hour bus ride runs through fields and orchards with views of rolling hills and medieval villages. Here and there are converted oasthouses and an old wooden windmill.

Hastings

The bus makes the long descent into the middle of Hastings, right through the middle of the old town. This road is called the Bourne because once it was a river, and the streets flanking it were on its banks. This is a good place to get off in order to wander in the old town. But first I strolled round the nearby fishmarket and among the teetering black wooden sheds on the beach in which, for some two hundred years, fishing nets have been hung to dry. The pebbly beach is covered with fishing odds and ends between the colourful boats drawn up above the tide (for there is no harbour: it silted up centuries ago). Behind rise many-coloured sandstone cliffs hewn into odd shapes by centuries of weather. There is a fisheries museum in a disused chapel.

At the start of All Saints Street, once the east bank of the Bourne, is a gigantic winkle (symbol of Hastings' Winkle Club, a fishermen's charity, one of whose members is the Queen Mother). The street itself has pretty houses with low oak doors, windows of leaded panes or bottle-glass, and half-timbered overhangs. There are beamy inns such as the Stag, which has a collection of mummified cats, and curiosities like the wedge-shaped cottage called the Piece of Cheese, sometimes open to the public. One of the pavements is raised high on a bank, presumably once a necessary precaution against flood and mud.

All Saints Church, at the end, is majestically enthroned uphill. Its main claim to fame is a medieval 'doom' painting high on the wall dividing nave from choir, with a lively devil casting souls into hell, but the much later Catholic church across the Bourne is arguably more beautiful inside though it has a plain exterior. Next to it stables have been converted into a theatre on the other side of which runs the old High Street. Of the many tiny cottages, number 118 is the quaintest – sheer Hansel-and-Gretel, with a chimney almost as big as the cottage.

Nearer the sea, St Clement's 14th-century church is oddly designed to fit the shape of the land (it was perched here because an earlier church on level ground was destroyed by the sea). It is a place of space and light, dedicated to the saint of fishermen. From here I went puffing and blowing up Coburg Place – narrow twisting stairs that run behind, between and even under houses to get to the top of West Hill, where William the Conqueror built his first castle.

A vast network of tunnels in the hill was originally gouged out by underground streams, but humans have had a hand since – most recently with figures of Churchill and others carved in the soft sandstone. No one knows how long ago the caves were first put to use, but they have often been used for refuge – from Vikings and from bombers in the Second World War, for example. Smugglers found them extremely useful hideaways, as did Wellington's soldiers when garrisoned in Hastings. Eventually the entrance was walled up. (Was one truant soldier inadvertently walled in? Some years ago a skeleton was found, said to be nearly 200 years old.) The caves were then more or less forgotten until a gardener digging a hole fell into them, and after that they became his life's work. He carved many of the figures and miles of pillared 'cloisters' with niches for candles. Occasionally candle-lit processions are staged there. Young people have a weekly disco, and the TV play 'King's Dragon' was filmed down there. All events are presided over by the custodian's cat, who never loses her way in the labyrinth that is her home.

Hastings was the most important of the Cinque Ports until Dover overtook it a century ago. This was in spite of the fact that it had to be recreated three times after the sea swept over it. Now the picturesque old town, with its antique shops and restaurants, is a very small part of the whole. Modern Hastings (go down West Hill to it by means of the lift) is a bustling holiday resort, full of entertainment. On the other side of the old town is East Hill and a country park with picturesque glens and nature trails. (There is more about Hastings on pages 164–5.)

If you do not want to go back to Sandwich or Dover, there are plenty of other options as Hastings is well served by coaches (to London, for instance).

7
The South Hams

Totnes – Dartmouth – Kingsbridge – Plymouth

'Ham' means 'sheltered', and the South Hams area of Devon is so sheltered that it has one of the mildest climates in Britain, which makes it a good choice for a few days' break even when other places are still wintry. It is entirely a farming area with no industrial ugliness to spoil the idyll, and because no fewer than five rivers run hither and yon, indenting the coastline where they reach the sea, any bus ride is full of interest as it goes up hills and down into valleys. Farming and trading have always prospered here, so towns contain handsome houses and the thatched cottages of the villages have been kept up well.

Totnes

I chose Totnes (on the River Dart) as a good base from which to explore the area by bus, and right by the bus park found the Royal Seven Stars Hotel, a coaching inn which dates from Charles II's day. The coachyard is roofed over to make a stone-flagged entrance hall with an imposing staircase descending from a gallery, and a long row of old room bells, now silent, hangs on one wall.

The inn stands at the foot of steep Fore Street, which is spanned halfway up by an immense blue-and-white gateway beside which are steps leading up to the ramparts of this ancient borough. Founded in Saxon times, it was once an important town, and at its quay merchandise has been loaded for nearly a thousand years.

Fore Street is lined with houses in pastel pinks and yellows, some with bay windows, some with little courts that can be glimpsed between them. A characteristic of Totnes is the use of slates decoratively hung like fish scales on the upper storeys. In the streets are the kind of small, old-fashioned shops which still have evocative smells – of toffees in a sweet-shop or leather in a shoe-shop, for instance – almost vanished from memory in this packaging-and-plastic age.

The rampart walk leads past the old stone Guildhall (now a museum) in its picturesque, colonnaded corner and to the 15th-century church with a really spectacular rood screen, its delicate tracery of carved stone amazingly intact after all these centuries and with some of the old gilding still surviving. On the elaborate monument to Christopher Blackhall, who died in 1633, are his four wives (successive not simultaneous), each in the fashion of her day, whether ruffed or lace-collared.

Beyond lies the castellated castle on a mound, neat and round as a child's sandcastle. It remained undamaged, I was told, because the burghers of Totnes were always quick to change sides in any war when the going became really rough. From here there is a good view over the tumble of rooftops below. The High Street beyond is where the most interesting shops and small restaurants are, many in columned arcades, some decorated with black-and-white fancywork and some with carved grotesques. In Totnes a great variety of building stones has been used, including red sandstone, granite, limestone and tufa (a stone formed from volcanic ash).

Plenty of bus trips are possible from Totnes – out on to the moors, for instance, or to lovely Dartington Hall nearby (set in exceptionally lovely gardens – the great lawn, flanked by grassy terraces, was once a tiltyard for jousting). I lunched from the hot buffet served at the Cott Inn near there, ducking my head at each low doorway. This is one of the oldest inns in the country, its thick white walls made of cobb (a mud-like mixture), its roof of dense thatch. Torquay, Buckfast Abbey and Paignton are all within an easy bus ride, too.

The bus route to Dartmouth runs between high hedges, pines and oaks, with views of fields where brown Devon cattle graze or ploughed earth shows up red among the green. It is a winding road, punctuated with streams and picturesque inns, rising and falling, often with trees meeting overhead. Descending steeply into Dartmouth, there is a lovely view across the water with its swans and bobbing boats to Kingswear: colour-washed houses are piled up on the steep bank, and a steam train puffs slowly along the shore.

Dartmouth

Dartmouth is one of my favourite places by the sea, perched precariously on steep cliffs beside the estuary, a little harbour at its heart. Picturesque and historical, it is a place of coves and cobbles, old houses and sub-tropical gardens, waterfront castles and trips on the river through spectacular scenery. Well worth visiting are Bayards Cove Fort and, further seaward, Dartmouth Castle itself: both early Tudor, and the latter one of the earliest castles built to house guns. From there one can take a further bus along the sandy coast to Kingsbridge, or Kingsbridge can be reached direct via Totnes by an inland bus ride that offers distant views of Dartmoor's smoky-blue hills and close-ups of the steep banks so characteristic of Devon lanes, with primroses, moss, hart's tongue ferns, celandines, holly, ivy and occasionally violets.

The Dartmouth–Kingsbridge bus route is particularly attractive, going close by the Slapton Ley nature reserve with a good view of waterfowl on the lagoons, and the sea on the other side of the road. American servicemen practised their D-Day landings here.

Kingsbridge

Kingsbridge is a little town on another estuary. Like Totnes it is on a steep hill by the river, and like Totnes it has an arcaded Butterwalk or Shambles that goes back to Tudor times. On Wednesdays, market days, it hums with activity, and the old King's Arms inn does a busy trade.

Plymouth

From there it does not take long to get by bus through more pretty villages to Plymouth. Drake's voyage round the world started from Plymouth, his home town. There is the famous Hoe (where bowls are still played) overlooking one of the most beautiful natural harbours in the world; beaches of sand and rock; brilliant gardens; the cobbled streets and fishmarkets near the steps from which the Pilgrim Fathers embarked on the Mayflower; and old lanes and little shops (big ones, too – Plymouth has a vast shopping centre). Much-bombed Plymouth does not have many old buildings. It is a big holiday resort now, with sights, excursions and restaurants enough to occupy one for a fortnight. Open-top bus tours and a viewing platform at the top of its Municipal Offices skyscraper make the most of one of its greatest assets: the views. Whether inland or out to sea, every prospect pleases. (Plymouth is more fully described on pages 249–53.)

Plymouth Youth Hostel

8

England's Only Prairie

Salisbury Plain

Salisbury – Amesbury – Marlborough

Wiltshire is a county often underestimated by tourists, who hurry in to 'do' Salisbury Cathedral, Longleat or Stonehenge and then dash on elsewhere. It is worth spending longer and, using Salisbury as a base for a couple of nights, one can make very varied bus trips in each direction. This is an account of just one, crossing Salisbury Plain from south to north and climbing up into the Marlborough Downs for contrast.

The Plain is a vast expanse, still holding many ancient secrets. People have lived there for at least 4,000 years, and the traces of far-off occupation are numerous yet often mysterious even to archaeologists. The great circles of which Stonehenge is the most famous remain the subject of argument. Were they temples? sundial-calendars for farmers? No one knows for sure, and it is even uncertain how such colossal stones were raised into position. There are literally hundreds of prehistoric burial mounds and traces of Iron Age forts and earthworks on hilltops – each adding to the landscape's distinctive contours. Some ancient tracks may well have been trodden by the feet of Stone Age people, and the famous white horses of Wiltshire's hills, cut through the turf to reveal the white chalk below, were in some cases created over a thousand years ago (others date from the 18th, 19th or even 20th centuries).

Salisbury

But first there is the starting point, Salisbury itself (described more fully on pages 277–81). The cathedral's 400-foot spire is known world-wide through reproductions of Constable's famous painting of it, and this is unquestionably its most beautiful feature. The soaring and lengthy interior is impressive, yet rather bleak. The spire was added a century after the cathedral was built early in the 13th century, and its 6,000 tons added such an extra strain to the foundations that there have been problems ever since.

Salisbury Cathedral

Within the cathedral is the oldest clock in the world, and its clacking iron mechanism attracts a bigger group of sightseers than any of the monuments. Having been working for 600 years it is quite possibly the oldest bit of 'living' machinery in the world. The cathedral has the largest cloisters in England, an octagonal chapter house with biblical scenes carved in stone, and a tiny chapel with exquisite fan-vaulting. Children may enjoy spotting one of its special though not very conspicuous features (binoculars are a help): some 60 stone faces very high up in the nave and elsewhere. Each is a portrait of somebody once notable, but very few have been identified. Some may also enjoy picking out (with the help of a booklet sold in the cathedral) the hundred or so saints and kings in their niches on the west front. With the largest cloisters, oldest clock and highest spire Salisbury cannot but be one of the most impressive of cathedrals.

Around the spacious green that is the Cathedral Close are old houses such as the medieval bishop's palace, canonry and deanery (some open to visitors), and to the north of it lies a network of historic streets, churches and inns. The most interesting shops and eating places are in the High Street.

Five winding rivers meet in a tangle at Salisbury. On the banks of several are gardens or meadows, so the countryside seems to penetrate right into the heart of the city. It is worth taking a bus to Harnham and walking down to the Old Mill, the spot from which Constable got his famous view of Salisbury's spire (one can then return to the city by a short walk across meadows and bridges over two of the rivers). The mill is now a small hotel and restaurant.

The bus ride to Amesbury (see also page 276) was brief but attractive, through unspoilt countryside, and the wintry sun burnished every stream and puddle so that the watery landscape was illuminated here and there. New calves were sparkling white. Looking backwards before entering Amesbury, one can still see the lynchets on the hillside – strips that were ploughed, seeded and harvested by generations of medieval villagers – and two old tollhouses, now cottages. Then come the lovely cedar trees that mark the approach to the town.

Amesbury

When Amesbury celebrated its millennium, Prince Charles planted the whitebeam now growing up among the ancient yews in the churchyard. One day it may be a noble tree some 60 feet high, the undersides of its leaves pure white. I wandered across the nearby footbridge over the Avon as it hurries on its long journey to Salisbury and the sea. This metal bridge spans the river alongside a stone one bearing the date 1775, waterweed clinging to its cutwaters. The only sounds were the rush of water over a little weir known as Tumbling Bay, the raucous rooks and mellow chimes from the church.

Amesbury's history goes back to the Stone and Iron Ages, with legends to match (Arthur's Queen, Guinevere, was reputedly buried here). The Vikings raided it. It later prospered, being on the junction of main coaching roads – hence the many inns that line the High Street – but it is a quiet town now.

The bus route to Marlborough follows the Avon upstream through the valley it has carved out of Salisbury Plain. On the way out of the town the bus passes, on the left, two curious buildings of dressed flint – a skilled technique almost forgotten now – with octagonal towers (one is named 'Diana her hous' and dated 1600). They were once gatehouses to the park of the long-vanished abbey. At the crossroads, Countess Farm has a fine collection of great 18th-century barns, evidence of the agricultural riches of the area.

Along the twists of the valley road were cottages of thatch and half-timbering or of brick alternating with flint bands, views of hills bare except for clumps of trees, swans on the river, and in the air two parachutists floating down and a glider. At Pewsey, King Alfred's statue stands in the street – a reminder of battles long ago when he repelled the invading Danish Vikings. Opposite one of the inns is a narrow hill called Brunkards Lane, and I wondered at whose genteel behest that 'B' had replaced what was once no doubt a 'D'!

The road to Marlborough crosses the Kennet and Avon Canal where pleasure boats idled below. Many of the thatched roofs are topped with a straw pheasant (some thatcher's personal trademark). The road climbs high, rounds a bend and suddenly the towers, spires and roofs of Marlborough were at our feet. The bus swooped down, crossed a lovely river, ran alongside a very lengthy copper beech hedge, passed Marlborough College and drew up in the vast main street – exceptionally wide and long, with a church at each end.

Marlborough

The town was devastated by a great fire in 1653, which is why so many of its houses show an 18th-century front to the world – but Tudor or medieval remains can still be found behind the many alleyways that are threaded between the buildings. Some shops are sheltered behind arcades. There are lovely lamplit courtyards, old coaching inns and the tranquil lawn and spring flowers of the old priory gardens tucked behind a modern cloister-like building in the middle of the street, which slope down to the River Kennet.

Other good bus trips out of Salisbury include, for example, Stonehenge; Tidworth (reached through the valley of the River Bourne); Shaftesbury (a hilltop town with abbey, ruins and cobbled streets, with fine scenery along the way – see page 125); and, for a longer trip, the seaside resort of Bournemouth (pleasant countryside, and the interesting villages of Breamore and Downton with half-timbered and thatched cottages are along the route). And there are lots of others. The Wilts and Dorset Bus Company has published a useful leaflet 'Out and About' (available from the bus station, or telephone 0722 336855).

9
East Anglia's Heritage Coast

Colchester – Ipswich – Orford – Woodbridge – Felixstowe

I had arrived at Colchester by bus through water meadows where cows grazed near a winding stream and hawthorns blossomed in the hedges. The bus strained up into the town via North Hill (where antique shops, bookshops and restaurants are located) and along the arcaded High Street with its resplendent Edwardian town hall and coaching inns.

Colchester

The bus station is at the end of the High Street and conveniently near the main places of interest – castle, museums, and so forth. But I did not head for them immediately, preferring to seek out Colchester's oldest remains first: the massive encircling wall the Romans started (down Priory Street, to the east). It is both impressive in scale and, with yellow ragwort and wallflowers springing from its crevices, beautiful too – but scarcely a pleasant walk, because there is a car park along its entire length. I was glad to turn aside to the ruins of the Norman priory (itself built from stones and tiles taken from Roman buildings). There is a spectacular doorway, its huge arch outlined with row upon row (twelve in all) of axe-hewn decorations. A pigeon had rather lowered the tone by building a nest in a crevice, loosely incorporating a large plastic bag that flapped in the breeze, but pigeons are always untidy builders, with little appreciation for ancient monuments.

Threading my way through Vineyard Street and another car park flanking the southern stretch of the Roman wall (exit of Roman sewer as clearly labelled as any nobler relic), I came via the quaint houses and little shops of Trinity Street to the rural crafts museum (housed in a disused church, partly Saxon) where lifesize exhibits show how thatching is done, how a windmill works and so forth. The recreation of an old laundry was fascinating – it had everything from wooden pattens (footgear to keep one's feet clear of puddles on the stone floor) to a box mangle, a huge box filled with stones that was rolled to and fro over the wet linen. 'Operating the mangle was tiring work' said the caption – the understatement of the age.

Colchester Youth Hostel

It was a short walk to Balkerne Gate (in the west wall of the city), the greatest Roman gateway still surviving in Britain; the modern Mercury Theatre (where I had a good, inexpensive lunch); and Jumbo – an extraordinary water-tower which has dominated the city for the last century or so. By the time I'd had a good look at the town hall and the old byways tucked behind it, I was glad to reach the gardens surrounding the castle and sit on the grass in its shadow.

The very early Norman castle is, in every sense, Colchester's high spot. It covers a vast area and was once immensely tall, too.

The huge stump of it that is left houses an extremely clear and well-devised museum, with models that vividly interpret all one has seen while walking about. The 1648 siege of Colchester by the Cromwellians is clearly explained in a vast panorama of fortifications and troops. There are models of how the city was in Roman times (where the castle now stands was once a temple to the Roman emperor, Claudius). Even the plethora of statues from the town hall façade are reproduced in plaster and explained. There are, of course, a lot of archaeological exhibits, the oddest of all being a horse's coffin from the Iron Age.

Nearby are two other good museums in interesting buildings. In an old church, children clustered round the ichthyosaurs and iguanodon that are among the dioramas and other displays of local wildlife, and in an early Georgian mansion surrounded by beds of violas and wallflowers is housed a collection of old furniture, costume, toys and so forth. A child's lesson book called *Reading Disentangled* was full of precepts like 'My dear children, I hope that you will never swear like some poor boys in the street.' Another social comment could be read into the caption to a portrait of Mary Wates who, by the time she died in 1620 at the age of 93, had 367 grandchildren and great-grandchildren (having herself given birth to 16 children). I suppose if you were tough enough to survive all that child-bearing (and the Tudor doctors), it was a simple matter to go on surviving into your nineties.

Before returning to the nearby bus station I walked past the handsome Jacobean plasterwork of Alderman Winstanley's home and into the light and elegant 15th-century church where his ornate tomb stands. The church has a dark oak roof adorned with bright angels, painted and gilded, a typical East Anglian touch. (Incidentally, in summer an open-top bus does a $1\frac{1}{4}$-hour tour of Colchester and its environs.)

My bus swung out and down steep East Hill – lined with Georgian or half-timbered houses, walls leaning and roofs at odd angles – over a bridge of blue-and-white ironwork, with a weir to the left, and past Siege House, pocked with bullet-holes from the Civil War and masked in dust raised by the passing traffic. Once clear of the suburbs, the route passes through 'Constable country', though East Anglian fields are often prairie-like in size now. It goes by pool and stream where upended ducks were plunging to find food, rises and falls as pink and thatched cottages are succeeded by orchards and then skirts the gold-and-silver of gorse and hawthorn hedges, until the busy county town of Ipswich is reached.

Ipswich

A beautiful park is one of Ipswich's outstanding features, in complete contrast to the opposite edge of the town – the quayside of the River Orwell. Here among the working ships from all over the world are moored others in honourable retirement. On my visit these included the great old sailing barge *Phoenician*, being converted for disabled people to sail in, an ex-Navy steam tug being restored by enthusiasts, and a scarlet lightship with seemingly top-heavy lantern. On land heavy lorries belt by old houses that were once the homes of sea captains and merchants, the handsome Custom House and Wolsey's Gate – sole relic of a college founded by the cardinal, an Ipswich man.

There are interesting old shops, wine bars, craftsmen, mullioned windows and courtyards to be found up St Peters Street and Silent Street. ('Silent'? Even at 8 am Ipswich has motor cyclists buzzing about as if a wasps' nest had been disturbed.)

Then I found a total surprise. Whereas some business houses have tried to blend their new premises into old Ipswich by designing in a traditional style (Barclays Bank, for instance, has built itself an imitation of a riverside warehouse), an international insurance company has gone to the other extreme – and with great success. Ipswich's most exciting building (in Friar Street) is the biggest glasshouse in the world, accommodating over a thousand workers. It is low (only three floors); it has a flowing, curved shape; and it is of a tinted glass that reflects the church spires and other old buildings around. Its roof is made of grass – an acre or so of lawn which (along with the swimming pool, gymnasium, restaurants and suchlike) helps to make this a very agreeable workplace. Curiosity, as always, overcoming discretion, I walked in and was given a handsome brochure about this striking building.

Though there is more to see in Ipswich, there was only time before catching my next bus to walk along the Buttermarket to Hatchard's big bookshop, a riot of carved wood outside and in. The façade is covered with pilasters, swags of fruit, lions' heads, oriel windows, pelicans in plaster and representations of the four continents (Australia was the as yet undiscovered fifth when the house was built, in Tudor times). From the bus station, in the curiously named street of Dog's Head, there is a view of three church towers – all beautiful in the morning sun, but in completely contrasted styles. One is simple, flinty and rectangular, beyond it is a slender spire, and finally the third is a chequerboard tower topped with lacy stonework of great delicacy.

The bus threaded its way out through narrow streets, past a new Sainsbury's with a wall textured in cobbles, bricks and mosaic; pleasant little early Victorian cottages; suburbs; and then a heath of gorse and birch with the morning haze still lingering on it. Further on, householders have planted the road's verges with spring flowers. Then came an imposing group of almshouses in hot red brick, a narrow street packed with ancient homes, and abruptly we found ourselves in the great, quiet square at the heart of Woodbridge (to which I would return later), dominated by the Tudor Shire Hall and courthouse in the middle and a century-old pump in a pumphouse, and ringed with old houses painted buff, terracotta, dark or pale green. I changed buses here, enjoying the Suffolk voices of the women who exchanged local news with the bus driver as we went steeply down, only just missing the overhead sign of the 15th-century Bell and Steelyard Inn – an astonishing weighing-arm that stretches out across the road (for the inn was once a steelyard).

The journey then became really rural – heath alternating with big ploughed fields, across the wide river at Melton (the tide right out), running by woodland and pools, past an air force base and through a pine forest where signs warned that deer sometimes wander out of the shadows and onto the road. Great barns and walls of knapped flint are characteristic of this area. A tractor hauling bales of hay slowed us to a crawl behind it in the narrow lane that approaches Orford and then, just as suddenly as at Woodbridge, a turn released us like a cork from a bottle into a great open square.

Orford

Everything of interest is close to this square or down towards the now distant quayside (as on much of this coast, the shoreline has shifted its position over the centuries, so Orford is no longer a port). There is the partly Norman church, impressive in its own right and also used to house various local relics. The wooden roof has carved bosses and, like many East Anglian churches, there are poppyheads at the ends of the choir stalls. Under floormats are a number of brasses – one shows a mother and the 12 children she bore who all died before they grew up. Stone coffins, the village stocks and old bells from the tower are dumped in one corner, near an ancient board detailing the terms of Brett's Benevolence, a fund for 'deserving poor Widow Women of the Parish'. The church's greatest treasure is a painting by one of Raphael's pupils. The church was cold, and I returned gladly to the sunny churchyard and the ruined arcade behind it, lingering over ancient epitaphs, telling of ancient griefs.

Orford Castle

Small though Orford is, it has a huge castle, many attractive houses, a choice of old inns and good eating places, picturesque corners and many stories to tell – of ghosts, floods, mermen and shipwrecks (it's worth buying the local guidebook, sold in the church). In fact, the village deserves an overnight stop, for from it one can visit the bird reserve on the island of Minsmere and watch oyster-catchers and other waders close up (from a hide). Details from the Warden; 072 873281.

If you have breath to climb 90 feet to the top of the castle (built for Henry II about 1170 as a defence against invaders from Europe) there are spectacular views of sea and countryside.

All the inns are interesting. I sampled the local brew at the King's Head, a coaching inn which was also a smugglers' base, then walked across to the Buttery for a fish lunch (oyster soup followed by eel-and-salmon mousse) eaten at a marble-topped table. Orford's Buttery is famous for its smoked fish and local oysters.

My next bus took me back to Woodbridge again but by a different route, colourful with the faded reds of last year's bracken and oak leaves, and with pheasants' copper breasts iridescent in the sun. The pheasants strut boldly at this season when shooting is over, scarlet and green heads showing up bright above their white clerical collars. There were partridges about, too. A row of dead moles hung along a fence – destined perhaps to make a velvety moleskin waistcoat?

As usual, there were few people on the bus and all but me were well known to the driver. His remarks floated up to me on the top deck: '. . . if I see Jack, I'll tell him you asked after him . . .', and, to a child getting off, '. . . and wait there till Mummy comes; don't you go running across the road.'

At Melton the tide was in and the moored pleasure boats bobbed happily. We passed a disused rail station, squeezed tightly through Woodbridge's narrow streets again, and ground to a halt.

Woodbridge

Woodbridge is famous for its 200-year-old tide mill down beside the River Deben, its wheel worked by the ebb and flow of the tide. All round here are cobbled lanes leading to quays and a scene of boats and boat-building. This is a town of great charm. Up its steep streets are many old houses (all porticos, fanlights and iron balconies), and it has some interesting shops. The Music Shop sells antique instruments; there is an art gallery; furniture, book, rod-and-gun shops abound, and so do inns.

The next bus chugged along, gently rattling and squeaking, on a straight road between fields of sheep (now a far less common sight than a century ago, when Suffolk was one of the great wool counties). There are picturesque inns along this route as well as cottages with immaculate thatch capping their dormers and shaped into eyebrows over bedroom windows. A pheasant strolled casually in front of the bus.

Primroses on a river bank, periwinkles tumbling down a wall, pink cottages, a field of chestnut mares with newborn foals – such pictures seen through the big bus windows came and went in swift succession. The earth hereabouts is reddish, some fields deep-furrowed and others ploughed to a fine tilth. At a colony for delinquent youngsters (a constructive alternative to prison), we passed a boy leading a great carthorse, others loading cabbages and some busy in a blacksmith's shop. There are many huge water-towers in this region, because of the chronic lack of rain on the eastern side of England.

Another aspect of east-coast life, however, has less pastoral charm. As in every century, England is on the defensive here. Much of the land belongs to the Ministry of Defence. Rotating scanners came into view, and suddenly we passed near a row of great missiles, lined up and pointing their sharp warheads out seawards and to Europe.

After another sharp turn red sails and then hundreds of little boats at anchor sprang into sight. We drew up by a small sandy beach at Bawdsey where children were playing. I, by that time the only passenger, got out to await the ferry which would take me from Bawdsey to the Felixstowe side of the Deben estuary.

Felixstowe

Mr Brinkley, the ferryman, told me that he came from generations of local fishermen (I had noticed the name in accounts of Orford's history), some of whom still brave the North Sea in their eighties. Listening to his anecdotes of people he had encountered on the ferry, I lost track of the time, missed my bus and so had a long walk into Felixstowe – along the sea wall, past bathing huts and Martello towers and across a golf course. A lark was singing high out of sight and a peacock butterfly alighted at my feet. Golfers were out in force and a salt breeze flicked the wiry grass as it passed. The only other sound was the sea on the shingle until I reached the outskirts of Felixstowe.

That was the end of my two-day tour, in a town very different from the others I had explored – a sedate seaside resort with magnificent, manicured gardens in which every lobelia and every bachelor's button knows its place, the palm trees grow straight as lamp-posts, and no one ever moves faster than wheelchair pace. Within two hours I was at home in London.

10

There's Something About Islands

I. The Isle of Wight

Ryde – Bembridge – Sandown – Shanklin – Ventnor – Yarmouth – Freshwater Bay – Newport – Cowes

Any island is bound to have a character all of its own, no matter how narrow the strip of sea that separates it from the mainland, and islanders are known for being stubbornly independent. The Isle of Wight is no exception: even the usual 'Keep Britain Tidy' posters are missing, and in their place hangs 'Keep the Island Tidy'.

For a bussing-about holiday on Wight there is an extra inducement: the local bus company (Southern Vectis) has fixed up a special ticket for road-rail travel connected with 'breakaway' holidays on the island at off-peak times of the year (since the island is so far south its spring starts early and its autumn goes on longer than the mainland's). This ticket enables you to travel free all over the island's 150 square miles. You pay an all-in amount for the holiday which covers rail fares from your home town to Portsmouth, the ferry from there to the island, accommodation (with breakfast and dinner) and the ticket for unlimited bus travel within the island. The road-rail day-ticket (or its weekly equivalent) is also available to people not on a breakaway package holiday.

Wherever one goes on bus journeys round the island there are beautiful shorelines and sea views, woodlands, rolling hills, historic buildings or unspoilt towns that still recall the days when the island was a favourite retreat of Queen Victoria and of the Prince of Wales' fashionable yachting set. Much of the island is owned by the National Trust.

Ryde

I arrived at Ryde on a Friday evening and stayed there for the first night. I spent the second night in Shanklin.

As soon as one steps onto the ferry from Portsmouth (see pages 270–274) there is an instant feeling of getting away from it all: the engine throbs, the wake makes a shining swathe in the Solent as the catamaran sweeps round, and the golden egg of the setting sun vanishes below the horizon leaving behind a pearl-pink sky. There is plenty of interest on this brief voyage – a quick glimpse of *Victory*'s masts as we pull out of Portsmouth, medieval ramparts and the old forts (Spitbank, Horse's Sand and No Man's Land) that have stood guard in the sea for two centuries.

The Portsmouth lights twinkled in the twilight behind us and then the spires of Ryde came into sight, above its jumble of sparkling white Regency and Victorian houses piled up steeply above the shore.

Next morning, after wandering briefly among the shops in the Royal Victoria Arcade and the seafront gardens, I watched the passing scene while waiting for my first bus of the day. Across the road from the bus-stop stands the Royal Esplanade Hotel, its façade rich with grapes and hops among lacy cast-iron balconies. From the sandy beach a hovercraft (like a large and noisy frog) took off across the sea.

The bus clambered up among stucco villas and stone mansions, every turn bringing into view different glimpses of the turquoise Solent below, its forts now tiny specks. Azaleas, camellias and all the other flowers of spring were out. We passed a willow-fringed pool, and there were views of hills inland and, on the other side, vast sandy beaches and a silver sea dotted with tiny sails.

St Helens is a village with a huge green. In summer one can take a ferry from near there to Bembridge harbour, but I stayed on the bus until it reached the centre of Bembridge and then, after fuelling myself with a cup of coffee, I slowly walked *back* to the harbour we had just passed (doing it this way meant that I walked downhill, not up).

Bembridge

Bembridge has an old windmill, cottages named for the plants around them (Woodbine, Bay, Fuchsia) and several inns – one built to look like a boat. I visited the little Maritime Museum (it has finds from wrecks, models of ships, and two colossal anchors outside) where I bought a plate with the old saying 'It is better to travel hopefully than to arrive' – good advice for bus riders! I decided to give the more distant lifeboat station a miss. Down by the harbour pleasure-boats were moored and the skeleton of a great old hulk was slowly rotting. Round the once-grand memorial fountain of porphyry and granite, just by the bus stop, came a cavalcade of children on ponies.

The bus goes by Whitecliff Bay, near which is a good view of the hilltop obelisk that is a memorial to the first commodore of the Royal Yacht Squadron (founded in 1815), and through Yaverland village with its Jacobean manor house, a route that passes fine Regency and later houses set in beautiful gardens, and cottages or farms of stone and thatch. Cocks strutted in a farmyard, ducks dabbled head-down in a pond, and lambs with black faces and socks frisked in the sunshine. The bus wound its way between hedges and trees lining narrow lanes, slowing to a crawl when we caught up with a solitary horse-rider. Then suddenly the whole sea was before us, bright and shimmering – Sandown Bay.

Sandown

At Sandown I relaxed in a deckchair on the vast sandy beach with a view of distant sandstone cliffs and read *Reptiles on the Rocks*, which I bought at the library where the bus stops. Above the library I had found a frowsty little room, full of sun and dust, that dignifies itself with the name of museum – but what a treasure house it is. Fossilized bits of local crocodiles and Oligocene rhinos, mammoths' teeth, the colossal backbone of an iguanodon and even fossilized pearls were amongst its hoard. The Isle of Wight is rich in prehistoric finds from 30 million years ago when this part of England was steamy jungle: it is only in the Isle of Wight that rocks from the Oligocene period are exposed.

Shanklin

Sandown runs into Shanklin, with small hotels and guest houses all along the way. I stayed on the bus until it got to the old village on the far side of Shanklin. This is certainly picturesque (all white-washed walls and thick thatched roofs) but, even out of season, it is very touristy; almost every cottage is now a restaurant. However, the famous chine that leads off it was deserted. 'Chine' is local parlance for a narrow ravine cut deep into the soft sandstone by a stream making its steep descent to the sea. Shanklin's chine runs down from the cliff-top village to the esplanade 150 feet below. On entering at the top, one's senses move into another world of cool, earth smells from the wet cliffs spangled with ferns, moss, ivy and primroses and of fresh sounds such as the splash of water and the song of birds. The first waterfall drops sheer for 40 feet. Wood or stone bridges cross each turn of the winding stream, and there are rustic arbours at every viewpoint. Towards the end a lookout platform provides a tremendous view over Sandown Bay, the pier, sailing boats, bathing huts and windsurfers scudding quickly over the waves. There are various curiosities along the way such as the marble-lined brine bath with steps, in which many Victorian health-faddists half-boiled themselves in heated sea water.

On leaving the chine I walked beside a hedge of hebe, along the esplanade and past the pier, and then took the lift up the cliff (here hotels face the south and the sea, with glass verandahs so that one may bask even in winter).

The short, serpentine bus journey up and then down to Ventnor is very lovely. There are streams, duck-ponds, thatched stone cottages with sparkling white window frames and doors, or slate-tiled with decorative white bargeboards, and – above all – stunning views back to Sandown Bay, with Shanklin itself a mere toy town on its edge and cattle looking like crumbs on the green billiard cloth of fields far below the road. At the top of the steep hill a horse trough (now planted with tulips) bears the message 'Be kind and merciful to all animals', and one's thoughts turn to the time when these wretched beasts had to haul loads uphill on hot days.

Along the bus route is a little pumping station in a field; there are views of white cliffs and then one looks down onto the roofs and into the gardens of Shanklin. Though the cottages are very crowded together, every one finds room for a rock garden, window boxes or glassed-in porch crammed with pot plants.

Ventnor

I spent a pleasant couple of hours in Ventnor before returning to Shanklin for the night. Ventnor, like Ryde, clings precariously to steep slopes that go right down to the sea. Its houses are like the audience in a Roman amphitheatre looking down upon the spectacle of the sea. After dawdling pleasurably in Mr Keen's well-stocked bookshop, I walked down past the cascade and the pier, and then up to the top of cliffs where teazles and pink campions grow in profusion. Surf was breaking on the rocks far below and children's voices floated up from the distant beach.

It was pleasant to stroll in the park where a stream gushed, ducks dashed and a spaniel paddled. Glass frames were full of geraniums waiting to be bedded out later. Further along a road of verandahed, gabled and slated houses (many of them hotels now) lie the Botanical Gardens. Their tropical plants and palms make it plain why Ventnor calls itself 'the Madeira of England'. In one corner is a museum of smuggling.

Next day, because I was a week too early for the coastal route to Freshwater that runs during some months only, I took a bus inland and northwards to Newport (and thence to Freshwater). The route through leafy, winding lanes was much more enjoyable in the big-windowed bus than it would have been in a low car, from which one could not have seen over the hawthorn hedges. The patchwork of fields (grassy or ploughed), coppices and gorse heaths was dotted with farms, streams and pleasant houses surrounded by lawns or magnolia trees in bloom. Godshill, like old Shanklin, is a once-picturesque village now mainly an enclave of thatched tea-rooms.

The bus crossed the river Medina and entered Newport, the island's capital, from which I got another bus westward – passing, as we went out of the town, the mayor with the mace-bearer and mace parading to church. The bus ran alongside an attractive terrace of iron-balconied houses raised up on a bank, a tiny green with colourful little villas, a roadside brook and the turning that leads to Carisbrooke Castle, a ¾-mile walk. (This is the Norman castle where Charles I was imprisoned by the Cromwellians, and where donkeys still work the great wheel that hauls buckets of water up a 160-foot well.) Past the dark mass of Parkhurst Forest the landscape opened up, and then a great expanse of the Solent came into view, lively with the white sails of small boats on the choppy waters.

Yarmouth

At Yarmouth (where there is one of Henry VIII's castles) the bus drew up by the harbour – a forest of small boat masts, their burgees flicked by the wind, with gulls wheeling overhead. A crowd of youngsters got on (standing room only then), filling the bus with their cheerful chatter as it crossed the harbour bridge and went over salt flats with a view of constantly changing sea, now dark, now light, and blue, green and grey in turns. A lighthouse, a huge green, a thatched church and then we were at Freshwater Bay, back on the rocky and dangerous south coast of the island that is so very different from the sheltered north, which has only the Solent between it and mainland England. Tennyson, who lived near here, said the air was 'worth sixpence a pint' – what price the dramatic scenery, I wondered? One can bus even further to fantastic Alum Bay, with its multi-coloured sandstone cliffs and its view of those rocky pinnacles, the Needles (to which boat trips go). This is the place for unusual souvenirs such as glass models filled with patterns in 21 different hues of naturally coloured sand. A chairlift goes down to the beach if you want to gather the sands yourself.

Yarmouth Castle

Freshwater Bay

At Freshwater Bay I went to see what six burly young men in orange overalls were doing with their huge inflated powerboat. They turned out to be lifeguards engaged on their weekly practice. Each is a volunteer who pursues trades quite unconnected with the sea during working hours. They even raise the money needed to keep the boat going. It is the sole hope for anyone in trouble along the next 20 miles of treacherous rocky coast, subject to the worst of Channel weather.

The next bus, a double-decker, took a deep breath and staggered up the exceedingly steep hill that leads to a heath, golf links and cliff tops owned by the National Trust. Here there are tremendous views of the sea (looking like shot silk), cliffs (white chalk changing to yellow sandstone), bays, surf and hills. In some respects the scenery reminded me of Cornwall. Inland are downs (tracks show up white where topsoil has been worn down to the chalk), with farms nestling at their feet; the hummocks on the horizon are prehistoric burial mounds.

A friendly passenger pointed out to me the hilltop mansion where J. B. Priestley used to live, and enlivened the journey with local gossip. The whole of this ride was picturesque and very typical of the Isle of Wight at its best – flint-capped walls, very pretty cottage gardens, quaint little churches, thatching in progress (from the top of a bus one gets a good view of that), an impressive 16th-century manor house (it originally belonged to Edward VI's tutor) and little inn at Mottistone, a barn perched on mushroom-shaped staddle stones to keep rats out, and a particularly fine farm just before Shorwell.

After passing under a rustic wooden footbridge the road turns inland between banks of wild garlic – always winding, rising and falling. The ploughed fields are pale with chalk. When Carisbrooke Castle came into view, spread out along a hilltop, I realized we were approaching Newport again.

Newport

I cannot say much in favour of Newport on a Sunday except that it is quiet. Or it was, until suddenly the air came alive with the sound of music – trombones, drums and bugles, to be precise; all the youth organizations of the town were parading to church. Fortunately I'd already had a look round the church which, though little more than a century old, has a very beautiful (and colourful) interior. It also has one outstanding memorial, a poignant marble sculpture of the 15-year-old Princess Elizabeth (daughter of Charles I) who died in Carisbrooke Castle. Queen Victoria had this beautiful memorial erected when the girl's lost grave was accidentally discovered by workmen in 1856.

There is much more to be seen in the island. For example, I had no opportunity to visit Osborne House, home of Queen Victoria and largely the creation of Prince Albert, where she died. The rooms are kept exactly as they were in her lifetime, and in the grounds are her bathing machine, the Swiss chalet where the children were given lessons in such useful skills as carpentry and cooking, and a miniature fort built by the ten-year-old Prince Arthur. There are also Roman remains, more mansions and museums, a working watermill, a steam railway, a model village, glass-making studios, nature trails, a working forge and much else.

As I wanted to reach the mainland by hydrofoil to Southampton, I took a bus from Newport to Cowes. We passed the grim walls of Parkhurst Prison, ran alongside the Medina estuary and went past a field full of radar scanners in every size and shape (oddly contrasting with the adjoining field of sheep).

Cowes

Cowes is above all a yachting centre, but the season had scarcely begun and there were few people in its steep old streets. I wandered in and out of alleyways, onto jetties, along the esplanade (which leads to the castle housing the Royal Yacht Squadron) and under the arcades behind the Fountain Inn. Half the town (East Cowes) lies across the mouth of the River Medina, which is crossed on a 'floating bridge' – a ferry that hauls itself across on huge chains that make a hellish rattle and rumble all the way. It is on this side that Osborne House lies, Queen Victoria's very splendid rural retreat (where she died in 1901).

I sat on the esplanade looking back towards the colourful houses piled up on the steep flanks of West Cowes. The waves slapped the sea-wall, buoys bobbed wildly and gulls battled hard against the stiff wind which had flung water and seaweed up onto the promenade. I headed for the ferry, hot tea at the Fountain Inn and a snug crossing back to the mainland, home and bed.

II. The Scilly Isles

St Mary's

Another island-bussing possibility is on one of the Scilly Isles off Cornwall. The Scillies are only 20 minutes from Penzance by helicopter; and on the main island, St Mary's, it is possible to bus about.

One's first view of the Scillies is of a scatter of rocky islets in the blue sea below, punctuated with lighthouses, for the history of the Scillies is a roll-call of ships wrecked in every century. As the helicopter approaches the main island, St Mary's, it comes in low over a shore of cliffs and coves, great sandy bays and a patchwork of granite outcrops, windswept pines and stone-walled fields.

A bus takes one to Hugh Town within minutes. Though the centre of activity on the island, this is not much more than an overgrown village of fishermen's cottages round a harbour, small hotels, a lifeboat station, a few shops and a particularly good local museum. Another bus departs from Hugh Town several times a day for a circuit round the island (which takes only $\frac{1}{2}$ hour). Its route is inland, but the island is so small that from any stop it is easy to walk to the coast and back, perhaps picking up a bus further along the route.

The island is kept firmly unspoilt and uncrowded, its population a mere thousand or so. Growing narcissi and daffodils is the main activity but, as these are sent to market in bud, the fields are never full of flowers. No matter; the cottage gardens and the wildflowers more than make up for this. I was there in April, when gardens were brilliant not only with red-hot-pokers, jonquils and marigolds but semi-tropical plants, too. Mesembryanthemums poured over the walls.

In the hedgerows was a profusion of flowers. Palm trees, cacti, crassulas and saw-tongued aloes grow wild, and the New Zealand flame tree blazes with scarlet flowers in December. Even the hedges have a tropical look with red-blossomed escallonia, glossy-leaved euonymus and magenta pittosporum (a New Zealand shrub) providing the dense windbreak so necessary in these islands where, mild though the climate is throughout the year, formidable gales can play havoc with the crops. The Scillies' great pride, however, are the enormous blue spires of echeum, some nearly 10 feet high.

The bus route is through narrow lanes as rural as it is possible to find. Every viewpoint is incomparably lovely, and the only sign of human activity is the occasional cottage, a group of wicker lobster pots or some churns of milk awaiting collection by the roadside.

I also had time to walk along one of the island's three nature trails (picking wild fennel, samphire and sea spinach as I went: 'food for free'). A linnet rose, singing, into the sky, and an oyster-catcher probed the wet sands for molluscs. There are less familiar wildflowers here, such as dwarf scurvy-grass – a pale-flowered plant clinging to granite walls that is rich in vitamin C (hence its past value in warding off scurvy). Strange whiskery lichens (a synthesis of fungus and algae) grow in profusion, a sure indication of the purity of the air, for lichens die in a polluted atmosphere but live for hundreds of years in fresh air. I saw some of the first butterflies of the year – holly blues, speckled woods and peacocks.

The nature trail, marked by planks and stepping stones through a marsh, led to rushing streams and reed beds frequented by frogs, and to a hide from which to watch swallows skimming a pool to drink on the wing. A sedge-warbler, yellow throat pulsating, sang non-stop on a bush declaring his ownership of this territory. Every year these little warblers, returning from their winter in Africa, always make for the same group of bushes. On through a copse of sallow willows draped with honeysuckle, past a thicket of another exotic settler, Japanese knotweed, and so onto the road again to catch the bus back into Hugh Town.

The whole Scillies story – archaeological, historical and ecological – is most clearly told in the little museum, which not only displays ancient finds but has produced a really clear exposition of local wildlife. Small details linger in my memory: from the wreck of the famous ship *Association*, sunk in the 17th century, a posy ring (i.e. 'poésie', poetry) was poignantly engraved with the rhyme 'God above Increase our love'; there were smuggler's tongs for retrieving kegs hidden underwater and 78 vases, each with a different fresh-picked local wildflower, clearly labelled.

The Scillies are, of course, an enchanting place to stay for days or even weeks, and between the islands 'bussing' is by boat. A uniquely romantic hotel is the Star Castle, where Prince Charles (later Charles II) stayed while fleeing from the Cromwellians. The small fortress, built like an eight-pointed star, is a maze of zigzagging corridors and odd-angled bedrooms. Even a guardroom out on the ramparts is now a bedroom, the musket holes glassed in and the interior comfortably furnished but otherwise just as it was four centuries ago.

11
The New Forest

Southampton – Lyndhurst – Brockenhurst – Lymington – Beaulieu – Hythe

It was bluebell time when I found myself in Southampton on business. Though summer was scarcely in, England was enjoying its longest spell of non-stop sunshine for half a century. What better than to tack on an extra day and go bussing in the nearby New Forest (though Bournemouth or even Salisbury are suitable bases instead of Southampton)? Later in the year the roads of this area would be packed with cars and caravans, but as yet there were relatively few visitors around to disturb its peace.

The Forest's 93,000 acres are not all tree-covered. The scenery varies from woodland to heath, farmland to riverside, with small

Queen's Bower, the New Forest

towns and isolated houses along the way. When William the Conqueror hunted there ('he loved the red deer like his own children', wrote a contemporary chronicler rather ambiguously), the heaths and woods must have been even wilder – a veritable jungle of undergrowth. Now not only ponies and some deer graze freely, but cows, donkeys and even pigs. All have owners and are rounded up when required, for under ancient rights 'commoners' are entitled to let their animals feed in the Forest (except where, to protect areas of young trees, wire fences have been put up to keep the animals out by the Verderers who manage the Forest). These animals are one of the many attractions of any drive through the Forest; the bus has to avoid them, not vice versa, when they stray onto the roads, and most are quite unperturbed by the presence of traffic.

Although there are a lot of conifers too, the woodlands through which the buses go are mainly of broad-leaved trees – ancient oaks and great beeches, in particular. I only once caught a glimpse of a herd of roe deer in the gloaming beneath them; these and fallow deer account for the total population of about a thousand (there are only about 30 of the great red deer left). The ponies and cattle are far more numerous, as well as less shy, and are seen everywhere, occasionally turning up among the village shops despite grids and gates intended to keep them out.

The Forest has been designated a National Nature Reserve because it is so rich in rare plants and wildlife. Great care is taken to arrange the recreational facilities (camp sites, car parks and all the rest) in such a way that, despite the millions of visitors every year, the Forest suffers a minimum of disturbance or damage.

Lyndhurst

A bus from Southampton took me to the 'capital' of the New Forest, Lyndhurst – the name means a wood of lime trees – through woodland where dappled sunlight fell onto moss-green trunks and a floor carpeted with rusty leaves. The brilliant light green of new oak leaves contrasted with the softer colour of graceful birches, well-nicknamed 'the ladies of the woods', and an occasional gnarled stump of ancient grey.

At Lyndhurst the Forest's Verderers hold their court to settle any disagreements among the commoners. Their hall, in Queen's House, is said to be very fine, but it was closed when I was there because the entire Queen Anne house was shored up awaiting repair.

I went instead to the nearby church which makes up in beauty what it lacks in antiquity (it was the masterpiece of a Victorian architect, William White, who got the job mainly because he charged less than his more celebrated colleagues). The interior is a colourful pattern of bricks in various reds and yellows, with clusters of dark slate columns topped by capitals carved with forest foliage. The red timber roof has a dozen huge wooden angels playing on trumpets, lutes and tambourines – in fact, the church is particularly rich in carved figures and heads of Protestant martyrs. There was quite a to-do when the eminent Frederick Leighton offered to paint a fresco, unheard-of since the Reformation. Despite objections to such a 'Papist embellishment', the offer was accepted and there it is: a dozen life-size virgins, wise ones with bright lamps and cheerful faces, foolish ones dejected in the dark. The church has other assets, too, such as Burne-Jones windows and a clock which, for technical reasons that are beyond me, horologists consider a national treasure.

Behind the building lies a simple grave, easily missed, where 'Alice in Wonderland' is buried, its only decoration the little daisies and birds-eyes which embroider its turf. 'Alice' grew up to become Mrs Reginald Hargreaves and president of a local Women's Institute; she died in 1934.

Before walking down the High Street I called in at Mr Strange's strange shop – dozens of antlers hang from the ceiling, and the huge head of a red deer presides over the counter. Mr Strange is a butcher, and his speciality is the produce of the New Forest, particularly venison. I added to my small baggage a joint and some venison sausages, well worth the effort of carrying them home to London.

Lyndhurst's main street runs downhill, flanked by shops and houses, tile-hung and some with pretty hexagonal chimneys and lattice windows. Wisteria rambled over a porch, and lilac and laburnum brimmed over fences.

'Do you go to Brockenhurst?' I asked the driver of a bus that drew up at the bus-stop. 'If I have to,' was the lugubrious answer. The bus whisked through Goose Green and then into the cool of overhanging trees. Brick houses came into sight along with a few half-timbered ones.

Brockenhurst

Brockenhurst village is pleasant, if undistinguished. There is a watersplash where the road fords a small, sparkling stream, and here I sat by the footbridge on a seat hot from the sun, listening to the gurgle of water, a distant woodpigeon and the soft movements of a mare and her foal grazing by the waterside. Every private house in the Forest has a cattle grid at its gate to prevent the ponies from eating the tulips and pansies; level crossings, too, are guarded by grids to keep animals from wandering along the railway lines.

My next objective was the railway station. No, I'd not lost faith in the buses, but I'd heard there was something of interest in the 'down' waiting room – and so there was. It is a collection of autographed photographs of eminent Victorians – Tennyson, Longfellow, Darwin, Browning and others, whose splendid, be-whiskered faces recall a time when great men really looked the part. The pioneer photographer Julia Cameron had lived nearby, and she made the waiting-room a present of the portraits because it had been the scene of an emotional reunion with her long-absent son.

The next bus ride went across heath as well as through woodland blazing with gorse (later, red heather would take over). There were occasional thatched cottages, and many solid late-Victorian houses set well back behind their pink rhododendrons or their flowering cherries. We had to slow down and detour round a donkey that was rooted in the road with oak-like permanence, its sides taut and round as a tennis ball, its eyes firmly closed in its indifference to the bus.

Lymington

Lymington is an enchanting town on the estuary of a river named after it. It is entered by a road with an attractive terrace of early Victorian houses, fanlights over the doors and shutters at the windows, leading to the very wide High Street, thronged with market stalls on Saturdays. There are many fine Georgian (and earlier) houses. Some of the most attractive have been taken over – as so often happens – by solicitors for use as offices, including the beautiful Ivy House (curiously named since it is covered by a very ancient Virginia creeper, its stem well over a foot thick).

It took my eyes some minutes to adjust from the brilliant sun to the gloom inside the church. It is an odd mixture: rugged old stone walls on one side contrast with a white pillared and panelled gallery, on the front of which black-and-gold panels chronicle various benefactions. My eye was caught by the Blakiston memorials. When Anne died in 1862 she was 81; her husband had died, aged 45, in 1806. His memorial, for which she presumably chose the words, says, 'To those who knew him the Enumeration of his Virtues would be superfluous: To those who knew him not it might be tedious.' Hers, on the other hand, goes on at length about her virtues. Georgian restraint contrasted with Victorian pomposity?

Many of the shops in the High Street have a pillared frontage. Up above project bay windows or canopied balconies with decorative wrought-ironwork. Between are alleyways with glimpses of green beyond or courtyards with flagstoned paths leading to cottages and beds of wallflowers or pansies. Wine merchants and antique shops are numerous, giving way – as the street starts sloping down towards the river – to yacht stores and shops or restaurants with names like Limpets or Shipmates. In the distance, above the trees, rises an obelisk (a memorial to some long-forgotten admiral), precisely placed to provide a focal point as one looks down the High Street.

A cobbled, pedestrian-only street twists its way steeply down, and suddenly I found myself on the quayside (a good place to picnic, incidentally, with cold meats or a quiche bought from the delicatessen on Quay Hill). Most of the moored craft were small yachts, but there were a few fishing boats, and the little black-headed gulls, of which there is a huge colony on this coast, were keeping a sharp eye on them. Further along, hundreds of slender masts stood like a marine coppice against the cloudless blue sky. Young men with high boots and tanned faces were busy doing complicated things with ropes or were perched up in the rigging, which the wind plucked like harp strings.

To return to the High Street I strolled up picturesque Nelson's Place, past the colourful houses of Captain's Row and along Grove

Road. Grove Road was surprisingly rural for a street in the centre of town – clover, meadowsweet and dandelion clocks brightened the grassy roadside. There are fine houses along there and the only crinkle-crankle wall I know outside Suffolk, its sinuous brickwork warm to touch, the mellow red tinged with grey lichen. Clumps of pretty toadflax on it were in flower. Further along, the road lived up to its name – a grove of blossoming trees, shrubs and creepers with bees busy on the tiny pink flowers of cotoneaster and butterflies on the lilac or wisteria of the cottage gardens.

My bus swung out of town past cottage gardens with clematis, elderflowers dancing in the breeze, and snow-white washing on a line. At a bus-stop by a stream there was time to enjoy bluebells, new fronds of bracken, pink Herb Robert and campions. I suddenly realized what a very decorative plant the common nettle is, a plant on which we rather pointlessly wage a war that the nettles always win in the end.

The road to Beaulieu crosses Beaulieu Heath, with a view of the Isle of Purbeck to the right (one is nearer the sea than one guesses) across acres of gorse and heather and of Hatchet Pond where anglers wait, ever-hopeful. There are some particularly immaculate examples of the thatcher's skill along the way. The decorative treatment of the roof ridges is a thatcher's trademark, and each has his own pattern. Some add a reed pheasant, owl or peacock to distinguish their work.

Then came the clear, tranquil water of Beaulieu river (among the reed beds that provide the thatch) and Lord Montague's vintage motor museum, stately home and grounds, and the remains of a Cistercian abbey founded by King John.

Beaulieu

Beaulieu village is extremely beautiful, with superb views of the very lovely river, the abbey walls and rural peace. In the distance great trees crowd down to the river edge, their boughs sweeping low to the sunlit surface of the water. The grass is lush, cows wander right into the quiet village street, the only person in sight was a man slowly walking his Sealyham and the only really busy individual a coot paddling rapidly by.

The bus climbed up through cool woodland and then across more heath. The imminence of Southampton is hinted at by pylons striding across the landscape and a distant prospect of factory chimneys. Suburban gardens flashed by, bright with azaleas, and then we were at Hythe, an old boat-building town.

Hythe

The ferry to Southampton waits at the end of a long pier built a hundred years ago. A primitive train carries passengers to it, a two-minute journey of jerk, squeak, rock and roll all the way. The train is about 60 years old and may be excused its arthriticky state. Onto the ferry (*Hotspur IV*) streamed businessmen with briefcases, housewives with shopping baskets, schoolboys with their bags – and a girl clutching a large melon. It takes ten minutes to cross the River Test. All kinds of craft pass by or are moored there: naval ships, a car ferry to France, cruise liners, a fireboat, landing craft and pleasure boats *Solent Queen* and *Island Scene* waiting for day-trippers.

At the other side a long queue was already waiting to board for Hythe. We all streamed off and dispersed to buses that go to the centre of Southampton. I ended my journey where I had begun.

12

Through Hardy's Wessex

Salisbury – Wilton – Shaftesbury – Sherborne – Yeovil – Chard – Ilminster – Taunton

Within minutes of leaving the bus station in Salisbury (see pages 93–5, 277–81), we arrived at Wilton House and the pretty little town of Wilton where a stream trickles by the roadside, there are lanes of colourwashed houses and pollarded limes stand on the green. A lot of houses along the start of this route combine flints with brick, in chequerboard or banded patterns, but later there were cottages of half-timbering and thatch or fine stone houses. The River Nadder stayed with us for a while, and across its valley I could see hills with military badges cut into the chalk (mementoes of the First World War) and a huge map of Australia.

This is a rural route, far from any motorway, with peaceful scenes as we passed by – brown hens scratching in an orchard, swan with cygnets on a lake, creeper-covered inns, old cottages half hidden behind fruit blossom, and trout streams sparkling in the sunshine. The road winds up and down, eventually making the climb up to Shaftesbury, an old market town perched on a hilltop.

The road into the town is lined with old stone cottages, and the coach paused to pick up passengers right outside the 13th-century church, its walls of soft stone weather-worn and much in need of restoration. Shaftesbury has a castellated town hall, secretive alleyways, pillared coaching inn and old cobbled courtyards. To the abbey used to come pilgrims seeking the shrine of St Edward, the martyr king who was murdered at Corfe in 978. Little remains of it now. The Grosvenor Hotel is worth a visit to see the great, carved 'Chevy Chase' sideboard.

As we turned out of the town and started downhill, I glanced backward for a spectacular view – mile upon mile of plains, fields and hills stretching into the distance.

The rest of the journey continued as before, with many streams to cross, verges occasionally colourful with campions and bluebells, and great old barns – their slate roofs gilded with lichen – soon to arrive at Sherborne, one of England's most beautiful yet least publicized ancient towns where a long visit is a 'must'.

Sherborne

From The Green, itself an attractive spot with Tudor houses close by, it is only a short walk to reach the famous Abbey. Strolling down Cheap Street, one passes medieval and Georgian buildings (many with bow windows or timber framing) and the entrance to Swan Yard which won a conservation award for its conversion

Sherborne Abbey

from stables to a little shopping precinct, lined with antique and craft shops. Because, here and elsewhere, there is a story to many of Sherborne's houses, it is particularly worth getting the 'Town Walk' leaflet before arriving – it tells you about the literary or other associations, and inside which shops you can discover such things as a painted ceiling depicting the four seasons.

At the bottom of the street is the Tudor 'conduit' (the decorative little building where the monks used to wash); and down tiny Church Lane nearby is the excellent local museum – well worth an unhurried visit.

But it is, of course, the great abbey church which is the centrepiece of Sherborne. Its stonework, which has only recently been cleaned and restored, seemed to glow in the morning sun and I needed no guidebook to assure me that this is unquestionably one of the most beautiful churches in England. Its great interior is equal in splendour, with some of the finest fan-vaulting in the country. The elaborately carved bosses in the roof have been restored too, and are now brilliantly coloured and gilded. Some of the fan-vaults are nearly 30 feet wide. As to their bosses, there are over a hundred in the nave alone – so detailed that every feather or leaf or petal is individually carved. In complete contrast is the reredos of shining glass engraved by Laurence Whistler in 1968, with symbols of glory and fruitfulness.

The precincts, too, deserve a visit, and I threaded my way amongst the twists and turns of the old walls to emerge among the buildings of Sherborne School – a monastic school until Henry VIII closed it when he turned the monks out of their Abbey in 1539. It was re-founded, as a grammar school, by his son Edward VI.

Sherborne's Old Castle was built in the 12th century by the great Bishop Roger of Salisbury, second only to Henry I in power and prestige (see p. 277), who was also Abbot of Sherborne. The New Castle was begun by Sir Walter Raleigh in 1594. Although both can be reached from the Abbey by walking up Long Street, which has some historic houses, it is easier to take a bus to the Black Horse inn.

The Old Castle's ruins are perched on a hilltop: a windswept and romantic site, worth the steep walk. As at Old Sarum, the castle was seized by Stephen but later reverted to the bishops, who then used it as a residence. It was reduced to ruins by the Parliamentarians during the Civil War.

At its foot is the village of Castleton (= castle town), with an unusual little Georgian church and houses. In the church is a memorial to the old lady who gave money to build it: for 70 years a domestic servant at the New Castle in the service of the Digby family, who still live there.

This castle is in complete contrast to the dramatic ruins on the hill – although it, too, is a fine sight from a distance, with towers, chimneys and stone beasts creating a memorable silhouette. It stands in a park (landscaped by Capability Brown) so huge that a small map is provided for those who want to explore its copses and pleasure-grounds, lake, orangery, Roman mosaic, rare trees, tea-room and so forth. The house itself is full of treasures from four centuries – the hall is Elizabethan, the oak room Jacobean, the library Georgian and the solarium Victorian.

Sherborne deserves a long visit because, in addition to its abbey and these two castles, there are a great many minor buildings of interest, too numerous to describe in this chapter. It stands comparison with many old cathedral cities and, like them, is well supplied with good eating-places, antique and craft shops. And because it has eleven schools, there are plenty of bookshops and cultural events (it is the home of the Dorset Opera Company).

Chard, Ilminster

A fast road sped us to Yeovil after which the journey on to Crewkerne became more attractive. Many cottages in this part of the world are of sandstone, or else colourwashed and thatched, with leaded panes in mullioned windows. The scenery is pastoral, often with great views laid out at one's feet like a map. High hedges enclose rich fields where cows graze.

Down the road swooped, through leafy valleys, and then up once more to the high hilltops with those distant views again (on a clear day, it is said to be possible to see both the Bristol Channel to the north and the English Channel to the south): the name of one, Windwhistle Hill – 750 feet up – tells its own story. The sunlight flickered on the road wherever there were stretches with trees meeting overhead, and then would follow miles of open country and, at Cricket St Thomas, an avenue of beeches beside the fine park of a thousand acres surrounding the Georgian mansion (and wildlife park) where *To the Manor Born* was filmed. There were flint lodges, handsome gateways, many wayside inns and hedges of holly and laurel along the way.

Chard swiftly came and went: an old lace-making town with a mile-long High Street which has a Tudor courthouse (used by Judge Jeffreys during the 'Bloody Assizes' after Monmouth's rebellion) opposite a very imposing town hall with Doric colonnade astride the pavement and a great clock-tower above, where the bus stopped to pick up passengers. The church is embellished with gargoyles, the houses with verandahs or bay windows, their stone walls pleasantly varied in colour.

As we continued westward a vast panorama stretched out ahead of the road: a rather bumpy, zigzag road that set all the ashtrays in the bus jingling in anything but unison. Farms looked prosperous, with huge centuries-old barns awaiting the harvest to come. When we turned off towards Ilminster, there were streams threading their way through the fields, willows weeping into them, and a pond of swans and ducks. Ilminster is a low-lying town, once a market for wool, with a Perpendicular church of particular grandeur (housing the Jacobean tomb of the couple who founded Wadham College, Oxford), its pinnacled and crocketed tower soaring high above the grass and tombs of the churchyard. A butter-cross stands in the middle of the small market square. The Ham stone used for the church tower – which is copied from the central tower of Wells cathedral – and for other buildings, is very orangey in colour, quarried from Hamdon Hill.

Up and down the road we went, past a field of tethered bulls and others of sheep or wheat, over more streams and by more thatched cottages, until we began to move into cider country and a succession of orchards. Wisteria was coming into blossom against old stone walls, and a group of horse chestnuts standing in a field of buttercups was beautiful to see. The summer sunshine was now streaming in from the west, so I moved over to the shadier side of the bus and opened the window. The traffic was increasing now, and already the great tower of Taunton's church was in view. We passed under a flyover and on through dreary suburbs – not a very congenial first impression – to draw up right in the middle of the city.

Taunton

A traveller hurrying through Taunton might easily suppose it was not worth a second glance: just a hustling, traffic-laden county town. For Taunton keeps its many charms tucked away behind the main thoroughfares, in parts that the pounding traffic never reaches.

Taunton Castle

The bus station, however, is ideally placed for discovering many of these secret places: it occupies what was once virtually an island surrounded by marshes, at the very centre of the original Saxon settlement from which the town grew. Right by it is the Winchester Arms with sun umbrellas outside, and there are lawns for picnicking. To one side of it are the remains of the medieval castle (now housing the extremely good Somerset County Museum); a short footpath leads to the very lovely lawns and trees bordering the River Tone only a few yards away, well populated with geese and ducks; to the side of the Castle Hotel is the flowery and peaceful Norman Garden on the site of the keep; and just across the way are the Municipal Buildings including more parts of the castle (round the other side of which is the Tourist Information Centre). I have yet to find a bus station which has so much of interest all around it, and so many quiet spots close at hand in which to wander or relax.

To explore any further afield than this, it is helpful to have obtained, before arriving, the free town plan which shows footpaths as well as roads. With the help of this, it is easy to find the short waterside path that leads north from close by the coach station to French Weir and a little park beyond. Or the one that follows the River Tone east and soon arrives at the bridge from which boat trips start, and at the Brewhouse Theatre and Arts Centre, a very good place to have an inexpensive homemade lunch.

South of the bus station is Bath Place (little more than an alley, but lined with cottages, antique shops and suchlike) at the end of which a stroll southward along the pedestrianized High Street leads one to the colourful great iron gates of Vivary Park. This park (named for the medieval vivarium or fishponds which used to be here) stretches a mile out into the countryside. (If you don't want to walk all the way back from the far end, buses can be picked up to take you back to the coach station.) The park has something for everyone – the flowerbeds, fountain and gaily painted bandstand give way to less formal acres, a stream and lake; followed by sportsfields and a children's play area (with a little railway). Overlooking this park are the elegant backs of Regency houses and the exotic red towers of Jellabad Barracks, a masterpiece of elaborately decorative brickwork.

Collections of pots can be pretty boring: not so at the Somerset County Museum, inside what is left of the castle that was built by King Stephen's brother, partly destroyed by Henry II, rebuilt in Henry III's reign, besieged in Henry VI's and again in Charles I's. Here Judge Jeffreys sentenced some 500 participants in Monmouth's rebellion of 1685. Where so much violence occurred, all is now serene.

As to the pots, I found them so absorbing that I had scarcely enough time for the other galleries. Here at last were displays that vividly explained the differences of earthenware, stoneware and porcelain, and their glazes. Styles moved on century by century, with examples from sites all over the county. Potters congregated in Crock Street, from a well in which 26 medieval water-jugs have been retrieved. There is a case full of puzzle and joke pots, and another of the unique Elton ware made in the 1880s with metallic and crackle effects.

But there is a lot else in this museum. 'And So To Bed' is a still-life of patchwork quilt, nightcap, candle-snuffer and chamber-pot. There is a huge collection of horse brasses and bells; an entire military museum upstairs; and down below a 20-foot Iron Age canoe gouged out of a single oak. A huge Roman mosaic of Dido and Aeneas. A Saxon loom recreated from stone weights dug up some years ago. And, a small sensation when it was unearthed in 1980, the Taunton hoard. When Taunton was under attack during the Civil War, some man of wealth hid his all in a clay pot and buried it. He did not survive to retrieve his cache, but over 300 years later it came to light: a treasure trove of 275 silver coins. And another treasure: a 14th-century stone reredos with angel and saints, found (upside down) in use as a floor. From the sublime to the ridiculous: a bar of workhouse soap that has survived the years, albeit chewed by mice; and a moustache cup, shaped to keep those Victorian whiskers out of the tea.

There is even more to Taunton than this. In busy North Street, the Post Office has a Telecommunications Museum which illustrates, with working exhibits, the history of the telephone and telegraph (you can phone a friend via a 1920s switchboard). The whole area behind this street is gradually being restored: alleyways lead to a network of neglected terraces well worth conservation and which will one day be a pleasure to explore. One of the first parts to have been completed is The Courtyard in Middle Street, where a cluster of small craft studios and speciality shops are now trading, with a restaurant. St Mary's church dominates this quarter, set in a peaceful churchyard with yews shading its daisy-filled lawns. Built early in the 17th-century, it has the most outstanding Perpendicular tower in Somerset – a county well endowed with such towers. High up inside the church are angels, and an exceptionally fine wooden roof.

In another direction (south of the bus station) is the Georgian part of the town. The Crescent is an impressive and handsome street, comparable with some in Bath. Taunton has Somerset's county cricket ground, too (just beyond the theatre mentioned above), and a huge cattle market. The more energetic can walk twelve miles from the town centre to Bridgwater on the canal towpath and then take a bus back. Altogether, this is a town of great variety, with plenty of pleasant surprises for anyone willing to search them out. And, above all, it is an ideal town for a visitor who arrives without a car.

13
England's Big Toe

St Ives – Land's End – Penzance

In Cornwall I decided to base myself on one place and spend a few days radiating out and back – making loop bus trips like the petals of a daisy and sleeping every night in the same centre (with my family). Instead of avoiding tourist spots, I went into the thick of one and, instead of going out of season, I went in summer.

My base was St Ives in Cornwall. It was seething with summer tourists and I wondered whether the buses would therefore be packed and hot. But there was no need to worry! Though coach tours were booked out for a fortnight ahead and car parks early each day put out 'Full' placards, the buses remained half-empty – airy, comfortable and roomy. We on the buses could go to all kinds of beauty spots, on or off the beaten track, and never have to turn away for lack of parking space. Only in Penzance at rush hour were we held up in a traffic jam – but, while the red-faced car drivers fumed, bus passengers took their ease.

The disadvantage of an in-season bus journey is not, therefore, the crowds – they stick to their cars and coaches – but the fact that one does not experience places in their everyday, real-life wear. Also, out of season, one may come across some of the old traditions that still survive in Cornwall, lost to the rest of England long ago: hurling, an ancient game that was the forerunner of rugby and is still played on the dedication anniversaries of some churches; guise dancing before Christmas (when disguises are worn); or rituals with corn dollies at harvest time.

However, summertime brought two bonuses. In a tourist area like Cornwall the bus company runs some extra services not operated out of season, and those stately homes that open only in summer are all available to visit.

Cornwall is a huge county. My chosen area was Penwith, the big toe of England. It is roughly diamond-shaped, with St Ives, Land's End and Penzance as its best-known centres. Penzance has the most bus services, but even St Ives had more than enough for the few days I was able to stay.

Bussing options can be much extended by planning a short walk from one bus route to join up with another. Examples are the easy mile walking downhill from Paul (an interesting church) to Mousehole, or Mousehole to Lamorna Cove along the coast ($2\frac{1}{2}$ miles), or Sennen Cove to Land's End (a breathtaking $1\frac{1}{4}$ miles of cliff-top scenery).

St Ives

The fishing village of St Ives was first 'discovered' in the 19th century by artists such as James Whistler and Walter Sickert, who were attracted not only by its picturesque cottages and steep, cobbled lanes around the bay, but by the very special light. There is said to be more ultra-violet in it than usual, and the sky and sea can certainly be incredibly clear and beautiful at times.

The artists are still there (and writers, too). Many open their studios for visitors to wander in and out, and there seem to be art galleries or craft shops round every corner. A number of the traditionalists exhibit together in a former church, the modernists in a former fish warehouse. In a recently created undercover market behind the famous Sloop Inn busy craftsmen are open to view in workshops producing pottery, leatherwork, silver, enamels and textiles. The building is an excellent example of how modern design can incorporate time-honoured natural materials such as slate, granite and timber. Upstairs is a gull's eye view down into the market from a gallery café serving home-made salads and pastries.

Barbara Hepworth's house (where the sculptor died tragically in a fire) has been turned into a permanent gallery for some of her work, while other pieces stand in her rambling, semi-tropical garden. This is right in the heart of St Ives, completely hidden behind 20-foot stone walls. Her studio is full of poignancy: not only are her tools and work clothes still as she left them the day before she died, but half-worked blocks of marble attest to what might have been.

There are lots of pleasant things to do in St Ives, but doing nothing is the pleasantest of all – and, oddly enough, one of the best spots for this pursuit is the bus station. St Ives might well claim to have the best bus station in Britain so far as its site is concerned – it is high on a cliff overlooking the bay and the so-called Island (really a peninsula) which has a tiny ancient chapel, sometimes floodlit, topping its grassy hump. Tradition has it that the chapel stands over the original grave of St Ia or Iva, the 6th-century Irish missionary after whom the town is named. One looks down from the bus station onto the roofs of St Ives, a higgledy-piggledy geometric pattern of ridges and troughs – old slates weathered, sagging and encrusted with lichen; newer ones still shiny enough to turn silver when the sun catches them; and contrasting warm terracotta ridge tiles and chimney stacks. Squeezed between the houses are tiny courtyards crammed with green shrubs or leafy pot plants.

Gulls nest in the angles between chimneys and roofs, preferring this centrally heated accommodation to slumming it on the cliffs. The chimney pots, too, are used by the gulls, who find them ideal lookout posts from which to spot shoals of fish in the bay (like the huers, human lookouts of old).

Tucked into the cliff under the bus station I found one of St Ives' nicer cafés, bistro in style but producing the very best of English breakfasts. I have found no better start to a day's bussing than one of Tilly's huge breakfasts eaten *al fresco* at a balcony table while watching the birds and boats below and the bright lollipop sunshades beginning to sprout on the sandy beaches.

It's a good spot in which to read the short history of the town by Sparrow and Williams (*About St Ives*), with the places they write about laid out at your feet. Straight ahead is the stone pier built in 1770 by Smeaton (designer of the Eddystone lighthouse), and one can imagine it heaped in the past with stacks of tin ore or barrels of salted pilchards for export, or with landed coal and wood. Time and again this harbour was raided by pirates, for until the 18th century all trading was by sea – there were no roads over the moors and the railway did not come until 1877. Farther off is Godrevy lighthouse which inspired Virginia Woolf (who spent memorable holidays in St Ives as a child) to write her novel *To the Lighthouse*.

The steep contours of St Ives have kept it quite small, but every bit of its limited space is used to maximum effect. Houses are built on any rocky surface that will take them, and others are crammed in every whichway. Fish cellars now house shops, and attics restaurants – there are plenty of good cafés and the upstairs ones have the bonus of marvellous views over the sea. But the restaurants have strong competition from *the* original take-away food, the Cornish pasty – a meat-and-two-veg dinner packaged in pastry, just right for today's bus travellers.

St Ives has much to enjoy: fine gardens, cliff-top walks, the famous Bernard Leach pottery, a lifeboat station open to view, a magnificent 15th-century church with unusual gilded carvings in the roof and others on bench ends, boat trips to watch seals, a fascinating pre-cinema museum of cinematography (Victorian peepshows, optical illusions and magic lanterns) and another of local history. But above all there are the twisting zigzag lanes, a mapmaker's nightmare, their crazy angles dictated by the rocky outcrops on which the houses jostle one another like seabirds' nests on a cliff. Tourists wander as if in a maze. But one hardly hears a Cornish voice among all the babel of accents in the summer. One must go elsewhere to find the Cornwall of the Cornish.

Land's End via Pendeen

To visit Land's End is an obvious 'must' when in Penwith, and the route from St Ives is superb. It runs along the narrow strip between Penwith's backbone of granite hills and the untamed Atlantic coastline to the north. Nothing lies between those cliffs and America but 3,000 miles of ocean, which has pounded them into one of Britain's harshest winter coastlines – a place of storms, and jagged rocks – and one of its most beautiful in sunny summers.

It was a freak summer that year and, up on the open top of the bus, huddled in my raincoat, I got a taste of Cornwall's savagery during the day's ride. The rain lashed down in torrents, the wind howled, and spray wrapped the granite headlands in invisibility. Nearly all the tourists had gone to earth and the wild, wet solitude was in total contrast to my previous day in St Ives.

It is easy to understand why Cornwall abounds in eerie legends of ghosts and goblins, wizards, mermaids and other harbingers of doom. The Atlantic gales whip the sea into a boiling hell and flatten the crops; cattle huddle miserably in the lee of any shelter they can find. Years of this kind of weather have contorted the gorse permanently into witch-like shapes. Almost no trees grow on this side of Penwith: the salty gales are too much for them. The few stunted ones that do survive are bent and wizened. The wind found the stitch holes of my walking shoes and nipped my toes.

The ruins of an old building or some great prehistoric stone would suddenly spring into sight as the mist cleared, only to vanish again in a second as it swirled back again. Solid shapes appeared and disappeared as lightly as any spectre.

Yet the bus also brushed by high banks gay with pink campion and Herb Robert, celandines, violets and wild garlic flowers, and passed beneath the occasional palm tree – tokens of Cornwall's sunnier side that flourishes despite such extremes of rain and wind. It is these contrasts that give the area its fascination – the bright and the dark, the smiling and the cruel coexisting. One moment the view is of wild, bleak moors and the next of a cottage garden neat as a picture postcard. The barren rocks loom menacingly above; look down and, hidden among the small ferns, a tiny stream gurgles.

The Round House, Sennen Cove

There are lots of interesting places at which to break one's journey for a couple of hours, for example Gurnard's Head, Morvah or Sennen Cove – especially the last, with its silvery sands and view of Cape Cornwall. For walkers the coast is easy to reach in kindly weather from the bus and there is a coastal path all round it. The National Trust owns many of the headlands with the most spectacular views (a large part of Penwith is protected as an area of outstanding natural beauty). A large-scale Ordnance Survey map, coupled with booklets available locally giving guidance on walks short or long, will indicate any number of good routes.

My choice of stop that day was Pendeen, to visit the working Geevor tin mine, part opened to the public. (This side of Cornwall is littered with the ruins of old tin mines identifiable by gaunt chimneys on the horizon and crumbling walls.) Wearing miners' safety helmets, visitors are shown round the surface works (not underground), the winding gear, the ore-crushers and the filtering sheds with one of the miners as a guide. Everywhere water is running – water red with traces of iron particles that have to be filtered out from the tin particles. Through shed after shed, from one great wooden tray sloping down to another, the particles are rinsed and rinsed again until the two metals gradually separate, the heavier iron eventually sinking away from the thin ribbon of tin that is left. Only four tons a day is thus yielded, but it is worth thousands of pounds.

The mine has an exceptionally interesting museum attached, telling the mining story from the Stone Age, when flints were prised out of chalk with animal bones, right up to compressed-air drills and electric detonators. Life-size models viewed from dark passageways give one the illusion of being in a mine; miniature models show how the whole complex network of galleries and shafts is at that moment operating half a mile beneath one's feet and for two miles around. Some galleries stretch below the seabed.

Just along the road is Botallack, peppered with disused mines; the mines' Count House where the miners drew their pay is now a restaurant (Pendeen itself has the Miners' Country Kitchen and a mining museum).

Another stop, involving a mile's walk down a lane rosy with pompoms of thrift, enabled us to visit the Pendeen Watch lighthouse, sited there in 1900 (and converted from oil to electricity in 1926) because so many ships broke up on the nearby rocks. As in all lighthouses, the interior is like the dream homes which polish and paint manufacturers show in TV commercials, all gleaming brasswork and immaculate mahogany with green paint that looks – well, fresh as paint. Notices ask you not to fingermark the metal fittings and I climbed apologetically up the dustless stairs. The lighthouse keeper refers to his responsibilities as 'mostly housework'.

'Well now, me darlings,' he begins in true Cornish style as he explains the workings of the great lantern. Prisms of the purest glass so concentrate the light from a 3.5-kilowatt lamp that its beam can be seen nearly 30 miles away unless obscured by fog, in which case a horn with a blast audible for 10 miles comes into operation (so dense are the fogs that, a few days after our visit, two ships collided nearby and sank with the loss of four lives – in *June*).

And so, onward to Land's End. Out to sea one should be able to spot two more lighthouses. A dozen of the 92 lighthouses round England and Wales are near Cornwall's deadly shores. But on a day like this, even the weirdly shaped rocks – named Spire, Knight, Kettle-Bottom and Shark's Fin – are hidden in spray.

Before the lighthouses, wrecks were so numerous that the locals made a good living plundering them. The lighthouse on the Longships Rocks was built in 1795; so primitive were conditions inside that the lighthousemen had to cook their meals on the oil lamps themselves. The first tower was too short (stormy waves engulfed the lantern) so in 1875 the present 120-foot tower replaced it. The equally tall one on Wolf Rock, which replaced iron beacons, is a few years older.

Out there beyond the rocks and foam lies, perhaps, Lyonesse, the lost land of so many King Arthur stories. Just here the Atlantic meets the English Channel, and when these two giant waters collide in an exceptional storm, anything is possible: in Cornwall, drowned churches and trees, and the shifting of mountainous sand dunes, are realities not legends.

With the wind making it hard not to lean at a 45-degree angle, I soon retreated to the well-upholstered lounge of the Land's End Hotel, an excellent Cornish pasty and, joy of joys, rum-and-shrub, the best remedy for icy toes and nose. Shrub is an alcoholic cordial peculiar to the West Country. It has been made (from a concoction of herbs) for at least three centuries, and it is said that its affinity for rum was first noticed when barrels of rum hidden underwater by smugglers got salty and the shrub was added to mask it. Lovage makes another such cordial, often mixed with brandy.

To return via Penzance, taking buses through the southern half of the peninsula, shows how different Penwith is south of its granite backbone. There is a wider area of fertile land sheltered from Atlantic winds, where flowers are grown for the London market – fields of daffodils, irises and tulips at the start of summer. Broccoli, cauliflowers and new potatoes are grown here, too. This side of the coastline has more sandy beaches and sun-trapping coves, more little fishing villages and more trees.

The Cornish hedgerow is basically a dry-stone wall topped with turf which soon attracts wildflowers, gorse and shrubs so that it rapidly becomes a high bank, cutting off the car driver's view – but bus passengers, even on single-deckers, can see over the top. Buses travel slowly enough for one to enjoy and identify the multitude of wildflowers in the banks as one goes along. At one halt I counted over 20 varieties just outside my window.

Few bus rides in Penwith do not pass reminders of Cornwall's great antiquity. Wayside crosses are typically Cornish and usually medieval, put up beside roads that led to churches or perhaps to commemorate someone. Many are stones with disc-shaped tops inscribed with a crucifix or other carvings. But these are comparative newcomers to the scene. Thousands of years before Christ, Stone Age people were building great tombs and temples here made from massive slabs or boulders. Particularly common are long stones (menhirs), of which many can be seen along the bus routes – single upright slabs which may have been primitive tombstones. Though it lacks both index and map, a useful booklet to take along is the Cornish Archaeological Society's guide to these local antiquities – shops and tourist offices sell it for a few pence. It also explains some of the Penwith place names, which are pure Cornish. The language is related to both Welsh and Breton and died out nearly two centuries ago. Crows-an-Wra, a hamlet with a stone cross on this route, means 'the witch's cross'.

There are old churches, too, but few have interesting interiors because Victorian 'improvers' unfortunately ripped out much that gave them character. In many places they are outnumbered by Methodist chapels. Cornwall has always taken religion seriously, even to the extent of rebelling against the Reformation in 1548, and John Wesley repeatedly visited this area during the 1740s. He was indefatigable, riding from hamlet to hamlet over moorland tracks, and made thousands of converts (and a good many enemies). All these chapels sprang up in his wake.

From Penzance (to be explored on a later day) the principal

route back to St Ives, via Crowlas, turned out to be neither the prettiest nor even the shortest, but it has more buses and they nip along the main road quickly. This road has attracted to it various entertainments such as the vast outdoor 'Age of Steam' railway exhibition, Lelant's model village and leisure centre, and other well-planned activities for children in particular.

From the top of the bus just outside Penzance one can see helicopters taking off for the 20-minute joy-ride to the Scilly Isles. On the other side of the road, over the railway lines, is Mount's Bay with St Michael's Mount and its castle perched 300 feet up (easy to reach on another bus, then by ferry or walking over the cobbled causeway if the tide is out). It is now in the care of the National Trust. Like Mont St Michel off the Normandy coast, the steep mount is an island only at high tide. For centuries it was topped by a priory under the authority of the abbey on Mont St Michel, but in 1425 it became a fortress. Perkin Warbeck, pretender to the English throne (he claimed to be one of the two princes murdered in the Tower of London), used it as his base in 1497. It was held during the Civil Wars by the Royalists, as were most of Cornwall's strongholds. The castle is now a mixture of every architectural style from the 12th century onwards. At the foot of the Mount is its own small harbour and fishing village.

On many bus routes St Michael's Mount suddenly pops into view unexpectedly and each time it looks quite different. It is not just a question of the angle from which one sees it. The sky and sea are always changing, and the castle changes with them.

Another of the advantages of this route is the view of the Hayle estuary before entering St Ives. The Hayle is wide and shallow here, ambling among pools and sand dunes known locally as towans. But once it was deep and tidal for four miles inland, in the days when Bronze Age miners bartered their tin with foreign ships. One of the few havens along the rocky northern shore, it was the landing place for many of St Patrick's missionaries from Ireland, now remembered as saints peculiar to Cornwall and after whom so many Penwith churches are named.

As the bus approaches Carbis Bay the horizon is suddenly bisected by an immense granite needle on a hill, the Knill monument. Knill was an 18th-century customs collector (his house can still be seen in Fore Street, St Ives) who built this 500-foot steeple, now in a grove of rhododendrons, with the intention of being buried inside it at his death. He left money for a ceremony that still takes place every fifth year on St James's Day (25 July), when ten girls and two widows dance round the steeple to a tune played by a fiddler.

Near the finish of this route is an even more welcome sight at the day's end: John Beck's fish-and-chip restaurant at Carbis Bay. The queues outside tell their own story. If this is not the best fish-and-chippery in Britain, it must surely be the best in Cornwall.

It is also possible to leave the bus at St Erth and finish the journey on the very scenic railway line that runs into St Ives along this estuary and the coast.

Zennor and Penzance

Zennor is quickly reached by bus. It nestles just off the main road, in one of the innumerable valleys carved out by streams tumbling some 800 feet down that granite backbone to the Atlantic shore. The church is famous for its mermaid, carved on an ancient bench end. The story goes that she lured a young man, one of the church choir's sweetest singers, to the sea and his death. Very Cornish, too, is the notable eccentric who created Zennor's Wayside Museum, which is something really special – yet mercifully the crowds have not invaded it.

A lifetime ago, a Colonel Hirst happened to notice some curious old implements among a heap of scrap-iron about to be shipped abroad. He decided to buy them. From this chance acquisition began a long pursuit of abandoned tools of vanishing trades and old household utensils. In his garden he displayed and labelled his finds with admirably large, clear explanations, and he threw open the gates to any passer-by who cared to enter – without charge.

And what an extraordinary collection it is: there is a wheeled barrow from which water was sold for ½d a bucket; strange tools for gathering fuel from the moors; and an oven like a huge clay pot in which smouldering faggots of wood were placed to heat it and were then removed so that the food could be put in.

Stones, so freely available here, were turned to innumerable uses – smugglers tied their loot to a stone with grooves or holes for the rope and sank it in a pool or the sea. Querns are round stones between which wheat was ground into flour. And what a variety of arm-aching irons for washdays: box-irons, heated by putting a hot coal inside; solid flat-irons; charcoal irons with chimneys; and goffering rollers to pleat frills. Then there are models of fishing and mining cottages and ancient hill forts, tombs and other antiquities. The watermill beside the garden's hurrying stream is also open to view, as is the restored miller's cottage.

After seeing so much, a restorative visit to the nearby Tinners' Arms was obviously necessary. This old pub, with ceiling of varnished boards and big stone hearths, was temporarily the home of D. H. Lawrence until he found High Tregarthen cottage (not far off, downhill between the farms of Tregarthen and Tremedda, which the bus passes).

Zennor Head (National Trust) is only a half-mile walk away but I wanted to see the other Cornwall, the moors inland that are less celebrated than the coast but have a wild beauty of their own. There were several ways to get from Zennor to Penzance across the moors. The road to Morvah and via Madron was tempting – Lanyon Quoit, a 4,000-year-old tomb, the carvings and monuments of Madron church, the ruins of one of the oldest tin mines – but I chose the quicker Newmill route on an open-top bus in order to have more time in Penzance later.

At Penzance (the name means 'holy headland') the bus deposited me near the harbour. The quay leads out over a decrepit bridge to the sailors' end of the town. There is a big Aladdin's cave of a shop selling shells from all over the world which takes bookings for shark fishing and other sea trips. Then, round a corner, I came to a yard where monsters loomed: colossal navigation buoys of all shapes and sizes, each with its name painted on it – Knight Errant, Montamopus, Udder Rock, Exe Fairway. As I stared and wondered, a uniformed officer came to see what I wanted and ended by giving me a private tour.

It turned out to be one of the Trinity House depots that look after all the navigation buoys, lighthouses and lightships round England's coasts. Trinity House was chartered by Henry VIII as a semi-religious body charged with responsibility for ensuring safety at sea. It was given a coat-of-arms incorporating four galleons, and its flag is the Red Ensign of the merchant navy with the four Tudor galleons added to it. It was not until 1836, however, that Trinity House took over control of all lighthouses and brought efficiency to a previously haphazard situation.

Although a lot of sophisticated automation now goes into these buoys, some give their warnings as effectively as ever by means of simple devices invented long ago. The doleful moan of buoys like the one at Swithian (listen to it just before the last bus goes, when most visitors have left the miles of sand dunes desolate) is achieved by a giant iron tube like a vast whistle: air is let in or kept out by four rubber balls pushed in and out of sockets by the waves. A loose length of chain, continually swishing, is enough to keep the ironwork free from marine growth.

Only a few yards beyond the Trinity House depot is the Barbican (barbican means a town's outer defence), once a stone fortification, then a warehouse and now imaginatively restored as a crafts centre with workshops, gallery and coffee bar. It was designed by Percy Williams, who created the equally inspired Sloop crafts centre at St Ives.

The rest of the waterfront is promenade. Turning uphill, I soon came to the parish church, set in a particularly tranquil graveyard of lawns, old tombstones and trees in which to sit and watch the sea below. The church itself has an unusual 'gothick' interior dating from 1832 – full of space and light, with a gallery round it and a blue-white-gold colour scheme. The font is made of polished serpentine, a stone peculiar to Cornwall.

Beyond lies Penzance's most beguiling road, Chapel Street. There is so much of interest in this single road that the tourist office (opposite the Guildhall) has – in addition to its leaflet with a complete town trail to follow – one on Chapel Street alone. Antique, craft and book shops are sandwiched between restaurants and historic inns – each with its ghost, minstrel's gallery or what-have-you. Most famous and colourful of all is the Admiral Benbow. The owner, once a diver and collector of bits from wrecks, has written a small book about it. Its interior is crammed with his finds, and painted figureheads guard every corner. It was truly a smugglers' inn, and the exploits of one man who dealt with the customs men by climbing on the roof and firing from there is well commemorated: look up outside and you will see his effigy clinging to the slates.

Chapel Street also has its Museum of Nautical Art, with a full-size section through an 18th-century man-o'-war as well as models, old ships' carvings, elaborately decorated cannon and treasure recently retrieved from the *Association*, which sank off the Scilly Isles in 1767. Strangest building of all is the Egyptian House, built as a museum about 1835, which looks as if it would be more at home on the Nile than displaying local crafts for sale.

West of Chapel Street lie Georgian houses. Regent Square is particularly attractive, the houses unconventionally laid out around a dog-leg street. By St Mary's Terrace, a gate leads into the very pretty Morrab Gardens, a few sloping acres punctuated with fountain, bandstand and flowering shrubs. Leaving by an opposite gate I found myself facing the entrance to the larger Penlee gardens, which surround the town's museum with tree ferns and other semi-tropical plants.

The museum is unpretentious, but its local exhibits are well displayed. The bird room helped me to identify a number of the plants as well as birds I'd seen from buses, while other rooms explained the fishing and mining history of the area. One display is devoted to the life of Sir Humphrey Davy of miner's lamp fame, who was born in Penzance just over two hundred years ago. His statue dominates Market Jew Street, the big shopping centre that runs down from the handsome domed building of Lloyds Bank (once the Market House).

I went by the library, pausing not only to look at an Armada cannon outside it but to scoop up some bargains in their used book sale. I then went along North Parade, a quiet backwater of terraced Regency houses, slightly faded and with gardens slightly neglected but no less attractive for that.

Every so often one comes across chunks of granite said to be the largest ever cut (Queen Victoria's tomb at Windsor is among the candidates). The 18-foot top step of the Law Courts in the nearby main road also makes this claim. I found *The Guinness Book of Records* silent on the subject of granite, but at least where length is concerned Penzance's slab must be hard to beat. (There is more about Penzance on pages 258–60.)

I chose a different bus service this time to return to St Ives, one that trundled up and down small lanes, past almshouses and over streams, winding between little gardens rich in lilac and laburnum. This bit of Penwith is nicknamed the Golden Acres because it is so fertile. We went by Suttons' seed trial grounds – a rainbow of pansies – and by fields full of new potatoes.

Gulval is a picturesque village celebrated for its flowery churchyard and vicarage garden, with interesting monuments in its church. It was a spot worth lingering in (though one can walk down to the main road with its more frequent bus service).

Then the bus strained uphill to Ludgvan with its stone cottages around a tiny triangular village green (not an unusual layout in this part of England). The tumble of mixed flowers in small cottage gardens was as colourful as a kaleidoscope. One more village sheltered in a valley with an old watermill (now a garage) by its stream. This was a very Cornish route with a little of everything along the way.

Porthcurno, Newlyn and Mousehole

For my third day's trip, after the usual drive to Penzance, I chose a bus route that would take me to some of the sheltered coves and fishing villages within a short distance of Penzance, a particular feature of the south coast of Penwith.

So, out through the western suburbs of Penzance we went. At first the bus was full of shoppers, but they soon alighted leaving only a few of us to jog on past the bowling green. We went past a thatched farmhouse sunk, it seemed, several feet below road level (or had the road been built up?) so that only the top half of the front door was visible; along the Esplanade and by the Bolitho Gardens (the Bolithos were – and are – a wealthy banking family of civic benefactors). The bus strained up steep Chywoone Hill to where Adit Lane runs down towards the sea. Adit means the lowest drainage level of a mine, often in a cliff just above sea level, so presumably there were once mine workings below us. We drove through Paul, which has a church with box pews, a barrel ceiling, handsome monuments and the grave of the last speaker of Cornish as a native language (who died in 1777). We passed a garden walled entirely with old tombstones. There are views over the moors and then the bus dips into leafy valleys – down and then up, all the way. The turning to Lamorna Cove runs through a tangle of bent tree trunks thick with ivy, birch saplings and sycamore.

Lamorna has its cove, granite cliffs, jetty and a few cottages and is a good spot to linger in, but I decided to press on inland with the bus. Huge rounded boulders lie half-buried in the fields, looking like the humped backs of whales in the sea. To the left is a ring of 19 great stones, 'the merry maidens', and not far off their two 'pipers', each nearly 15 feet tall. Stone Age and Bronze Age people erected these circles of (originally) 20 stones in a number of places.

Their purposes are not now known, so stories grew up to explain them; it was said that people who danced on Sundays were turned to stone. A burial chamber is usually found near each such circle and Tregiffian is no exception.

At a wayside cross the bus turned, passing fields with typical Cornish stiles of stone steps. St Buryan (another cross here) has a shop specializing in things made from serpentine, and a church with a fine interior and a wood screen carved with a notable menagerie of beasts.

A precipitous road snakes its way down the steep sides of St Levan's valley. One can walk into Treen and from there to some of the National Trust's beauty spots on this colourful coast – half a mile to Treen Cliff and the Logan Rock, a mile to Penberth Cove. 'Logan' means 'moving' and this delicately balanced, 66-ton rock could be rocked with little effort until in 1824 a high-spirited young lieutenant pushed it right off its perch. He had to have it replaced, but it has never been quite the same since.

After miles of countryside Porthcurno took me by surprise, because one's first impression is of the overwhelming presence of the telecommunications industry, which has a training college and other enterprises in this remote spot. At Porthcurno the trans-

Minack Theatre

atlantic cables enter the sea. But once the bus has parked (for motorists there was not one space left in the huge car park) it is easy to leave all that behind and wander down to the beach – one of the most remote in England, though only an hour from Penzance.

On this beautiful and romantic coast a circular open-air theatre – the Minack – has been carved out of the cliff-top where once there was nothing but a depression filled with gorse. The theatre developed gradually over the last 50 years, but it is now superbly equipped. Stage and backdrop are of stone – or, rather, the backdrop is the sea and the sky, for the audience sits with its back to the land. It is worth seeing even when no play is being performed.

The same bus service returned me to Newlyn, where a different scene awaited. This is a busy little town with quite a big harbour; a 'meadery' where one can eat as well as enjoy free samples of this very ancient Cornish wine made with honey (the name 'mead' comes from the Cornish word for honey); and fish warehouses at which great juggernauts from France call daily to load up with lobsters. I walked from the bridge spanning the roadside stream as far as the church to find Harveys' warehouse and buy two very big crabs, freshly caught and cooked. Newlyn was the centre of a celebrated group of artists at the turn of the century, of whom Stanhope Forbes is the best known. They painted the harsh life of the fisherfolk and villagers as it really was in those days, and the quality of the Cornish light and water as it still is. I was lucky to find an exhibition of their work showing at the town's art gallery, collected together from all over the country for a few weeks. The Queen's Hotel always has examples on view.

Mousehole (pronounced Mouse'l), a few minutes away by bus, was called by Dylan Thomas 'the loveliest village in England', and there he spent his honeymoon. He stayed at the Lobster Pot, which is still a delightful spot to choose, its dining room hanging right over the harbour. Mousehole is less lovely than it used to be, because its popularity has brought too much traffic for its narrow and twisting streets – the bus driver's task was about as easy as squeezing toothpaste back into the tube, even though special narrow buses are provided for the Mousehole service.

A good place to start exploring Mousehole is in the Penlee bar of the Old Coastguard Hotel, dedicated to the nearby Penlee lifeboat and to one of the most tragic lifeboat disasters ever, a few years ago. The walls are covered with mementos and photographs of local lifeboat work. The aerial pictures of ships breaking up or gone aground on this treacherous coast sent me back to the RNLI's collecting box in the bar. Britain is the only country in which such a heroic force is manned by volunteers and financed only by what the public gives to support it. Looking at these photographs of local storms, one understands why Mousehole's harbour is almost completely enclosed in granite walls with a gate to close off even its very narrow entrance when the weather is at its worst.

The village is picturesque. It has old cottages, almshouses, cobbled lanes, and an ancient inn with a porch hanging half across the road. Sitting on the harbour steps, I ate a Cornish pasty, while watching and trying to identify the different kinds of gulls – black-backed, herring, black-headed – and their youngsters, still in the brownish plumage of the first two or three years of life.

On the quay a table bore a collection of sea urchins. The absent diver who was offering them for sale (at far less than the shops) trusted one to put the money through the outsize keyhole of his front door, moneybox-style. Sea urchins, which seem to have been designed by the Almighty for the express purpose of making into lamps, are a relative of the starfish, covered when alive with 600 little plates bearing sharp spines that move this way and that as they browse on seaweed. The Cornish call them zarts, or mermaids' eggs.

It is worth the steep climb up the other side of Mousehole not only to see the spectacular view but to visit the bird sanctuary. The Yglesias sisters, having acquired a reputation for the care of injured wild birds, were brought so many that eventually their house and garden were turned into a hospital and convalescent home, particularly for seabirds and the crow family which flourishes in Penwith (magpies, ravens, jackdaws and so forth). Eventually the enterprise grew so big that the RSPCA stepped in to finance it for over twenty years. Then, a few years ago, this support was withdrawn. The sisters, by then in their 80s but undaunted, started a fund-raising campaign that allowed the bird sanctuary to survive – but only just. Its story has been told in a book by one of the sisters. Every year about 1,500 birds are treated, though only half can be given a new lease of life. Many are dying from oil spilled by tankers (after the *Torrey Canyon* disaster, 8,000 birds were brought here). Others have broken wings, broken legs or eye injuries. Some are choking on fish-hooks. Orphaned chicks need feeding every half hour round the clock.

I walked through the old-fashioned garden of wallflowers, columbines and forget-me-nots to find a multitude of wire enclosures containing birds on their way to recovery and freedom. It was fascinating to see at close quarters wild birds such as divers, not to be found in zoos and too shy to encounter in the wild except through binoculars.

By the time I started on my homeward journey (back to St Ives via Penzance) it was milking time, and the bus had to wait for an unhurrying herd of cows in the lane ahead. The grass on the verges is evidently much sweeter than that of the fields, and the stone walls are ideal for scratching on – if you are a cow, that is – regardless of the bus timetable. On the cows waddled, unflustered by the growing queue behind. It was pleasant to pause and enjoy the ivy trails on the walls, a solitary palm tree, primroses, violets and new little fronds of bracken bright among the grass: just a very ordinary Cornish evening.

14
In the Steps of Dickens

Gravesend – Cobham – Higham – Cliffe – Chalk – Strood – Rochester – Chatham

A good choice of book to take when bussing about in Dickens country would be *Great Expectations*, *Pickwick Papers* or *Edwin Drood*. The last is particularly full of references to the area. This part of Kent played a large part in Dickens' life. He spent his childhood in Chatham (1816–21), honeymooned in Chalk (1836) and died in Higham (1870). He wanted to be buried here rather than in the glory of Westminster Abbey.

Gravesend (see page 58) he knew well, travelling regularly from its station to London during the 1860s, but he had no great liking for it ('Muggleton' in *Pickwick Papers* was based on Gravesend), though its waterfront inns, old fort, covered market, lanes on Windmill Hill and church where the Indian princess Pocahontas was buried in the 17th century are all worth visiting. (The local library has produced a leaflet on 'Dickens in Gravesham', the name for Gravesend and its surroundings.)

Cobham

A bus from Gravesend takes only a half hour through a beautiful area with fields of daffodils in spring to reach a village he liked much more – Cobham, named after an ancient family. Here the old, timbered Leather Bottle Inn is full of Dickens mementoes. It, too, appears in *Pickwick* along with the church (famous for its brasses), adjoining medieval almshouses and the great park of Cobham Hall, a Tudor mansion that is now a girls' school and is sometimes open to the public.

A $\frac{1}{4}$-hour's ride back as far as Chalk enabled me to pick up another bus for a journey in the opposite direction through very different scenery. Instead of woods, marshes stretch towards the North Sea on a little-frequented peninsula between the Thames and the Medway estuaries. There are glimpses of ships passing or, in autumn, migrant wading birds arriving. The first chapter of *Great Expectations* describes this wild place:

> ... Ours was the marsh country, down by the river, within, as the river wound, twenty miles of the sea. My first most vivid and broad impression of the identity of things seems to me to have been gained on a memorable raw afternoon towards evening ... the dark flat wilderness intersected with dykes and mounds and gates, with scattered cattle feeding on it ... the low leaden line beyond was the river ... the distant savage lair from which the wind was rushing was the sea ...

But in May the scene was different. At the start of the ride, after the domesticated gardens lay flat fields hedged with hawthorn or with long rows of towering poplars protecting the blossoming apple orchards from east winds off the North Sea. Some fields were green with wheat, others brilliant yellow (full of rape, grown for the oil-rich seeds). Ploughed, baked earth alternated with pastures where young lambs grazed. The honeyed smell of meadowsweet was in the air. There were scattered farmhouses, weatherboarded or tile-hung, some with handsome Georgian doors or windows. In every cottage garden wallflowers were growing abundantly.

Higham, Cliffe and Chalk

At Higham the road crosses the railway, and alongside it are reeds and the vestiges of the canal that ran along there long before the railway was built in Dickens' time. The canal went through a long tunnel in the chalk hills and one can see its entrance still, with the railway line disappearing into it, below the brow of the hill where four oast-houses stand. Its purpose was to provide sailing barges with a short cut between the Thames and Medway estuaries, but tidal delays made it a longer route and so it fell into disuse.

Further on, towards the marshes, a great container ship seemed to slide among the fields (an optical illusion – the Thames on which it sails is hidden from view). Birds sing, butterflies flutter and there is a cloudless blue sky above the chalky tracks that lead off to the marshes. This is one of the few wildernesses left near London, though it is under constant threat of exploitation for oil refineries or even as a dumping ground for London's refuse. One has only to look across the Thames to what has happened to the Essex shore, a mass of chemical tanks, to see how serious a threat this is.

When Dickens took his long, solitary walks around this area, smock windmills were his landmarks – several dozen dotted the peninsula (one was still working until about 40 years ago). Now electric pylons stand out on the skyline.

Cliffe is a village of weatherboarded houses, much neglected, and a very splendid 13th-century church. Once, as its name suggests, it was on the edge of the estuary, but silt built up the miles of marshes that now separate it from the water.

I returned to Chalk where, at Forge Lane, the picturesque original of Jo Gargery's forge (Pip's early home) still stands, a tumbledown, weatherboarded cottage with yellow roses rambling above faded blue shutters. More disputably, a cottage nearby bears a plaque stating it is where Dickens spent his honeymoon (he wrote part of *Pickwick* while honeymooning in Chalk and the landlady of this cottage, Mrs Craddock, appears in the book); however, there is no conclusive proof.

Buses from Chalk to Rochester are frequent and quick. They pass by Dickens' last home, the 18th-century house at Higham called Gad's Hill Place (now a girls' school, not open to the public). It stands opposite the Falstaff Inn, where he used to take an active part in the local cricket club meetings (the inn has a very good buffet). A tunnel under the road, its entrances still just visible among the ivy, linked his front garden with another where for many years he had a big chalet that had been sent to him in prefabricated parts by a Swiss admirer. In this he used to write, and that is what he was doing on the day he died. It can now be seen outside the Dickens Centre in Rochester.

Rochester

I went on past the old Crispin and Crispianus Inn, one of Dickens' favourite haunts (described in *The Uncommercial Traveller*) and then over one of Rochester's triple bridges to alight and walk along the High Street, lined with old buildings, tea-rooms, inns, antique and

Rochester

book shops. The Tourist Information Centre is there and, among much else, it has a leaflet explaining all the Dickens' place references to be seen in or near the High Street, such as:

- Royal Victoria & Bull coaching inn (mentioned in *Pickwick* and *Great Expectations*)
- Guildhall: 18th-century rooms and museum (*Great Expectations*)
- Corn Exchange: spectacular clock (*Uncommercial Traveller*)
- College Gate (*Edwin Drood*)

Watts Charity: old hostel, sometimes open (*Seven Poor Travellers*)

Nos. 150–154 (Uncle Pumblechook's shop in *Great Expectations*)

The Dickens Centre: 15 rooms recreating scenes from the books and from his life (the Nun's House in *Edwin Drood*)

The Norman castle and the Norman cathedral, Minor Canons Row and what was once a monastery vineyard – all these occur in *Edwin Drood* and other books. Many of the names Dickens used in his stories can be deciphered on tombstones around the cathedral. Restoration House (where Charles II stayed on his way back to the throne) became Miss Havisham's house in *Great Expectations*. On the outskirts is 13th-century Temple Manor, once an outpost of the Knights Templars.

Chatham

Rochester and Chatham are almost one now: a few minutes on a bus and Chatham centre is reached. Dickens' father worked in the old part of the naval dockyard on the river, where Nelson's *Victory* had been built. The modest family home at 11 Ordnance Terrace is still standing, near the railway station, and Fort Pitt is where the famous duel in *Pickwick* took place. High over the town are the 'Great Lines' – walls, moats and crumbling forts strung along the hills, mostly built during the invasion scares of Napoleonic times – one open to visitors. At the former naval dockyard are historic buildings, a visitor centre and a museum. Near it (in a former church) is the city's heritage centre. The 'Chatham Sheds' are now a national monument: built in the 18th century, their purpose was to house timber for building the Royal Navy's ships.

There is much more to see in the Medway towns. Dickens doubtless knew the Huguenot community (they have their own square in Rochester still, called La Providence), the huge sailing barges (once river cargo ships, a few dozen are now preserved and sailed for pleasure or in races), the Tudor seamen's hospital founded by Sir John Hawkins, and the summer shipboard 'court' and cruise of the mayor.

Between May and August are held a Dickens festival, a street fair, and a regatta. This is Royal Engineers' country, too, and their museum at Brompton Barracks on the edge of Chatham is far more interesting than most regimental museums – with a splendid statue of General Gordon on a tasselled camel outside. Threading through everything are the winds of the Medway, semi-industrial but well worth a paddle-steamer trip.

15

Apple-Blossom Time

Maidstone – Hadlow – Tonbridge – Tunbridge Wells – Matfield – Maidstone

This is a journey for late springtime, but to be sure of doing it when the pink blossom is at its best, first phone the South Eastern Tourist Board (see page xx) to ask whether it is fully out yet. There are many possible routes. Mine took in historic towns, many pretty villages, and miles of orchards (and hop fields) in between. It can be done in a day but deserves two.

Maidstone

I started at Maidstone, where the remains of the 14th-century archbishop's palace and the church (one of the greatest and finest of that period) stand by the river among beautiful gardens. The archbishop's stables now house an impressive collection of historic carriages, well worth a visit, and the gatehouse contains a Tourist Information Centre which can provide details of much else, including river trips. From here there are two bus routes to Tunbridge Wells, each taking about $1\frac{1}{4}$ hours, so that one can go out one way and return another.

The bus that goes via Tonbridge at first runs through the Medway valley, with occasional glimpses of medieval church towers and an ancient bridge at West Farleigh. Mereworth is memorable for its church – an unusual one to find in the countryside, copied from 18th-century London churches (its steeple imitates that of St Martin-in-the-Fields). Hadlow's landmark can be seen for miles: an octagonal 'gothick' folly tower nearly 200 feet high, built by a landowner who used it (the story goes) to keep watch on his errant wife. In fact, it was built in 1838 by an eccentric called William May whose *folie de grandeur* expressed itself in this attempt to outdo Beckford's great tower at Fonthill. It is not as tall, but at least it is still there (Beckford's tower collapsed).

Hadlow

I stopped off at Hadlow to investigate further. Through an ornate arch, romantically creeper-covered like some haunted ruin from a Tennyson poem, one can walk into grounds where modern houses are discreetly hidden among the conifers and bamboos. The tower itself is now a home, too, and its florid pinnacles can be admired only from a discreet distance. Its great height dwarfs the simple tower of the nearby church, at the end of a picturesque cobbled lane (Church Road) and a brick path through the graveyard. Two very small boys were hunting for something among the sunlit tombstones. 'Have you seen God?' the younger one asked me. This was not out of concern for my soul, it turned out – they were taking literally the proclamation on the church notice board that 'He who seeks God will find him here.' What *can* be found there is the very elaborate mausoleum of William May, the folly-builder, sadly in need of rescue from weeds and decay. Parts of the church are Saxon. In its shady interior the scent of lilies hung heavily on the cool air as I wandered round followed by the two small boys, who were then debating the whereabouts of heaven.

Hadlow, though only 30 miles from London, is a country village still, with a history that goes back thousands of years. It was one of the first Stone Age settlements in Kent, and it claims to be the birthplace of the printer William Caxton. It has survived many changes and hazards (including bombs in the Second World War).

Tonbridge

Tonbridge is an ancient town, but not particularly attractive now. The Saxons built a fortress on the mound by the river, and then the Normans used it for the same purpose. The ruins are medieval with the addition of an 18th-century mansion and pleasant gardens. The High Street and Bordyke have a few timbered and Georgian buildings and down an alley is an old church said to have brilliant modern stained glass – but I found the door locked because of vandals. So was that of the chapel in Tonbridge School: the sundial outside says 'Keep innocency, Do the Thing that is Right', but the school authorities evidently put more faith in locks than in exhortations.

One can eat at inns or, better still, picnic in the castle grounds; or sit, as I did, by the river, watching a brood of 16 tiny fluffy ducklings paddling determinedly against the tide. A new block of offices has been designed with sensitivity to blend into the waterfront scene and there is a walkway beside the river.

Back on a bus and along a main road that rides high on a ridge, I found fine views. Agreeable, unassuming houses lead to a wide, tree-lined avenue. There are lacy iron verandahs above the shops and early Victorian houses set well back from the road. A minute later we were in Tunbridge Wells.

Tunbridge Wells

I made straight for my hotel, the Wellington, which was outside the centre and right by the famous Wellington Rocks on the common – an extraordinary formation, rounded yet craggy and deeply fissured. The hotel, full of portraits and mementos of the Duke, is all that one might expect of a Tunbridge Wells hotel in the grand Regency manner: crimson velvet, solid mahogany, classical pillars and crystal chandeliers.

Early next morning I walked down into town across the common. The sunshine was on my face, birds were singing, dogs of every pedigree were taking their masters for walks. The white smoke trail of a plane bisected the clear blue sky, and the sun highlighted the fresh green of newly unfolded chestnut leaves.

Tunbridge Wells, all ups and downs, had its heyday as a spa in the 18th century. Between stately avenues, squares and crescents are intriguing tiled footpaths with picturesque cottages. The official guide includes a plan enabling one to thread a way through the town and hardly ever walk along a road. From the start many of the houses were built as visitors' lodgings, and there are still bed-and-breakfast rooms to be had near the famous Pantiles where the therapeutic spring is.

The water from the cool spring tastes faintly rusty. It bubbles up into marble basins a few feet lower than the paving stones, and an attendant with a dipper fills a glass for you to sip as you view the Pantiles before setting off to window-shop there. Named for the red roof tiles originally used (in contrast to the rest of the slate-roofed town), the street is a pedestrian promenade sheltered by a row of trees down the middle and by a colonnade in front of small shops selling antiques, hand-made chocolates, leather goods, books and suchlike. Some shops have wrought-ironwork, bay windows or weatherboarding above, with hanging lanterns or clocks. Steps go up and down; at a lower level are houses in fondant colours, Assembly Rooms where Victoria stayed while still a child-princess, a Corn Exchange topped by an overweight Ceres flourishing her sickle, and a muster of antique shops. 'Here health and social pleasures reign . . .' begins an 18th-century ode to the town. Both still do.

As the Stuarts were regular visitors to the Wells, it is not surprising that the parish church was dedicated to Charles I, martyr but not a saint. By comparison with most Kentish churches this is a parvenu – less than 300 years old – but a very handsome one; its elaborately domed and garlanded plaster ceiling is a work of art.

Both church and Pantiles lie at the south end of the High Street, which curves as it ascends north to Mount Pleasant Road, a wide shopping street with museum near the top. To the right lie the beautiful Calverley Gardens and Crescent Road, along which one is surprised by Calverley Park Crescent. Its houses have their plain backs facing the road, and only if one walks round to the other side is the almost Bath-like elegance of the Crescent revealed: slender white columns supporting delicately railed verandahs, and pretty half-moon gardens. There were deep pink camellias blooming against a warm stone wall when I was there.

The journey back to Maidstone starts through a very green route, with mansions concealed behind high hedges of cypress, laurel or holly, drooping larches and thickets of venerable trees. The bus goes past the greens and almshouses of Pembury, on through ploughed fields, by oast houses and great barns, and past views of sheep grazing.

Matfield

I broke my journey at Matfield, tempted by the tables in the sunshine outside the Wheelwright's Arms, a pretty weatherboarded inn with roses climbing round the windows and hanging baskets of flowers at the timbered porches. Matfield has a huge green. I walked across it enjoying the smell of mown grass and the tiny daisies spangling the turf. A large fish suddenly leapt in the small pond.

Among many attractive houses fringing the green is a formal mansion, its date declared on the old rainwater heads as 1728. 'Mind the Time' warns the ornamental, one-handed clock above its stables – good advice when there is a bus to be caught – so I did not linger much longer by the cottages, the quaint butcher's shop or the tea-rooms.

From here on the orchards multiplied, some with lambs under the trees, and the hop fields; with them the oast houses became more frequent, too – at Beltring there is a congregation of 30 in one group. We crossed one stream after another, rose high up for distant views and plunged down again. More barns, old wagons, white horses (there really do seem to be a great many white horses in Kent, and they are the county emblem, seen adorning village signs).

The journey was nearing an end. After Teston there is a tranquil view of one of the Medway's lovely bridges, the sharp spike of a church spire announcing the village of Barming, and then within minutes the bus is into the environs of busy Maidstone. Yet even there spring and nature have their way: my last memory is of a bird nesting within the broken glass cover of a tall streetlamp – 'mod cons' preferable to the hazards of life in the wild?

16

1066 and All That

Eastbourne – Pevensey – Hastings – Battle – Ninfield – Hailsham – Lewes – Eastbourne

A day on the buses makes a change when, during a seaside family holiday, swimming, sunbathing and sandcastles begin to lose their appeal. Eastbourne is one of the pleasantest seaside resorts I know and it also has the bonus of being on the coast where English history started – or, at least, where most history books like to start – in 1066. So, for the high spot of an Eastbourne holiday, I worked out a bus trail following in the steps of the Normans, along the shore and inland through the hills of the Sussex Weald. 'The Fortifications of East Sussex', a well-illustrated booklet published by the County Council, does much to bring alive the battles of long ago.

Pevensey

Pevensey Bay, lined with miles of shingle, is only a few minutes by bus from Eastbourne. The spot on this bay where William

Pevensey Castle

beached his Norman ships and waded ashore that stormy September is hard to recreate in one's imagination, for the bay is now crowded with bungalows (and two Martello towers). In any case, the shoreline has moved south over the centuries as the Atlantic seas have piled silt on it, so it is better to stay on the bus. It goes on to Pevensey Castle.

On landing William had found the remains of a ten-acre Roman fort, just one of many built to keep the Saxon tribes from landing 1600 years ago, and he madc use of it. He dug ditches inside the old walls as an additional defence for his camp. Later he handed the place over to his brother to fortify properly with a great keep. This castle – where the Roman walls, ditches and keep are still to be seen – continued in use right up to the Second World War. The remains of gun emplacements and lookouts camouflaged to look like ruins, are still there.

The castle stands on a mound that was once virtually surrounded by sea (the '-ey' in Pevensey is Saxon for island). One can clearly imagine this when approaching by bus, for it stands up high above the land over which the bus runs (once sea where ships sailed). It looked dramatically bright when I saw it against a sombre, rain-laden sky, with the downs dark behind. Before the waters receded, a little port had grown up outside the castle, and some of its old buildings still survive – the 14th-century Mint House (the Normans started minting coins at Pevensey), the Court House and the 13th-century church. At the adjoining village of Westham is a church of even greater antiquity and grandeur, said to have been the first the Normans built in England.

The first part of the bus ride to Hastings is over clay marshes (they were under the sea in 1066) called the Pevensey Levels. The Haven river and the rippling drainage dykes were fringed with reeds; black-and-white Friesian cows grazed beside them as well as sheep that looked picture-book white because they were newly shorn. Calves scattered and ran at our approach, grass still hanging from their mouths. Graceful willows bordered the road until the bus got to the 15th-century Lamb Inn, climbed a hill with sea views and then entered the outskirts of Bexhill. This is the more attractive side of the town, and the bus travelled along a surburban avenue where instead of hedges or fences there are roses all the way, their scent drifting into the bus. At Bexhill when the tide is low it is possible to see the remains of drowned forest exposed, a reminder that once land linked England with France. The further side of the resort is a boring suburb, but it is soon followed by St Leonards, where there are still many elegant streets from the 1820s when the town was first laid out (Warrior Square is particularly fine); it is virtually part of Hastings now.

Hastings

Hastings (described on pages 87–8) commemorates its place in the story of the Norman Conquest with a great 'Conqueror's Stone' by the pier. When William left Pevensey he marched to Hastings, and on its hilltop he erected a fort of prefabricated wooden parts shipped from Normandy. Later he had a stone castle built there, of which fragments still remain. It was not here, however, that the famous 'Battle of Hastings' took place but at Senlac (Norman for 'sandy lake') six miles inland, on a hill where King Harold had drawn up his foot soldiers to await the onslaught of the Norman cavalry. The place is now known as Battle. (Hastings commemorates the battle every October with torchlight processions and other junketings; a leaflet is obtainable from the town's Information Centre in Robertson Terrace (0424 424242).

Hastings castle (there is a lift up to it not far from the bus station) comprises impressive fragments of what was once a place of considerable pomp. The Norman kings used this, their first castle in England, whenever travelling between their two kingdoms in England and France. There was a church inside it and a college for priests of which Thomas à Becket was once the dean. The mound on which it stood was created from the sandstone hewn out to make the flanking ditch – a massive task, depicted in the Bayeux tapestry.

That famous tapestry inspired another effort in recent years, by the Royal School of Needlework, whose 250-foot panorama of English history hangs in the town hall next to the bus station. While parents settle down to Tusker beer at the Town Crier pub next door, children may enjoy this vast picture strip, but I thought it a pity so much effort should not have had the benefit of a good artist to design the figures, choose less garish colours and give the faces more character. There is a good model of the Battle of Hastings showing exactly how the opposing armies encountered one another. The town hall itself is a piece of high Victoriana with stained glass, font-like plant containers and so forth. The exterior (adjoining the bus station) is decorated high up with colourful panels depicting local history – and a couple of lively red devils.

Battle

The bus to Battle climbs out between verandahed and bay-windowed houses to a road with views across fields and into wooded valleys. I got off at the edge of Battle to lunch at the copper-topped bar of the ancient Chequers Inn, and then walked into the town centre along a road which has the abbey's immense, buttressed wall of stone on one side and pretty cottages on the other. Among these is the medieval house where, when Henry VIII broke up all the monasteries, the Abbot of Battle retired to live (it is now a bookshop). Nearby is the church which, among much else of interest, has an alabaster tomb on which the figures of Edward VI's tutor and his wife are gilded and painted in heraldic colours.

Battle Abbey was built by Benedictine monks from Normandy on the battle site. Although in ruins, the remaining stonework includes some fine examples of Norman craftsmanship. Not far off, the exact spot where King Harold died is marked by a monument presented by the French people in 1902; William himself commemorated his heroic enemy with a high altar on this spot, within a church that has long vanished. At what is now the Pilgrims' Rest restaurant monks used to dispense alms to poor travellers.

The town museum explains, with models, how the battle was fought. It also houses a replica of the Bayeux tapestry, in which can be found illustrations of horses being disembarked at Pevensey ('Pevensesae'), the fort being built at Hastings ('Hastenga'), and finally the death of Harold and flight of the English.

The museum also contains the historical bric-à-brac that gives most local museums their particular charm – as miscellaneous as a mighty axe head unearthed on the battlefield, deadly cock-fighting spurs and some 2oz coins that weighed heavy in the pocket in 1797. Worth two pence, they were almost immediately discontinued because their weight made them so unpopular.

Of more substance is the display explaining the Sussex iron industry, which flourished at many small sites in the Wealden forest from Roman times until 1820. One fine example of Sussex ironwork is a magnificent fireback in the old building that houses the Tourist Information Centre and a display of local crafts. The centre has a free leaflet about the town with the aid of which I found a footpath leading through fields at the back of the houses.

A punnet of strawberries added to the pleasure of the short ride into the hills of the Weald to Ninfield. Up and down went the road between beeches and sweet chestnuts and through a grove of huge rhododendrons in bloom. It was a beautiful route, winding this way and that, woodland alternating with golden fields of barley or occasional cottages with red roses splashed against white walls. Once or twice the skeleton fingers of a dead elm clawed at the sky, but in every other particular the countryside pulsed with life.

Ninfield

At Ninfield the need to change bus routes gave me time to stroll along an obscure path. Starting opposite the bus-stop, it led through woods and by hidden cottages to the modest church which has one or two unusual features – a minstrel's gallery and, below it, the mechanism of the clock face on the weatherboarded turret above, ticking steadily away behind glass. Up in the turret is a solitary 14th-century bell, and in the churchyard a vast convoluted yew looks almost as old. The church road leads to a clump of Scots pines, their fircones strewn all over the ground. Beneath the tree is a rather odd example of Sussex ironwork: the village stocks has four leg holes, one very much bigger than the other three. Just here, William raised his standard on the eve of the great battle.

The road to Hailsham lies through a landscape of tranquil prosperity with great farms and barns, stone walls bearded with moss, ancient inns and weatherboarded cottages. The delphiniums stood as erect and blue as stained-glass saints, bracken was as high as the hedges and water-lilies spread their waxy petals wide. Views were panoramic whenever the secret shades of the woodlands opened up: at this time of year, dense foliage screens much of what can be seen earlier. Many of the medieval houses along the way are now restaurants; the picturesque old forge was long ago turned (like so many others) into a garage when motors replaced horses.

The most interesting village on the way is Herstmonceux, a

Norman name, and if you want a gardening basket, this is the place to buy one. Herstmonceux is the centre of traditional Sussex trug-making ('trog' is a Saxon word meaning boat), and the baskets are made of overlapping willow boards like a boat.

Hailsham

Guidebooks tend to dismiss Hailsham as dull, but there are some ancient buildings and distinguished shop fronts as well as a pleasant churchyard with brick-paved paths and an avenue of variegated hollies clipped into neat little lollipop trees. Hailsham, which has a great market of three acres, used also to have the doubtful distinction of making ropes for the hangman.

From there it is a short run back to Eastbourne. However, anyone who preferred to stay overnight at Hailsham could go direct from there to Lewes next day. (This ride takes one through rich farmland and across streams, with views from its highest point across to Firle Beacon, a 700-foot landmark on the South Downs. Time and energy permitting, Ringmer's church is worth a visit. On the way to it is a tortoise, embodied in the village sign, known as Timothy; his mortal remains are now in London's Natural History Museum. Timothy belonged to the aunt of the naturalist Gilbert White, who wrote about him in his *Natural History of Selborne*.)

I returned to Eastbourne for the night, bussing along roads with verges 'painted all with variable flowers' and past attractive small houses, patches of woodland or open country. Polegate's windmill peeps over the top of surburban bungalows and their trim gardens, with Combe Hill (once an Iron Age stronghold) beyond; within minutes Eastbourne is in view again.

Next day I went to Lewes via Newhaven. This is one of the most beautiful bus routes I have found, and a double-decker gives one a superb view. The bus climbed out of Eastbourne between attractive old and not-so-old houses, flint walls and timbered inns (Eastbourne's excellent little art gallery lies on this road, set in a pretty garden, and so does the old church). Ahead lay the wooded downs, densely green as spinach purée, except where a chalk cliff stood out stark white. Ash and sycamore tapped at the windows, through which the fresh morning breeze streamed in. Looking backwards, I saw the great bay far off and bright as silver, with the golf course forming a bowl of shaven turf between it and the road.

Across vast acres of windswept wheat and barley the view receded into a far blue distance. Villages came and went, with flint walls and leafy lanes, until we reached one of England's beauty spots – the broad valley of the River Cuckmere, which glides in lazy S-bends through the water meadows. It is wide, shallow and brilliantly blue, with cows dozing on its banks.

Onward the hedges were full of flowers, and poppies brightened the cornfields until the once salty marshes heralded our approach to Newhaven. Soon its ships came into view. The tide was out leaving only a thin brown current in the estuary, and on the great timber posts in its banks the brown bladderwrack seaweed hung like frills.

The bus to Lewes goes inland from here, not from the town centre, travelling through the big level valley which the river Ouse has carved out between the hills – a region of marshland drained by brooks and dykes. It was in this river that Virginia Woolf (who lived at Rodmell) drowned. The wind was now very lively and people were struggling against it, heads down or clutching their hats. Even the gulls were battling hard, up amongst the splendid scenery of the sky.

Lewes

After William was crowned he rapidly started building castles to keep his conquered subjects under control and his continental enemies out. The English had seen nothing like them before – immense stone structures, almost impregnable. He allowed his nobles to build their own castles, too, in return for pledging their service to him. The usual plan involved an outer wall enclosing a bailey (courtyard) filled with huts where the garrison lived and where animals could be kept in time of siege, with a tall keep on a mound in the middle (the lord's dwelling place) into which all could retreat if the outer walls were breached by an enemy. There was such a castle at Eastbourne but it has vanished.

The one at Lewes, a very early example, still stands, built to an unusual design with two mounds and keeps. (The mounds were built from blocks of chalk.) Outside the wall of the bailey a great, dry moat was added, with a sturdy gatehouse to protect the entrance. Houses soon clustered around the castle and, in the 13th century, these too were enclosed within town walls of which fragments remain on the west side. From the battlements of the one remaining keep is a view down into the old lanes and twittens (alleys) or across to the Downs, the sea, chalkpits and a memorial to Protestant martyrs burnt at the stake in Lewes on Mary Tudor's orders. Lewes to this day celebrates Guy Fawkes Day with anti-Papist demonstrations.

William's son-in-law Warenne sited the castle to protect a strategic gap in the South Downs through which the River Ouse passes. At the same time he built St Anne's Church and a priory (which, like Battle Abbey, was later demolished on the orders of Henry VIII). Its ruins can still be seen (walk down cobbled Keere Street), and its hospitium, a hostel for travellers, is now a church in which Warenne and the Conqueror's daughter are buried. It stands in Southover High Street, one of the most attractive streets in Lewes, which also contains a museum of Sussex crafts, particularly ironwork (Sussex trees fed the iron furnaces of England centuries before the coke-smelters of the north took over). The museum is in a timbered house that once belonged to Anne of Cleves, fourth wife of Henry VIII. Southover Grange, where the diarist John Evelyn grew up, has pleasant gardens open to the public. Back towards the bus station and over the river just beyond it lies Cliffe High Street, with quaint timbered houses overhanging the narrow road and Harvey's, the local brewery.

The return from Lewes to Eastbourne on an express coach follows an attractive route through an area of outstanding natural beauty. The coach lumbers out through narrow streets with flint walls and houses that are half-timbered, weatherboarded or faced with coloured stucco; it passes over the river and near the old brewery. Then comes a vast panorama of meadows and hills. We passed flint barns, monumental oaks, briar roses and honeysuckle in hedges, as well as cottage gardens thronged with lupins, a river (the Cuckmere again) with yellow water-lilies and ducks swimming softly down, and Windover Hill, rising high. If you change at Polegate, this gives a chance to visit the milling museum in the 1817 windmill, two sails of which dropped off one day (narrowly missing me!). They're back on again now, rather more securely fixed. And so to Eastbourne once again.

17
The Lake District

Windermere – Wrynose Pass – Hardknott Pass – Coniston – Windermere

The Lake District and its bus services are unique. Strictly speaking, the area would be better called the Mountain District for, huge and numerous though the lakes are, the mountains take up most of the space. Necessarily, therefore, roads are relatively few, but buses run on virtually all of them. This means you can go almost anywhere by bus – along lake shores, through valleys and up mountain passes. There is one private bus company which even goes up and down gradients that make some car drivers blench. And just about every one of these roads has spectacular views: no one need depend on advice about which bus service to pick for a scenic ride, as all are good.

The Lake District surely needs no description here; its beauties are world-famous. Of all our National Parks it is the most outstanding, but this naturally brings tourists by the million. The many walkers soon disperse into the hills, but in July and August car drivers can be a menace when they crowd the narrow lanes and little towns. It's not much fun for them, either: stone walls and 'no parking' signs prevent them from pausing where they wish. The case for bussing about is therefore a particularly strong one in this area.

The best base from which to go bussing is Ambleside, followed by Windermere, Grasmere and Keswick in that order. A useful map of all services is obtainable from the Cumbria Tourist Board (Holly Road, Windermere; 09662 4444). There is a private company called Mountain Goat which runs some very unusual services. Its minibuses, run on propane gas not petrol, can get to all sorts of places high up in the mountains (one of these journeys is described later in this chapter). The little seats are not comfortable for the long of leg or the broad of bottom, but some of the routes are so exceptional that it is worth putting up with this for a couple of hours or so. Some Mountain Goat buses run on regular routes (timetables are available from the company at Victoria Street, Windermere); others do special excursions, details of which are also obtainable. It is necessary to book seats on their buses.

I went to the Lake District in June – perhaps not the best time, for the daffodils that inspired Wordsworth start in late March, while it is not until October that the spectacular russet bracken colours the hills. Nevertheless, June anywhere has great charm. It is the month of briar roses, strawberries, cream teas and village fêtes; of new-mown hay and new-shorn sheep looking oddly skinny; of foals and calves, ducklings and cygnets; of poppies in corn, dog-daisies on the banks, and honeysuckle in hedges. Thistledown is idly afloat and industrious bees are on the wing. 'The fields breathe sweet' in June, and it is a good time to travel about (even if wind and water are frisky and the sun coquettish) because it falls between the May bank holiday rush and the July–August school holiday pressures.

Mountain Goat minibus

This, above all months, is one in which to take picnics and a pocket-sized book to identify wildflowers, particularly in the Lake District where so many grow. When bussing about, it is the easiest thing to ask the driver to drop you off in any pretty area you see and then to hail a later bus as it comes by (not the kind of liberty you can take with a coach or a train). June can, however, turn showery – though usually not for long – and in any mountainous area a pocket mac is necessary.

Inside the Mountain Goat minibus we were snug enough, however, and what started as a grey day brightened later.

Windermere

The little bus set out from Windermere through a road fringed with larches and rowans, past Brockhole and the Stagshaw Gardens of the National Trust and past cows grazing among the ruins of a Roman fort. Houses were of grey stone with slate roofs or else whitewashed; over dry-stone walls, velvety with moss, hung clusters of elderflowers or the ruby trusses of rhododendrons. Through water meadows a shallow river wound its stony way and every so often the soft turf was thrust aside by rocky outcrops or rose up in mounds where the glaciers of the Ice Age had deposited their debris. This is a landscape of immense antiquity. We passed a slate factory, where great slabs – green or blue-grey – waited to be sliced in an old bobbin mill no longer needed by the once thriving woollen industry. The mill got its power from water, and just beyond can be seen the foaming source of that energy, Skelwith Force.

As we climbed into the hills roving sheep watched us curiously – the Jacobs, with multiple horns and black-and-white fleece, and the dark, shaggy Herdwicks, an oddity for they have fewer ribs than other sheep and are unique in their willingness to eat bracken. John Peel's 'coat so grey' (*not* gay) was made of Herdwick wool, and he hunted among these mountains.

Jack, our driver, paused beyond the gunpowder mill, now a hotel, to let us see . . . a sewage works. Or rather, to not-see it, for the whole point is that clever landscaping completely conceals what might have been an eyesore. Jack was a connoisseur of sewage works: 'There's another very nice one at Grasmere,' he told us with relish. Even new buildings have to be faced with local stone to preserve the integrity of lakeland architecture, and a brick house is a rarity.

The bus toiled upwards. Beech trees met overhead, tiny ferns sprouted from the walls and foxgloves thronged the verges. Beyond the Three Shires Inn a pillar stands where once Lancashire met Cumberland and Westmorland (before bureaucracy erased the ancient boundaries). There was a tarn fringed with yellow irises, and pied wagtails flicked their tails nearby. Tarn is a Norse word for a pool; when the Viking raiders settled in Cumbria they brought their own vocabulary, and it still lives on in local place names such as thwaite for clearing, beck for stream, gill for ravine and so on.

Wrynose Pass

'Extreme caution' warned a road sign; we were entering Wrynose Pass. Jack pointed up to a distant spot, once a Stone Age factory with a thriving export trade. There immense numbers of stone axe heads were hewn, taken to the seashore to be polished with sand and then bartered with traders from Normandy. The huge heaps of spoil up there show that the craftsmen operated a very strict quality-control system.

The mountain got steeper, its rocky side deeply grooved by a swift, silver thread of a stream rushing this way and that. Elsewhere more water spread wide like a shimmering cloak over great boulders. Here were fell sheep, black-faced and horned. Looking back, I saw that tarn again – but by this time it was just a bright dewdrop lying within the green bowl of hills far below us.

As we went still higher, the vegetation changed. White cotton-flowers and reeds grew in the boggy ground and lichen crusted the rocks. Clouds floated serenely behind a grimly jagged skyline. Far down, clumps of trees looked like mere tufts of moss, and the road we had just traversed was no more than a thin cord of brown idly dropped by some giant hand on a green velvet cloth. The tarn, perpetually changing, was a sliver of cold steel.

At last we reached the top, a place of wilderness and beauty. But was it unspoilt? Hardly. Some lout had discarded a cola tin and sweet packet in one of the little streams.

Hardknott Pass

Our bus pressed onward and down. Ahead of us lay a great valley, with road and river zigzagging through it like a couple stepping out some complicated dance together. This led us to Hardknott Pass, a 1-in-3 gradient with acute bends all the way – the shortest, steepest pass in all Europe. Cars regularly get stuck there, and even Jack (not helped by a cow ambling in front) ground to a halt, backed down and took a fresh run up. A sheep gazed in amazement at our performance while within the bus there was general sympathy for the laden, armoured legionaries who once marched this way – for beyond lies a Roman fort that is one of the most outstanding sites in Roman Britain, not just unusually well preserved but in a commanding position with magnificent views (someone called it a fortress in the air). Built in the time of Emperor Hadrian (of the Wall), the garrison consisted of Slavs who comforted themselves in this chilly exile with hot baths and central heating – the bath house is still there to be seen.

The head of the pass is a good place for a break. I sat by a tiny rivulet almost hidden in the wiry grass, watching a water boatman skim the surface and the pebbles shining bright below the little trickle. I could see the source of the small stream high in the mountain above me and follow its course for miles down below me, as it wound its way to a river and thus to a far distant ocean. A marvellous landscape: rocks jagged and fissured, lichen almost fluorescent green and bracken luxuriant.

All the way down were hairpin bends, leading to Eskdale and more pastoral scenes with buttercups, speedwell and foxgloves; there were wagtails again, birch trees; whitewashed farms and a group of back-packing youth-hostellers. Up in the hillside is a huge red scar where once iron was mined and railroaded to the coast (the old line is still there, with steam locomotives now pulling carriages of tourists).

Coniston

The journey continued up and down all the way through crags and bracken, a panorama of great peaks. Sheep were not yet sheared, their fleeces hanging shaggy and beginning to fall off naturally. The River Ulpha was strewn with mighty boulders and walls were made of colossal stones. A great slide of 'spoil' spilled down where once slate used to be quarried. Humpback stone bridges were succeeded by picturesque cottages with honeysuckle growing up their stone walls and lanes pink with foxgloves, briar roses and campion. We had a god-like view (backwards and down) of the immense sands of Morecambe Bay, miles away, and another of dense, sombre Drysdale Forest (far ahead and high up). There were a few patches of early heather brightening the roadside and then Coniston's shining surface came into view with cottages that still have the old spinning galleries once common in lakeland, and a slate memorial to Donald Campbell who died while attempting to make a new water-speed record on the lake. We made a brief pause to see the now celebrated *Gondola* steamboat, 120 years old (rescued by the National Trust from a watery grave and restored to all her former glory with bright paint and gilt), and so we returned to our starting point at Windermere. Of all the bus rides in this book, this was one of the most memorable, and it was made even more interesting by Hunter Davies' lively paperback *A Walk Around the Lakes* (Hamlyn). Even he took buses occasionally. He quotes another walker, Alfred Wainwright (whose fell-walkers' guides are now internationally famous): 'The slower the bus the better I like it. There's nothing more restful than a stopping bus.'

18

Real Ale Trail

Yorkshire Dales

Bradford – Bingley – Keighley – Skipton – Grassington – Aysgarth – Hawes – Richmond

There is no breathalyzer to face after drinking if your transport is a bus, and as CAMRA (the Campaign for Real Ale) publishes a *Good Beer Guide* describing hundreds of pubs where real ales are to be found, this makes the planning of a day's inn-to-inn bus route pretty simple. (CAMRA's address is 34 Alma Road, St Albans, Herts.) Most of its 150 local branches publish guides to their own areas, though some are more informative than others.

CAMRA has made a lot of headway in its efforts to persuade publicans to stock beers made by the traditional methods and not just mass-produced keg beer.

CAMRA defines real ale as beer which (after being brewed from unadulterated hops, malted barley and yeast) is kept in vented casks in the pub's cellar and dispensed by means of a tap or pump, not by gas pressure. Some is made by the big companies but most is from small local breweries distributing only within their own neighbourhood. This makes the exploring of unfamiliar territory particularly interesting for real ale enthusiasts.

Yorkshire is one county that has always taken its beer seriously, and here a 'real ale trail' through areas of scenic beauty is full of scope. In addition to the normal opening hours (see end of this chapter), pubs in towns with markets often stay open throughout the afternoon on market days. The local branches of CAMRA have combined to produce an excellent guide to North Yorkshire inns, and with its help I picked a Sunday route for early summer through the Dales National Park starting at Skipton (easily reached from Manchester, Bradford or Leeds, for example: my choice was

Bradford, well worth a few days' stay before heading for the countryside) and going up Wharfedale to Hawes in Wensleydale and thence through Swaledale to Richmond (from which it is not difficult to get back by bus via Scotch Corner to Leeds again). So, combined with travelling through three of the loveliest dales and passing some very attractive villages, one has a choice of more local ales than could possibly be sampled, allowing for the limitations of opening hours as well as one's own physical capacity. But avoid high summer and bank holidays, when crowds are attracted to the Dales, and winter or weekdays when some of the buses do not run.

The scenery is very varied – luxuriant grass, dry-stone walls, picturesque woodlands, turbulent streams and waterfalls (often aptly named 'forces'), rolling hills in front of rolling clouds, grey stone cottages, vivid village greens, gaunt crags and zigzagging ascents and descents. Wildness, isolation and drama contrast with the charm and dignity of gentler slopes with dairy farms.

Bradford

Bradford was first among the industrial cities to scour a century's soot off its gloomy buildings – to reveal them as they were when first erected in newly quarried sandstone that glows like honey when the sun is on it.

The city reached its prime in Victoria's reign, with fortunes being made (or sometimes lost) from the weaving of worsted cloth. The textile barons, like all wealthy Victorians, travelled in Europe, bringing home works of art – and new ideas about architecture. No longer would they be satisfied with four walls and a roof in which to store their raw materials: the first street I walked down, Hall Ings (which describes what it used to be – a hall by a meadow) is lined with wool warehouses each of which looks like an Italian palazzo. The Wool Exchange is straight out of Venice (except that the heads decorating its façade are those of Victorian wool merchants), the City Hall looks as if it has been transported by some colossal magic carpet from Florence.

Even after all this display of personal and civic pride, the wool merchants had more money than they could spend: many, therefore, set up their own banks, and these too were built in resplendent style, pillars rising around carved doorways, domes above the pillars. I found it worth popping in and out just to look at the ceilings and other detail of the interiors. Even when a Penny Bank was established, to encourage workers to save, it was given the full architectural treatment (the Penny Bank, though it is now the great Yorkshire Bank, still has its name incorporated in the wrought-iron arch over the big doors). All these are within a short stroll north of the coach station.

I went inside the Wool Exchange, largely idle now that dealings are conducted by telephone or telex, and looked at the vast 'hammerbeam' roof – made not of oak but of iron girders, and with kings up there where angels would be if this were not a cathedral of trade. Sometimes antiques fairs or flea markets are held here. Tucked inconspicuously below the great hall is – typical of Bradford's eccentric quirks – a small perfumery. The shelves are lined with herbal extracts, aromatic oils and men's hair-lotions in the kind of old-fashioned bottles likely to have been found in the dressing-rooms of those bewhiskered merchants who once thronged the Exchange. Here the staff are sadly disappointed if you do *not* settle down to a long session of sniffing this and that before making your purchases; and for £8 or so you can have 50 ml of scent blended to your own preference, or to a very near match of the most expensive names in perfume.

Anyone may wander through the marble corridors of power in the City Hall, and often the Council chamber itself can be seen – circles of leather seats under a ceiling of plaster vines encircling stained-glass skylights. The walls are of figured mahogany and coloured marbles: the best that the world could produce was sent to Bradford. From its high tower, bells peal out a carillon, with carols at Christmas echoing over the city. But June is the time to be here, when the new Lord Mayor is installed – complete with Lord Mayor's Show progressing to the City Hall. (The Tourist Information Centre is here.)

The oldest pie-shop (of many) in Yorkshire is just across the way, and Philip Smith's reputation for excellence extends far beyond Bradford. In the window, the versatility of the pig is amply demonstrated in the piles of black puddings, cooked pig-cheeks and shanks straight out of the oven, among a dozen other local porcine delicacies.

A bus takes one out to Moorside and an old wool-spinning mill which has been restored as an industrial museum. (On the way, I passed the great Victorian cemetery, itself a showpiece vying with the famous one at Milan in the splendour of its sphinxes, obelisks and even more elaborate monuments; and opposite it the lovely lawns and flowers of Peel Park spread downhill.) The museum also houses old trams, steam engines, broughams and other vehicles. The greatest of the wool merchants were inventors as well as traders, and some of their engineering 'firsts' are shown in displays which start with prehistoric weaving and tell the story of wool over the centuries; often exhibits can be seen in motion.

I lingered over a small display about children in factories (some only 5 or 6 years old), and reformer Richard Oastler who campaigned to end this terrible abuse. Further on, there is the indenture of an apprentice, signed with a cross because he (like so many) was illiterate. Yet just such apprentices as these ultimately became superb master-craftsmen, creating the complex and beautiful machines of brass and steel now given an honoured place in the museum.

Bradford is still, but less exclusively, a textile city, though techniques have changed. At the museum shop, one can buy mementoes of the old days in the shape of wood bobbins, no longer used, converted into a variety of souvenirs.

Adjoining the mill is the manager's house. In the early days, owners lived beside their mills. But as they grew wealthier and their mills grew sootier, they moved out to country mansions and installed managers in their place. This house is just the way it used to be. The parlour has its horsehair sofa, aspidistra, Turkey carpet and albums of sepia photographs; the bathroom its loo patterned with blue flowers; the maidservant's room its iron bed. Even the museum café is in period, with Victorian light-fittings and tables on ornamental cast-iron legs.

Most of Bradford's textile mills have shops (accessible by bus) which are a bargain-hunter's paradise: as I write, I am wearing a top-quality lambswool cardigan sold for £1.90 because a button was missing. The Tourist Information Centre has a list of these mill-shops, indicating which sells men's suits, which knitting-wool and so on. At least one is within walking distance of the coach station. A favourite is Listers (in another Italianate building of great splendour) for the superb curtain velvets, normally £12–15 a metre, which sell at under £4. This is in the Manningham area where once-fine mansions of woolmen are now, in many cases, good small hotels.

Nearby is an extraordinary museum, with shop, containing a collection of gemstones and rocks that is in certain respects more comprehensive even than London's Geology Museum. Its bearded owner, George Hinchliffe, is especially proud of his display of dull-looking rocks which, under a type of ultra-violet lamp unique in this country, glow with fluorescent life in a dozen colours and patterns. All around are fossilized flowers, 'pudding stones', petrified palm trees and much else (even, rather oddly, a collection of walking-sticks that includes Chaplin's and Gladstone's). Many of these rocks, Mr Hinchliffe told me, he had amassed on round-the-world trips in 'old bangers' such as a Ford pick-up bought for £35 which he flogged over the Andes and across the Sahara.

I had underestimated Bradford and should have allowed myself more days there. There was no time left for me to walk round Little Germany (the quarter where Jewish refugees settled, prospered and built their fine mills and warehouses: several are now wine bars); the museums (films and photography in one; kaleidoscopic colour and the story of dyeing in another); the Art Gallery (which among other world-famous paintings has Gainsborough's 'Blue Boy' – Hockneys and Henry Moores too); the many beautiful parks (the Lister Park claims to be one of the best preserved examples of a traditional Victorian park, with every detail of the highest standard); Ponden Hall (which is the Thrushcross Grange of *Wuthering Heights* and where, in weavers' old cottages, one can see weavers at work); Bolling Hall (a Tudor mansion with ghosts); or the clog factory.

That is only the beginning of the list. I had sampled Yorkshire pudding in the hotel's carvery but not a Yorkshire high tea nor Yorkshire ale. What about Yorkshire brass-bands (Black Dyke Mills' or Hammond Sauce Works', for instance) or music-hall? There are several theatres in the city, and at St George's Hall the Hallé orchestra or rock concerts play to packed audiences. Of course, Bradford boasts outsize shopping centres, markets and sports centres. It also has Harry Ramsden's, where fish-and-chips has the status of haute cuisine; canal trips with dinner on board; and a choice from a hundred other good eating-places. Some visitors enjoy tours to see textiles being woven, or the *Bradford Argus* being printed; or even to look around the offices that handle their mortgage – Bradford is a great place for building societies' headquarters and they, too, have their open-days, for Yorkshire ('Where there's muck, there's brass') is proud to show off its workaday life, particularly now that there's more money than muck around. Clearly, I would have to return again, perhaps on a 'heritage' weekend like the one I had so much enjoyed at Nottingham (see p. 239), but this time the theme would be either the Brontës, industrial archaeology or steam railways. Bradford, rightly labelling itself 'a surprising place', has so many different choices to offer.

Shipley, Saltaire, Bingley, Keighley

Bradford's high-tech bus station is shiny and modern as an airport: a vast interchange with buses, coaches, rail and underground converging. On leaving it, we went through the square where W. E. Forster's statue stands (the reformer who made free, universal education available for the first time). The great presses and huge rolls of newsprint of the *Bradford Argus* could be seen behind high plate-glass windows. We headed out to Airedale.

At Shipley we halted by the church, with an array of red-and-yellow-canopied market stalls all around a big modern square. A little further, I caught a fleeting glimpse of Saltaire, one of the very first (and most handsome) of garden cities, laid out by mill-owner Titus Salt who named the township after himself. Bingley has its old mills with tall chimneys and a green surrounded by antique shops (the famous five-rise locks were not visible from the bus). Along the valley the National Trust owns East Riddlesdon Hall (its tithe barn, lake and ducks visible from the road) but most of the buildings along here are suburban – though the wild hills are not far away, seen rising up from the other side of the valley.

After crossing the River Aire, we passed rows of back-to-backs and then went through Keighley – a town built with civic pride, when every building had its purpose clearly incised in the stone (public library, temperance institute, school board or the like), as if time would never alter the status quo; even the cycling club had its name carved on a substantial building. But now industrial smells hang in the air, and Keighley takes more pride in boasting that it has its very own radio station and big leisure centre.

It was only when we left it behind that fine scenery began, a taste of what was to come. And then the bus reached Skipton, to stop among old warehouses, rippling roofs and canalside buildings.

There were colourful narrowboats outside the lock on the canal. (How, I wondered, as the coach halted, was the name 'Bold Venture Street' acquired by such a tiny, modest lane?)

Skipton

Skipton has long been the centre of the southern Dales, for coaching roads and canal meet there. Some medieval buildings still survive the ravages of progress, including Lord Clifford's castle (which is completely intact, with parts still inhabited) and the church which has an outstanding roof and rood-screen. Market stalls are set up in the broad High Street on most days, and old wharves and warehouses line the canal banks. In the corn mill folk museum, working exhibits recreate the occupations of the past. Look out for Stainforth's Celebrated Pork Pie Shop, canal boat trips and many interesting little shops through archways or up alleys – especially near the mill bridge by the church.

Skipton Castle

The River Wharfe and its dale are claimed to be the most beautiful in England. Leaving Skipton, we soon overtook a bright-coloured throng of cyclists, legs going like pistons up the hill, and climbed higher towards a bright blue sky. The sun shining through the sycamores made a lively pattern on the road. In the fields bales of hay were stacked, and Swaledale sheep (black-faced and curly-horned) and shaggy, long-horned cattle watched us go by. The wet summer, which had meant late (or lost) harvests, had also made the grass richly green.

Early in the journey we passed pretty Cracoe (a small forest of red-hot pokers peeping above mossy dry-stone walls). Then came one of the loveliest villages anywhere, peaceful Linton, which has both a packhorse bridge and a clapper bridge (made of huge slabs of stone) over the stream that runs right through it, as well as a picturesque inn smothered in yellow roses and Nelly Moser clematis. Linton's big surprise is Fountaine's Hospital, almshouses designed in the grand manner by Vanbrugh – architect of Blenheim Palace – in 1720 with cupola, pediments and urns.

Grassington

Next is Grassington, built around a tiny cobbled square on a hill-side. It is a prosperous little town with good shops, a folk museum in a cottage, tea-room with crackling fire, and alleyways gay with flowers. This was a good place at which to take a break, where the beauty of the river contrasts with the stark hills around and every cottage is bright with pansies, petunias, lobelia or marigolds.

Even on Sunday some shops were open, including that of 'the toffee smith' who should surely be in *The Guinness Book of Records* for the variety of toffee he makes. I also found the blacksmith at work and, on sale, pebbles beautifully painted with birds – his blacksmith son is a gifted wildlife artist in his spare time. Opposite the bus depot is a National Park information centre with many useful booklets that interpret all there is to see in the Dales.

The view along the road through the hills is beautiful whichever way you look. Far off are blue mountains, a changing cloudscape, a patchwork of fields (green, yellow and gold) and rugged heights. Nearby the verges are blue with cranesbills or yellow with butter-cups. Slatey stones thrust through turf, mullioned windows decor-ate old stone houses and the river is wide, shallow and clear. As we pressed on, the bus overtook a white-haired couple pedalling steadily on a tandem bicycle and two young back-packers with a collie.

We drove by a trout farm and then almost underneath the overhanging Kilnsey Crag, a gaunt grey challenge to rock-climbers (though they are discouraged from climbing when buses are passing beneath the crag). A stream was bright with yellow-and-white-flowered water plants. We went on to pretty Kettlewell with its old stone bridge and grey houses, and then the road left the river and began to climb beyond Buckden, beautifully sited and with panoramic views along the way. Picturesque white-washed inns, great stone barns, waterfalls and rocky outcrops added variety to the scene, and through the window occasionally came pleasant country smells of hay, catmint, wild aniseed or wild garlic.

Aysgarth

At the head of the dale, where the descent begins, is a tremendous expanse stretching gently downward to Aysgarth. It is worth getting off before the bus enters the village (alight at Palmer Flatt Hotel) to walk down to the 400-year-old Aysgarth bridge and the famous series of waterfalls – shallow cataracts that are very beautiful (especially after a wet season). The water cascades in a white, roaring froth, forming pools and eddies among which young men in thighboots perch (with their fishing rods) on midstream rocks of pinkish stone tinged green by algae. A solitary tern swooped to compete with them for any fish that might have been going.

Nearby is a carriage museum in an old textile mill, and further on is another National Park interpretation centre, housed in what were once railway buildings. The disused track (on an embankment) makes a pleasant walk with an 'Aysgarth Trail' leaflet (not very well designed) to explain the distinctive scenery. The basic rock of the Dales is 300 million years old. Seas covered it and left deposits that became softer rocks of various kinds which eroded or weathered away at different rates. That is why there is such a great variety of landscape, soil and vegetation. Humans have added their variations: small fields are of medieval origin, large ones date from the time of the 18th-century enclosures of common grazing lands. Even the dry-stone walls vary in pattern, as do the shapes of the stone stiles set into them, though all are made on a similar principle – that is, two inward-sloping walls of big, carefully chosen stones (no cement), with rubble sandwiched in between, and a lid of large flat stones on top to bind both walls together and keep the rain out. Wire fences didn't come in until about a century ago; fortunately, the National Park authorities have seen to it that within their boundaries these have not ousted the old craft of dry-stone walling. The old wooden five-bar gates are vanishing though, for most are too narrow to admit modern farm machines. Even their first successors, of strip metal, are now 'antiques', for gates of cheap tubular metal have in turn superseded them.

The onward bus follows a road that rises and falls, with exceptional views at every turn. As it continues uphill it passes through Bainbridge, a village around a big green (complete with stocks), where the river flows down over flat steps of rock. Throughout the winter a horn is sounded at 9 pm to guide any traveller lost in the fells. The sunny morning had given way to a grey, misty afternoon with ominously dark clouds, a hint of how necessary that horn might be on a really bad night.

Hawes

Finally we reached Hawes, where the famous Wensleydale cheese is made (a perfect complement to Yorkshire ale), where sheep are brought to market, and where back-packing ramblers stride in from their marathon treks along the Pennine Way. This is now the highest market town in England. A cascade rushes among its streets of stone houses at one end of the town and Hardraw Force, the highest waterfall in the country, is about $1\frac{1}{4}$ miles' walk away. I was told that you get to it through the Green Dragon inn and can walk right behind the 100-foot fall of water (or clamber up and wade across the top of it). In Hawes itself you can watch rope being made, or read on the wall of a cottage dated 1668 (now part of Cocketts Hotel) the confident stone inscription, 'God being with us, who can be against us.'

The next ride is one which the local bus company considers its *pièce de résistance*, ideal on a summer evening. From Hawes the bus does a swift ascent to mountaineer its way through the Buttertubs Pass to get from Wensleydale to Swaledale. Some of this spectacular moorland road runs at a 1-in-4 gradient, passing through a gorge and then narrowing and zigzagging as it descends. There is an alpine tang to the air. The 'buttertubs' are seven curiously shaped holes in the limestone rock by the roadside, some of them 100 feet deep.

Beyond lies the very pretty village of Thwaite. Then comes tiny Keld, a lovely stone village among the hills right at the head of Swaledale.

Keld, once a Viking settlement, is a place of tiny, narrow lanes lined with foxgloves and bracken. There the bus turned back and retraced its route through Thwaite. In peaceful Thwaite, however, the biggest traffic jam in the Dales had built up. Two herds of sheep were being driven in for shearing. Shepherds in gumboots and cloth caps waved their sticks and shouted; sheepdogs ran hither and yon; the sheep bawled their indignation. We waited – and waited. Eventually the mêlée sorted itself out.

The road zigzagged down to Gunnerside, at the foot of a gorge, which has views of old lead mines (their tracks and tips) on the steep hills. All along this route the River Swale ripples or cascades its way down the rugged dale – so very different a valley from Wensleydale – and the road keeps crossing and recrossing it by old stone bridges.

The final stretch lay through woodland and fields, with a great ridge ahead on which trees clung precariously to the vertical rock face. The road wound its way through a glade with the occasional glint of water from the River Swale still faithfully running nearly alongside the road.

Richmond

The end of the journey was Richmond, a town of great charm built on a rock which is almost surrounded by a loop of the Swale. Curfew is still rung each night at 8 pm.

A Norman castle perches on a sheer precipice and in the town below is the second oldest theatre in England, built in 1788 and still in use. Altogether Richmond is outstanding among small towns – cobbled Georgian streets, twisting wynds (alleys), old inns, interesting shops, the largest cobbled market square in the country (with a church and an enormous 18th-century obelisk in the middle) – a place in which to linger. The Green Howards have their regimental museum in this church (the parish church is outside the town walls); horse races are held on a course two centuries old; and within easy walking distance are the ruins of Easby Abbey in a beautiful riverside setting.

The houses are made either of rugged limestone, hard and rough-textured, or of sandstone which, being softer, can be sawn smooth and fine. Some sandstone-slabbed roofs remain but often the weight brought collapse, so a variety of lighter tiles or slates replaced them including rippling pantiles, originally from Holland.

An excellent local booklet called 'A Look at Richmond' explains as much as one wants to know about the architecture and history. The best walk of all was at the foot of the castle, where a path winds round high above the river foaming noisily below, under a lovely Georgian bridge and over stones (riverbed pebbles were used to cobble the market square). Out of the massive stone blocks that make the castle walls, looming dizzily above, grew more than a dozen self-seeded country flowers. Seats are placed in angles of the walls to catch the morning sun, and there I sat to enjoy the view, the wildflowers and the activities of a curlew and other birds.

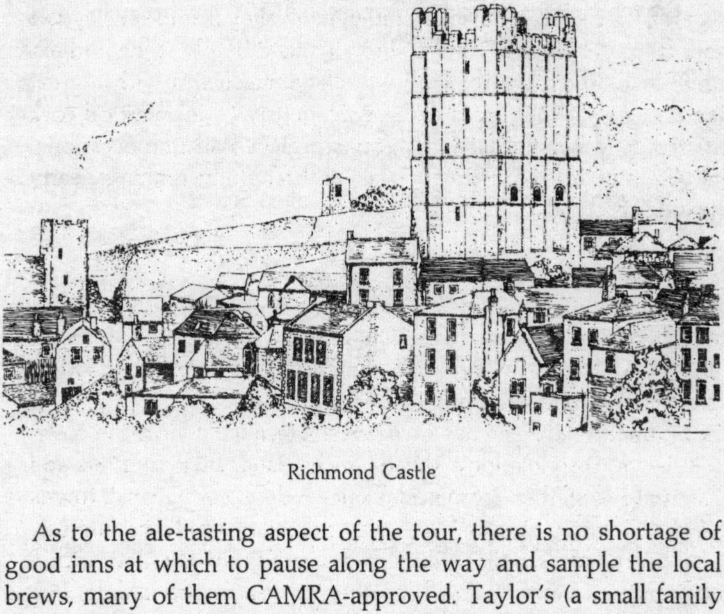

Richmond Castle

As to the ale-tasting aspect of the tour, there is no shortage of good inns at which to pause along the way and sample the local brews, many of them CAMRA-approved. Taylor's (a small family firm) produces distinctively hoppy milds and bitters. Cameron's make a bitter described as 'one of Britain's great beers', as well as the heavier Strongarm. Tetley's bitter or dark mild are widely sold. Theakston's have made a reputation with Old Peculier, strong and sweet. Webster's sweetish bitter and hoppy mild are recommended. Marston's bitter has supporters, but it is not to everyone's liking. Finally, there is strong Bass from Burton (CAMRA don't recommend the Tadcaster Bass).

I am indebted to CAMRA for help in compiling the following list of recommended inns.

Skipton

(11 am–3 pm, 5.30–10.30 or 11 pm on Friday and Saturday, and in summer. Open till 4 pm on Mondays, farmers' day)

Of the ten CAMRA-approved drinking places, here is a selection:

Black Horse 17th-century building, its yard now a market. (Taylor and Younger) Meals, snacks.

Devonshire Vaults Under 18th-century hotel. (Tetley)

Castle Inn Stone pub by castle. (Tetley) Outdoor drinking, snacks.

Chew's Bar One room, with fire. (Bass) Snacks.

Craven Heifer On road to Grassington. Open fire, farm pub. (Bass) Outdoor drinking, snacks.

Cracoe

(Hours as for Skipton, no farmers' day)

Devonshire Arms Stone floors. (Younger) Snacks.

Grassington

(Hours as for Cracoe)

Black Horse (Theakston and Tetley) Outdoor drinking.

Foresters' Arms (Tetley) Snacks.

Kettlewell

(Hours as for Cracoe)

Bluebell Hotel Old stone building. (Theakston and Tetley) Meals, snacks.

Buckden

(Hours as for Cracoe)

Buck Inn 18th-century hotel. (Theakston, Younger) Meals, snacks.

Thoralby

(11 am–3 pm, 6–10.30 or 11 pm on Friday and Saturday)

George Inn Georgian. (Webster) Snacks.

Hawes

(11 am–3 pm, 5.30–10.30 or 11 pm on Friday and Saturday. Open all afternoon on Tuesdays, market day)

Board Hotel (Marston) Outdoor drinking.
Crown (Theakston) Outdoor drinking.
Fountain Hotel (McEwans) Meals, snacks.

Gunnerside

(11 am–3 pm, 6–10.30 or 11 pm on Friday and Saturday)

King's Head Small bar with hand pumps. (Cameron)

Richmond

(Hours as for Gunnerside)

Bishop Blaize Hotel (Cameron) Snacks.
Buck Inn (Bass) Snacks.
Holly Hill Stone pub, beamed interior, ales from jug. (Theakston) Snacks, outdoor drinking.
Turf Hotel Georgian inn, racing connection. (Bass) Snacks.

More about the Dales

The three dales I travelled through on this journey are only a sample. (I did the whole trip one Sunday but wished I had spent at least two or three days over it.) There are all the other dales, too, and the West Yorkshire Road Car Company (East Parade, Harrogate; 0423 66061) has a 'Dales Bus' folder; possibilities include alternating walks and bus rides. One of the most beautiful and least frequented of the dales is outside the National Park – Nidderdale (it starts roughly halfway between Skipton and Ripon) and I went there later, undeterred by the fact that there is no regular bus service. For I had heard that a local operator ran a school minibus, mornings and afternoons, on which anyone is welcome to travel. In fact, he will make special journeys for groups (0423 711312).

Nidderdale has unique attractions. At several places the river Nid was long ago dammed to make a series of great reservoirs for distant cities. These now form a 'Lake District' of great beauty, and the multitude of birds (some very rare migrants) brings ornithologists from all over the world. About 200 different species have been recorded. Then there is the wildly romantic, or romantically wild, How Stean gorge where a stream cascades into a jagged cleft 70 feet deep. (In the modest café at the top, I encountered something even less expected: a superlatively iced birthday cake on the point of being delivered to Clarence House, London, for the Queen Mother! The café proprietor is a patissière of distinction.) And right at the head of Nidderdale is arguably the most spectacular churchyard in England, in the village of Middlemoor, with views to rival those of Cumbria's Lake District. There was not a tourist, except myself, to be seen that day.

19

Through Downs and Weald

Brighton – Lewes – Tenterden – Ashford – Canterbury

The bus route out of Brighton passes the Royal Engineers' barracks, Moulsecoomb Wild Park, then Stanmer Park and the very modern university buildings up on their hilltop. We were soon out into the countryside – sometimes passing among trees that made a leafy roof over the road, sometimes rising out of valleys to enjoy uninterrupted views far over the hills. Lambs, chalky fields and spring blossom made a typically Sussex scene. A couple of bold crows pottered on the grassy verge of the road quite unperturbed by the passing traffic.

Lewes was quickly reached. We entered past the flint-walled prison which looks like a castle, glimpsed beyond cherry blossom, and down a steep old road lined with a great variety of houses – tile-hung, flint or weatherboarded, some very colourful and many with elegant doorways or balconies. The Norman castle high on its mound is tucked away down a sidestreet – just one of many ancient buildings that it would take hours to explore in this most historic of towns. Leaving Lewes there was a quick glimpse of the old 18th-century brewery by the waterside, and then we were once more back on the fast road heading towards Ringmer where tile-hung or thatched houses stand around a large cricket green. Nearby is a well with a wheel to pump up the water.

The road ahead was one long, straight line stretching to the horizon and beyond – originally laid down by the Romans. Delicate mauve ladies' smocks thronged the sides of ditches outside the fields of Raystede animal rescue centre. Beyond farm buildings and streams near Halland, gliders were coming in to land. There was great variety all along this route – graceful trees of all colours, a medieval inn, hop gardens, rhododendrons and magnolias in full bloom.

Where the road runs along the crest of a ridge in the High Weald, views to both right and left stretch for miles. Already, although still in Sussex, the scenery was becoming rather Kentish with oast houses appearing here and there, many weatherboarded houses and a white-painted windmill. Drifts of forget-me-nots made a blue carpet; on the great chestnut trees spires of white flowers reached towards the sky.

Approaching the village of Burwash a signboard with the name Little Pook Hill was a reminder that we were now in Kipling country: in his Tudor house at Burwash (now a National Trust property) he wrote 'Puck of Pook's Hill' and many of his other stories or poems about Sussex. The village is attractive – here a Queen Anne doorway and bay windows, there a white façade smothered in wisteria, and everywhere gardens full of spring flowers. To each side of the road as it continued onward were narrow lanes stretching downhill. Hawkhurst was yet another village with a big green, Georgian houses and an ancient church at the foot of a street leading uphill and past arcaded shops.

On once more, through orchards now, to Rolvenden which, small though it is, has a museum of vintage cars run by the owner of one of the antique shops along its grass-edged streets. And still, wherever we went, the far views on both sides continued to be superb. Crab-apple trees were blossoming abundantly and ducks dabbled busily in lily pool and stream.

Tenterden, standing on a hill, can be seen long before one enters it. It is distinguished by the wide lawns which border its main road, and by the large number of Georgian houses that have survived the years unspoilt. Plenty of coaching inns here (the Caxton Inn has a particularly lovely cedar spreading its old branches wide just outside it), a half-timbered church and a town hall with its upper storey jutting over. The little town is a great place for markets: at one, you can buy anything from the freshest of fish to Shetland sweaters; for paintings go to the open-air market held on the huge green; and there is a cattle market too. Those who linger here can find a figure-of-eight footpath well worth following around the old mill-ponds; and there is the old steam railway (with museum) for a scenic ride to Bodiam. In autumn, the copper beeches are a blaze of colour.

After a while, the architectural styles began to change a little. There were quite a number of decorative Dutch-style gables, introduced by the Flemish refugees who fled to Kent after religious persecution on the continent. From the high windows I could see over hedges to the huge barns needed to house the abundance of this area and a paddock of grazing Arab horses. Some fields were brilliant with yellow oil-seed rape.

In and out of bustling Ashford, and then onward to Wye, an attractive spot surrounded by hop fields and the Wye Downs – beautiful hills owned by the National Trust. (Anyone stopping here for a while could go over the level-crossing and past a weir to explore this little Georgian town, its church and green. Wye Agricultural College has occasional open days and the gardens of Withersden Hall can sometimes be visited. Wye has several celebrated restaurants, and a good tea house.)

The road onwards repeatedly crossed the tranquil waters of the winding River Stour, before road and river apparently reach agreement to run harmoniously side by side. The green fields were at their brilliant best, woodlands at their freshest. Going downhill with trees arching overhead, it felt as if we were diving into a tunnel of green water. As we neared Canterbury, the Stour widened; the traffic began to increase; and we whirled over the top of the busy bypass carrying a procession of continental juggernauts from Dover to London.

We entered Canterbury via seedy outskirts (the terraced cottages were built for soldiers' families, during the days when the city was a military centre) and a modern roundabout, before sighting ahead of us the great Norman walls which still survive to enclose the ancient heart of the city. We followed them round, with a glimpse of Dane John (the great grassy hillock which is a prehistoric burial mound) as we went by, to come to a halt just within the east entrance, the one used for centuries by travellers from the continent and Dover.

Canterbury

Stone Age people lived here; and Celts built a fort near the spot used later by the Normans for their castle. But it was the Romans who created the city, constructed its first walls and houses (the mosaic floor of one can be seen in Longmarket, near the bus station), and, in their last centuries here, built the first Christian churches. These fell into decay during the Saxon period but when, in 597, Augustine was sent by the Pope to re-Christianize England, he restored a number of them.

So, to start Canterbury's story from the beginning, I did not head immediately for the nearby cathedral but went first to St Martin's Church (a ½-mile walk along Longport, or take a bus), which was originally Roman – and some Roman bricks can be seen, re-used, in its walls. It is the oldest church in England still in use.

It was here that Bertha, Christian wife of the Saxon King Ethelbert (a pagan), used to pray – and here she provided Augustine and his monks with their first sanctuary. Only after King Ethelbert was converted were they able to build and preach freely elsewhere. Standing in the chancel of this modest little church perched on a hillside, I was standing where Saint Augustine had himself prayed; and it was at the stone font, with its Saxon-style decorations, that Augustine most probably baptised Ethelbert.

Outside, I wandered up among the old tombstones, wood anemones and yews to a terrace from which there are fine views – of the abbey which Augustine then founded (in 602), and beyond it the later cathedral (begun in Norman times).

To reach the abbey ruins, I retraced my footsteps along Longport: on one side, pink and green almshouses built in 1657 as a thank-offering for the birth of a baby to a couple who had been childless for twenty years, and on the other the prison, railed in with Roman fasces of cast iron. I went through the pretty garden that has been created around a Roman burial mound, now colourful with heather, the top of which provides a good view of the city. Beyond this is the abbey – in its time, a university long before Oxford or Cambridge.

It was – of course – Henry VIII who in 1538 reduced this to ruins (all except the 14th-century guest hall, which he and later monarchs found a useful lodging when travelling through Kent – it now belongs to King's School, so named when Henry took this, too, out of monastic hands). Among the towering, broken arches and the remnants of great stone walls are the tombs of Saxon kings and queens and of the very first archbishops of Canterbury, including Augustine himself, which survived successive rebuildings of the abbey throughout the middle ages. This vast complex of buildings, and its significance in English history, place the abbey ruins among the most important in Europe; and the site has a powerful presence.

Leaving the quiet ruins and their lawns for Monastery Street (with the glorious 13th-century Fyndon Gateway to the abbey still intact), I threaded my way through narrow streets towards the cathedral. There was plenty to look at on the way: I lingered outside the house of James Chilton, whose daughter was the first of the *Mayflower* pilgrims to set foot on American soil; at the bay-windowed shops which, for nine centuries, have been leaning at a tipsy angle over the road; and by the flint-and-ragstone church of St Paul, parts of which go back to Saxon times. I emerged to face the city wall and one of the few great bastions to have survived from the twenty-one originally built to defend the city.

In the Middle Ages it was Sandwich not Dover which was the principal port for travel to and from Europe; and pilgrims coming via Sandwich would have entered the city, as I now did, along the ancient road of Burgate (its name means 'the way in to the borough'). By contrast with the holy places of Canterbury, this is a quarter dedicated to commerce.

Bombing in the Second World War devastated much of Canterbury, so Burgate is a mixture. It's a street of small shops and cafés (much of it pedestrianized). There are still some old premises with panelled doorways or carved grotesques and foliage. One has a plaque to Thomas Barham and his poem about the cathedral's ghost, Nell Cook. Barham, Kentish poet-parson and author of 'The Jackdaw of Rheims', lived here. There's a National Trust shop; a Catholic church with a mural of all Canterbury's saints and early archbishops (and relics of Thomas à Becket); and, by the 14th-century tower which is all of St Mary Magdalene's church that survived the bombs, a small garden in which to rest before pressing on. Even the modern stretches of Burgate are interesting – from decorative paving to the maple-leaf motif in balconies above a new parade of shops (a gift from Canadians, in memory of a Canadian killed by the bomb that fell here). Longmarket, to the left, has trees and seats among the shops: it is here that open-air carols are sung, with mayor and archbishop leading them, every December. Up Butchery Lane many medieval buildings survive (and a bull's head above what had for centuries been the butcher's shop – it closed only five years ago). Many of the older restaurants or inns in Burgate are known to have been pilgrims' hostels originally: Chaucer's pilgrims stayed at The Chequers of the Hope.

Burgate ends with what was once a bull-ring and before that a buttermarket. Behind its façades of Georgian plaster or imitation brick (actually 'mathematical tiles') lie medieval timbers and below are medieval wine vaults: you can visit one under Debenham's shop, as it is now a buttery.

Continuing past the great gateway that leads into the Cathedral precincts, I walked onwards up Palace Street (named for the archbishop's palace which was built on the right-hand side: another street of mainly 16th- and 17th-century houses and inns). On the corner of Sun Street, high up, is a scarlet pump marking the site of a spring from which flowed red water – reddened by Becket's blood, said the superstitious.

At the Mayflower Inn (a café now) some of the Pilgrim Fathers stayed in 1601 and here signed the agreement to charter the *Mayflower*. Between the houses there are arches through which coaches used to enter, and narrow alleyways (like flowery Turnagain Lane). The Priest's House, at no. 8, is decorated with big-breasted creatures that have cloven hoofs, carved and painted. All the way along, there are interesting architectural details: lozenge panes, decorative tile-hanging and pretty gables.

Opposite the big flint building which was part of the archbishop's palace (now used by King's School) is Conquest House, at no. 17, now a shop. This part-Saxon and part-Norman building was once an inn; and here the four knights who murdered Becket stayed on the night before the assassination. Their intention had been to murder him in the palace but when he fled for sanctuary to the cathedral they pursued him even there, the ultimate sacrilege. Over a fireplace is a painted coat-of-arms identical with one in the palace. The story goes that the artist engaged by the palace could not pay his inn bill and so discharged his debt by painting this replica.

No. 23 (now, like many others here, an antiques shop) was once the workshop of refugee Flemish weavers; and the Jacobean corner house – which tilts even more than the tower of Pisa – was a sweet-shop selling humbugs and 'lemon stunners' to the King's School boys. Here, where the city walls curve round, used to be the north gate of Canterbury; and just beyond lie St John's Almshouses, their half-timbered gatehouse, gardens and Norman remains well worth visiting – the very first almshouses built in England, and still serving the same purpose today.

To get to another of Canterbury's main historical thoroughfares (St Peter's Street) I walked along backstreets. Canterbury's Benedictine monastery was, like all the greatest ones, a commercial powerhouse in Norman times, and for finance it often depended upon Jewish moneylenders – who congregated here, around the King Street area (where there is still an old synagogue, with lotus-topped pillars). So close was the relationship that some 7-branch candlesticks and vestments in Jewish style were used in the cathedral.

My walk took me past the remains of the Black Friars' monastery and down Best Lane, where a recently discovered well and clay pipes from Canterbury's pipe factory can be seen in front of the Kingsbridge Well restaurant. Opposite is a tiny garden in which to rest a while.

In St Peter's Street itself are the 12th-century hostel for poor pilgrims (spanning the River Stour), the 16th-century weavers' house (above the shop, you can watch a weaver at work there, or do brass-rubbings), the old ducking-stool for scolds behind it, boats for hire (or boat trips), and 15th-century Queen Elizabeth House (a restaurant). It was in this half-timbered house with elaborate plastered ceilings and gilded bosses that Elizabeth I finally told her suitor, the Duc d'Alençon, that she would have none of him. The great museum, its porch writhing with carved griffins, is mock-medieval: apart from its own displays of local and military history, its visiting exhibitions are of a very high standard – for instance, Degas sculptures when I was there. But St Peter's Street does not reveal all at a glance – below there are cellars to visit where Canterbury had its own mint, and above one can see the big top-storey doors through which bales of wool were hauled, to be spun and woven on the first floor, for sale on the ground floor (where the weaver's family would have had living quarters too).

The Poor Priests' Hospital (with imaginative heritage museum) and the remains of the Grey Friars' monastery take some finding, but are well worth it. I turned out of St Peter's Street to walk down Stour Street until I saw an archway with a nurseryman's sign on it. Through here lie 13th-century ruins, their grounds now used for growing plants. As I crossed the footbridge over the Stour (shallow, with brown trout, green weed wavering in the current – 'stour' means fast-flowing – and ducks nesting on the bank), I could see the 14th-century bridge downstream – the earliest example of a brick bridge in England, the bricks being an innovation brought by Flemish refugees. A flowery path led to a quiet, sunny seat for a picnic beside the ruins and the mill-race. I could see the Franciscan monks' kitchen built across the river, with a trapdoor through which they could fish. Beyond the rows of plants was the Poor Priests' Hospital (part 12th-century and part Tudor; with café) and in the other direction the cathedral tower loomed above the rooftops. I knew that further along Stour Street is ancient St Mildred's church (more gardens) and the shell of the Norman castle in its green setting; but no place could be more attractive than Greyfriars for a restful hour – except perhaps West Gate Gardens. The West Gate is the only city gateway still standing (a small museum inside, and a fine view from its towers). The Stour, which is as tangled as a skein of wool, runs here too and on its banks a particularly pretty flower garden has been laid out: another of Canterbury's peaceful retreats from crowded streets.

And so to the cathedral. What can I possibly write about it within the space of a few paragraphs? I have visited nearly every

Canterbury Cathedral

cathedral in England yet still this remains my favourite – not only for its beauty but because so much history has happened here. It is, too, one of the warmest and most colourful of cathedrals. I have returned again and again, for there is no way in which a single visit of, say, an hour or two can be sufficient.

So I will write about one thing only: the Becket story. The earliest parts of the present building date from 1070 (a previous structure had been destroyed by fire) and so it was exactly a century old when Archbishop Becket, having persistently defied Henry II's authority, was murdered by four knights. Immediately, the martyr became the centre of a cult, with all the paraphernalia of shrine, miracles, pilgrimages and so forth. Kent is full of churches dedicated to him.

Another fire gave the opportunity for fresh rebuilding (though the site of the assassination survived), on a splendid scale, to house Becket's jewelled tomb – until Henry VIII made off with its treasures and erased every trace of Becket that he could.

Later the Puritans did away with many other tombs, statues and stained glass; but despite this vandalism Canterbury's remaining medieval glass is some of the most outstanding in the world. The windows tell stories, in 'strip cartoon' form, for congregations that could not read, and among them is a long series of 13th-century windows relating the story of Becket's martyrdom, and of miraculous cures subsequently performed at his shrine (one window gives pilgrims a broad hint: a supplicant is shown handing over a bag of gold to one of the priests before praying at the shrine).

The Becket windows were designed half a century after the assassination, and the clothing is therefore in the fashion of that period (the time of King John). To understand every incident – and, indeed, all the cathedral's windows – it is well worth buying the little 'Guide to the Stained Glass' sold, along with other excellent booklets (some for children), at the cathedral's bookstall. With its help one can pick out the crippled, the paralysed and the mad; those with toothache or epilepsy, recurrent nightmares or leprosy, swollen feet or the plague. All the miracle cures are shown in 'before' and 'after' pictures. But even more vivid testimony to the tremendous following that Becket's memory inspired are the dull stones beside the spot where his shrine stood, worn into hollows by the knees of the thousands who prayed there: a few years ago, the Pope himself.

This is a tremendous cathedral, its nave soaring 80 feet high, filled with monuments to the great and the good (or not so good). Even its Norman crypt is unique – the biggest in the world: a huge area skilfully covered with vaulting, some of its walls still painted with pictures of the same period. The delicate fan-vaulting below the tower, the elaborately carved effigy of the Black Prince lying on his tomb, the lovely cloisters, 'Bell Harry' tower (from which curfew is rung each night, the signal to close the gates of the precincts): any one of these would make Canterbury Cathedral worth a visit, and it has them all.

The 230-foot tower is a masterpiece. Despite its skin of stone, it was built from bricks – an almost unique achievement in 1498. Tremendously impressive at any time, it leaves an unforgettable impression if seen on a summer evening (or at Easter or Christmas) when it is floodlit: a grand finale to any visit to Canterbury.

Part Two

COACH JOURNEYS

20

Skipping Down to the Sea

London – Coulsdon – Pyecombe – Brighton

That ceaseless 18th-century traveller, William Cobbett, said of Brighton: 'It is so situated that a coach which leaves it not very early in the morning reaches London by noon. Great parcels of stock-jobbers skip backwards and forwards.'

They skip even faster on today's coaches; and it did not take me long to shed the industrial outskirts of London and, passing the old Croydon Aerodrome buildings which conservationists are now eager to preserve as part of aviation history, to speed out towards the countryside. From a leafy road that runs high up, there were far views ahead. The coach sped past suburban gardens at their spring best, with magnolias and pink cherry blossom bursting out all over, purple aubretia pouring from walls and rockery banks, or scarlet tulips standing to attention like grenadiers.

Once beyond Coulsdon and across the boundary into Surrey, the scenery became rural, with horses grazing in the fields. On a dual carriageway and with urban congestion behind, the coach picked up speed (overtaking everyone else on the road). We zoomed over the top of London's orbital motorway (M25) that crossed beneath us, and made our way south – following a route that wound its way up and down among green hills, golden gorse and silver hawthorn on the roadside banks, fields of grazing cows alternating with woods of larch and birch.

There is a colourful book, no bigger than a pack of cigarettes, which I often carry in my handbag: Collins' *Gem Guide – Trees*. Out it came along the next stretch of the ride, for the wide strip separating the two carriageways is full of chestnuts, conifers and other trees in great variety.

The ploughed fields that followed were chalky-pale (we were on the edge of the chalk hills of the South Downs) with pottering crows sharply silhouetted against them. Already the lambs in the meadows were half-grown. Ahead lay the Downs, their smoky-blue humps like the backs of whales. Farm buildings and churches hereabouts are (typically of a chalk region) flint-walled; and some houses are tile-hung in Sussex style. The road led onwards to little Pyecombe, the sign with its name bearing a shepherd's crook because once this village had a forge celebrated for making these crooks (and, later, for making bishops' crooks). Its tiny church stands on the brow of the hill. Past the Plough Inn (with old plough outside) are the white stone pillars that mark the boundary of Sussex – and of Brighton. The traffic began to build up here.

This leafy road makes a fine approach to the town. Houses with pretty gardens are succeeded by a particularly beautiful park with a row of delicate fountain-jets, and flowerbeds that produced gasps of admiration from several coach passengers. To the left is historic Preston Manor. Every summer, a design for each flowerbed in this park is sent in by a different town with which Brighton has associations – all vying to produce something even more attractive than the others. The rockery on the right of the road is laid out like the picture on willow-pattern plates, floodlit at night.

And so into the heart of Brighton: the Grand Parade. When the Prince Regent built his summer Pavilion here, this is where the court paraded in all their finery. Regency houses – bow fronts, lacy ironwork – fringe the area, and its centre consists of lawns, flowers and statuary: still an elegant oasis in the heart of what is now a considerable city.

There was a quick glimpse of the sea, of Palace Pier and of the Pavilion's oriental domes before the coach swung round to squeeze itself through a narrow lane and come to rest in Pool Valley, only a few minutes behind schedule.

Brighton

It was really Dr Richard Russell who, in writing his 'Dissertation Concerning the Use of Sea Water' (1785), put what was once a muddy little fishing village onto the map (he lived where the Royal Albion Hotel now stands), though it took the Prince Regent to make it fashionable – first by coming to Brighton in pursuit of the good doctor's 'cure' himself (he was a great believer in the properties of both bathing in and drinking sea-water); then by installing his beloved Mrs Fitzherbert in a house – now a YMCA hostel – overlooking the parade; and ultimately by building that most exotic of royal palaces – the oriental Pavilion. Around this grew up all the pleasures his courtiers could desire. The coach station (sited where the Prince had a muddy pool drained and paved) is right in the middle of all this, nicely sandwiched between the sea and the Pavilion, close by the famous Lanes. Therefore it is easy for a coach traveller to spend an entire day exploring these parts (and often this is all that tourists do, even though there is far more to Brighton).

Brighton Pavilion

The Pavilion is all fantasy: Indian without and Chinese within. Much of the original furniture is there, and what furniture it is! – carved into the shape of dolphins and sphinxes, dragons and birds, with hardly ever a simple chair- or table-leg to be seen. In recent years, grime has been removed to reveal all the original, dazzling colours. It was almost a relief after wandering through this succession of magnificent and exotic rooms to enter the kitchens where row upon row of huge copper pans and an enormous spit were standing ready, as if for yet another banquet that night. In summer the banqueting room has its gold plate laid out on its table, part of the annual Regency Exhibition.

From this dreamlike and brilliant world, I wandered to The Lanes, a cobweb of tiny, brick-paved walks (no cars) where little shops, pubs and restaurants jostle one another – selling antiques (Queen Mary used to hunt for finds here), crafts, pretty clothes or tempting food. The goods may differ from those of the Prince Regent's times but the atmosphere is much the same – vanity fair!

I walked up past the Theatre Royal (a pretty, plush-and-gilt Victorian theatre where, on a previous visit, I'd enjoyed Penelope Keith in a play later to become a West End success – Brighton is often one jump ahead of London's theatregoers) to the Indian-style dome that had once been the royal stables with riding school adjoining. Now part of this houses Brighton's museum – a very unusual one, and not only because of the splendid buildings in which it is housed, where even the entrance is a grandiose and golden Indian arch. It has probably the only major collection of *art nouveau* and *art deco* in the country (furniture, dresses and jewellery), and also galleries with other specialized collections. In one, the history of the seaside is the theme; in another (the most dramatic of all, I thought) is a collection of outstanding ethnic art, spotlit against a dark background; and one traces the area's history back to 100 million years ago, beginning with a fossilized mammoth tusk superimposed on a full-scale picture of the huge creature. Brighton is surrounded by hills where its earliest, Celtic inhabitants built their forts and villages: small-scale models recreate these vividly. The story is then taken on in other exhibits, with finds from Roman, Saxon and medieval times.

Back then to the coach and bus station, for a ride westward along the seafront. Buses go all the way to adjoining Portslade-by-Sea (3 miles away), following the seafront all the time. A ride like this is a good way to see what the resort has to offer, with the intention of returning later to chosen spots. In summer, there are illuminations all the way along to Hove.

Most people simply stay near the centre and Palace Pier, but beyond West Pier (at present closed) lies quieter Hove, and here everything changes.

But before getting to West Pier, I looked out for the Old Ship Hotel because it has an interesting story. When Charles II (then prince) was attempting to escape the Roundheads by fleeing across the Channel, he was aided by a Sussex skipper called Tettersell. He later rewarded him with money to buy the Old Ship and become an innkeeper. Every year, the Old Ship sponsors a cross-Channel yacht race to commemorate the royal escape, and nearly a hundred sailing-boats gather along this stretch of coast for the start of the race.

In Hove there are fewer high-rise flats and more splendours of early Victorian architecture, carefully conserved. Corinthian pilasters rise, three stories high, to stately pediments. After Regency Square, where striped canopies shelter the pretty balconies of the smaller hotels, there comes Brunswick Square, followed by the lovely curve of Adelaide Crescent which leads to Palmeira Square (now full of offices and English language schools for overseas youngsters). These have carefully tended gardens in which to sun oneself, or picnic, when the incoming tide has partly covered the pebbly beaches. Up in Palmeira Square, the time is told by a floral clock (the bachelors' buttons were doing so more accurately than the nearby church clock). Seafront lawns follow (with bowling, croquet and suchlike).

After that, it seems as if the seaside has vanished, and nose-in-air motorists zip by the next bit as fast as they can in order to escape the view of factories and power station. But appearances are deceptive, and locals know what lies behind and how easily it is reached if you get off the bus at the Schooner Inn (which, incidentally, has a bar with snacks that overlooks an absorbing water-front spectacle). For this is where the basin of Shoreham harbour lies, and it is easy to walk across the tops of the triple lock-gates to get to the other side of the basin and to the little-used beaches that are nearby. The basin is frequented not only by great tankers and cargo-ships, best seen when they move in or out at high tide, but by the small sailing-boats of the local yacht club. Alongside are bonded warehouses for sherry shipped in from Spain and stacks of timber from the Baltic. When the tide is out, the beach beyond is the place to be, for then the sand is revealed. Having only one café and shop, this beach is mercifully free of litter as well as crowds.

There is a view from here of Shoreham's harbour close by. Two stone breakwaters shelter the mouth of the River Adur (pronounced

Ada), and when I was there a dredger was busy shifting the river's silt away. It's an interesting spot with a lighthouse, lifeboat house (sometimes open to the public), old fort with ramparts to walk upon, and coastguards' lookout – you may be allowed in when they're not busy. The best part, the west jetty, is reached by a somewhat roundabout bus trip.

The best way to travel the eastward stretch of seafront is to go first to Rottingdean by the inland route, and come back along the coast by another bus (some open-topped in summer) which is then on the side of the road close to the sea. Half-way back (at the Marina), you could change onto Volks' quaint seafront railway if you prefer.

The quiet heart of this one-time smuggling village, tucked away from the main road, is charming: Rottingdean has smooth lawns with beautiful houses of flint or half-timbering, a pond and a wide green (suitable for picnics) overlooked by the old Plough Inn. Byways are cobbled; the main street has a number of hotels and inns. There is access to the beach through a gap in the cliffs beyond.

A number of celebrities have lived at Rottingdean. Sir Edward Burne-Jones was one (he designed the stained glass in the church), and his nephew Kipling later lived here too – perhaps it was Rottingdean that inspired his poem about smuggling, '. . . brandy for the parson, baccy for the clerk', because the local vicar, Hooker, is known to have colluded with the smugglers. Hooker, whose pupils included Bulwer Lytton and Cardinal Manning, has his bust in the church, and his house is now a museum of toys – with paintings by William Nicholson, who lived there later.

The fast ride back into Brighton is a splendid clifftop route, white cliffs contrasting with green tops. We sped past a windmill on the right and the huge buildings of Roedean girls' school, and then the Marina came into sight far below on the left – so huge it is almost a seaport in its own right. There are often historic ships there among the throng of small sailing-boats, and special events like a regatta or race.

Approaching Brighton from this direction, one passes architecture of a slightly younger vintage than on the west side. Lord Olivier is one of many theatrical people who have lived here, in the terraces of houses with bow fronts and canopied verandahs, big windows and delicate ironwork.

Within minutes, the bus was back in the centre of things again and I got out by the historic aquarium, where sea-lions and dolphins live an underground life, to take one last look at the seafront from Palace Pier. Things were much the same as in 1736 when a parson on holiday wrote home: 'My morning business is bathing in the sea, and then buying fish, and my evening occupation is riding out for air and counting the ships.' Thousands do much the same thing today.

21

Taking the Waters in a Regency Spa

Heathrow – Northleach – Cheltenham

It was a hot, hazy morning. The towers of Windsor Castle were just a misty and romantic outline glimpsed briefly beyond the trees before we turned off the M4 motorway to drive more slowly across Farnham Common, knee-deep in summer grasses and tall buttercups. Oaks and plane trees stretched across this road, and the air beneath their boughs smelt fresh after the fumes of the pounding motorway.

Then, via a roundabout that was gay with marguerites and clover, we joined another main route, the M40, and once more gathered speed, flashing by overgrown hedges where elders were in flower and, beyond these, the fields of wheat, grazing horses or sheep with lambs. The windscreen became spattered with the corpses of summer midges; and a steamy haze enveloped the far hills which we saw intermittently between patches of old mixed woodland or occasional conifer plantations.

Passengers dozed in the soporific heat. As the coach moved faster, a welcome breeze poured in. There were occasional streams, and a pool with a notice saying that carp and tench could be caught: I envied the fish their cool depths. The road passed through a cutting, chalk cliffs to either side, and emerged to a dramatic view of the great plain ahead which we were now to cross. Here groups of cows lay in the sparse shade of willows that traced the route of a stream, while the sun beat down on the vacant grass.

We left the motorway for a shadier road fringed with spruce and larch, then skirted Oxford to press on through an increasingly attractive summer landscape. Meadows brimmed with wildflowers, and even the rushy streams were colourful with the flowers of waterweeds standing up above the surface. The lacy heads of cow parsley were like a great cloud of foam along miles of road.

Already the fields of stiff and spiky barley were beginning to turn colour; there were scarlet poppies among the grain; and the lush green grass was being cut for silage.

We were now well into the Cotswolds and here, instead of hedges, dry-stone walls enclosed the fields – the honey-coloured blocks of limestone neatly laid, unlike the irregular stone walls of the Lake District. We were now high up and could see stone-built villages tucked away behind sheltering trees in the folds of hills, then the great spire of Burford's medieval church. Small cottages and great farms alike are made of the same beautiful Cotswold stone, so readily worked into a variety of attractive details – shapely dripstones over mullioned windows, porches and steps, cornices and columns.

For some time we were stuck behind a long, slow lorry, heavy-laden with building materials. Eventually, even mild old ladies got impatient to overtake it but this was a winding road and 'better safe than sorry' said the patient driver. We passed slowly into Gloucestershire, grateful for the cool leaves of trees arching across the road before once again we were out among the fields. At long last we were able to pass the straining truck. Swiftly we drove by hedges of pink and white hawthorn with traveller's joy scrambling over them, a noble gateway leading to a distant mansion, flocks of bright white sheep (newly shorn), and donkeys dozing in a field full of meadowsweet – the scent drifted into the coach. Clusters of flowers hung down heavily from the sycamore trees.

The coach pulled up briefly at lovely Northleach (see also page 56), in which every mellow stone house is rooted in the past. There was a good view, while we paused, of the church's spectacular windows, and its immense tower. This is one of the most glorious examples of a church built entirely in the 15th-century Perpendicular style, at the height of the Gothic period. It was erected when Northleach was a wealthy centre of the wool trade – as were most of the houses one sees in the streets. Just outside Northleach, an old stone prison has been turned into the Cotswolds' own Museum of Rural Life.

There was not much further to go – up and down, with distant views to both left and right. The sign of the Puesdown Inn shows a stage-coach stuck in the mire, with its passengers pushing it: probably a common enough incident on these hills when roads were little more than dirt tracks. We descended into the valley, fields of purple clover succeeded by a great manor house and the shining Dowdeswell reservoir with a solitary boatman and groves of pink rhododendrons right down to the water's edge. Here Cheltenham spread itself out across the valley floor, and it took the coach a little while to get through the outskirts of Victorian villas behind privet hedges – a mixture, on this side of the town, of the seedy and the splendid. There were flying glimpses of one of Cheltenham's most elegant spots (Pittville Circus, with the entrance to Pittville Park close by – of which more later); of the birthplace of the composer Gustav Holst, now a museum; and of elegant terraces among green squares.

And then we had arrived, at one of the biggest coach stations in England, where sometimes as many as 300 coaches can be seen manoeuvring in and out. Its size is the reason why Cheltenham's coach station is (unlike most) not close to the town centre. So, finding it too sultry to face even a ten-minute walk, I taxied to the centre of the Promenade.

Cheltenham

This is, par excellence, a town in which to stroll. It was laid out expressly for that purpose, and is on a level. Its pavements are wide, shaded by chestnuts planted in the Prince Regent's time, and plentifully supplied with seats. Lawns and flowerbeds are everywhere. And wherever you pause, there is something pleasurable or interesting at which to look: fountains, Regency architecture, elegant shops, sculpture, stucco or stone houses, lacy ironwork. It is one of the best of spa towns, created entirely because the fashionable world wanted to come and 'take the waters' when the excesses of London life had taken their toll, and to spend their summer in an atmosphere of elegance and recreation. Much of that original ambience still survives.

Further, Cheltenham being at the hub of a network of coaches (and buses), it is a good base from which to explore much of England.

The best starting point is the Tourist Information Centre (in the middle of the great Promenade, lined with sophisticated shops) where a 'walking tour' leaflet can be obtained, with notes about the architecture and history of the buildings in the Promenade; the

The Promenade, Cheltenham

famous Ladies' College; and – my favourite part – Montpellier Walk, with arcades of small shops, and dozens of caryatid figures copied from the Erechtheum of Athens. (It is around here that many of the good guest-houses lie.) The Montpellier Gardens come at just the right moment for a rest, before tackling Suffolk Parade and the antique dealers' quarter. Little Trafalgar Street is worth seeking out, with the pretty cottage of Thomas Hardy's retirement years; and the colourful Imperial Gardens, yet another of Cheltenham's many green oases, a park with walled garden, beer tent in summer, fishpool and bandstand. At the Town Hall, you can help yourself to the famous alkaline waters (ugh!) from a blue Doulton urn in the foyer (it's here that most of the town's festivals and other big events are staged). Close by is Regent Street, the best place to look for a bistro-type meal (the food at the Everyman Theatre is good, too).

This perambulation of an hour or two covers most of Cheltenham's centre, the only part that most tourists bother to explore. But I have been back to the town a number of times, because there is so much more to discover. There is street upon street of handsome houses – terraced, or set back in their gardens, each with impeccable detailing in its balconies, classical pilasters, doorknocker, 'gothick' porch, carefully proportioned lintels or frieze around the top – all best appreciated from the upper deck of a bus. There are ancient trees in the streets, and old 'piecrust' pillarboxes along the way.

For instance, a bus will take you to Pittville Park, through the town's most exclusive quarter (Pittville, named for Joseph Pitt who first developed it as a spa in 1825). Here are most of the very finest houses, and some excellent (yet not very expensive) hotels; and at their heart are 34 acres of informal parkland, flowers and lakes with ducks, with the magnificent Pump Room for concerts, which also houses an excellent museum of costume and jewellery. Children enjoy the aviaries and rabbit pens as well as the playground, and there is a nearby café. A boating lake and sports ground lies beyond – and a little further is Cheltenham's celebrated Gold Cup racecourse.

Sandford Park is more central. This has 14 acres with riverside paths, waterfalls, duck or fish pools, fountains, flowerbeds and an open-air swimming pool with café. (There are still more parks – the Tourist Information Centre has a leaflet with details about all of them.)

For anyone who wants to enjoy Cheltenham architecture away from the tourist-thronged hustle of the city centre, any of the buses which head down Park Place and return via Lansdown Crescent give a very good idea of the Cheltenham that only the residents know.

In complete contrast is the bus ride to the little village of Swindon, now almost a surburb of the town. This is where the huge recreation centre is, and a stadium (for squash, swimming, etc.). But Swindon is also a good starting point for country walks, described in a leaflet obtainable from the Tourist Information Centre.

There were two more things I wanted to see in Cheltenham – conveniently close to the coach station from which I would depart. One was the church with its tremendous 14th-century rose window, and the other was the museum and art gallery.

Cheltenham is the most complete of Regency towns. It is a garden-city, too, with trees and lawns everywhere; a town with every kind of shop or entertainment.

Public Transport to the Countryside

How easy and convenient did you find the bus (and coach) services on your travels? Was there always a bus service where and when you needed to travel? Was travel information easy to obtain?

If the answer is yes – that's fine.

If no – don't just grumble about it – tell someone. The chances are you probably aren't the only one dissatisfied. Only when the consumers' voice is heard will we ever get a public transport service we need.

Write to the nearest bus operator describing where you wanted to go and the problems you encountered. Ask if they could consider putting on a better service next year or improving the quality and availability of information.

Write to the County Council in that area telling them of the same story. They do have a responsibility for providing public transport information and services for visitors and residents whether for leisure purposes or for shopping or going to work. Councils often have an interest in developing their local tourism industry: tell them that extra services or a special effort with information could attract more visitors to the area.

If you want to find out more about designing and promoting public transport to the countryside there is a free booklet available from the Countryside Commission. It explains how to set about improving and promoting bus services. It also describes how some successful new services got going.

Write to the Countryside Commission, 19/23 Albert Road, Manchester, M19 2EQ and ask for the free booklet 'Public Transport to the Countryside'.

22

Roundheads and Cavaliers

Cheltenham – Worcester

The coach started its journey through an area of market gardening and greenhouses in the foreground, with the jagged outline of the hills as a backdrop – blue and hazy in the heat of the day. Midsummer's presence was all around: in the bales of hay that dotted the fields, the poppies by the wayside and the briar roses or creamy elderflowers of the hedgerows. The few clouds in the brilliant blue sky, reflected in a bright blue river, looked as if they had been painted on with a palette knife. Fields of wheat were a bluish-green (all the yellows and light greens of spring fields were long gone).

Part of the motorway was under repair, so the coach slowed down to weave its way through lanes indicated by thousands of scarlet-and-white 'witches' hats' for a while, before picking up speed. We whisked by rows of poplars, straight as grenadiers; and by willows trailing their silvery-grey skirts into trickling streams. The shadow accompanying our coach was pencil-thin, with the midday sun almost directly overhead.

And so, downhill through leafy suburbs of Georgian and Victorian houses, we made the descent into Worcester – its great cathedral tower dominating the skyline. There were quick glimpses of tipsy black-and-white houses, the Commandery (described on page 217), the red sandstone gateway to the cathedral precincts, old churches and the stone bridge with boys fishing and canoeing on the waters beyond.

The coach drew up in what is certainly one of the most attractive coach stations in England: right by lawns on the river bank. After a hot journey, what could be more refreshing than to sit here a while (with a cold drink from the café) to watch the boats go by? In fact, it is from this spot that boat trips start, an ideal way in which to view the town and its environs before exploring further on foot.

Worcester

Alternatively, a very pleasant way to approach the cathedral and all that surrounds it is by walking along the riverside, watching the boats and ducks go past. The path passes 'the glover's needle' and its terraced rose gardens (the needle is the slender spire, all that remains of St Andrew's church); and under rows of shady limes and beeches. If you were to continue far enough you would come to Diglis Canal Basin, lively with small craft.

I turned off, however, to visit the Royal Worcester porcelain factory where, apart from tours of the historic factory itself to see china being made and decorated, there is an excellent museum, with audiovisual show, as well as two shops – at one, 'seconds' attract bargain-hunters, particularly during the January and July sales. There is so much to see that the presence of a café is a welcome addition. Because the factory tours are very popular it is wise to book ahead (tel. 0905 23221).

Further on is the busy City Walls Road, along which the coach had entered. Among the antique shops in this area is The Commandery, one of Worcester's most ancient buildings (far larger than it seems from the road). Here Charles II had his headquarters during the Civil War and one room is filled with displays about the battle of Worcester, the Royalists' final defeat in 1649. Inside is a great hall with minstrels' gallery and hammerbeam roof, its bosses ornately carved. The house contains collections of armour, Jacobean furniture and reconstructions of old workshops (glove-maker, cobbler, cooper and blacksmith). Everywhere is the smell of beeswax polish. The Museum's range of booklets is particularly interesting, there are kits for children, a café, and a canalside garden with views of locks, narrow-boats and former glove factories. The Commandery deserves a visit of several hours.

The cathedral is only a few yards away. Through the great gateway of reddish-cream sandstone is quiet College Green, so-called because all the surrounding Georgian houses are now part of King's School. Worcester Cathedral has very lovely cloisters with windows looking onto grass, graves and white roses. The cathedral interior is richly decorated – rib-vaulting, angels, gilded bosses, colourful monuments of alabaster, a marble pulpit and a font with pinnacle cover rising roof-high. Its crypt and chapter house are both unique, and the great organ fills one of the transepts. This is the cathedral where King John chose to be buried, and from his tomb one gets the best view of the glorious east end. Prince Arthur (first husband of Catherine of Aragon) also lies here, in an elaborately decorated chantry chapel – too elaborate for Protestant tastes, which is why many figures of saints were deliberately defaced.

Outside the west door are terraces and a walled garden where catmint and valerian thrive, leading to the yews and lawns of another Georgian green beyond which stands a statue of Elgar (unveiled by the Prince of Wales in 1981) near what was once his father's music shop.

Friar Street, Worcester

Across the road is Friar Street. I lingered among its antique and art shops; peered into the Tudor House museum of social history and the wine bars; and sat a while in the cobbled courtyard of Greyfriars which is overlooked by a gateway with scarlet-and-gold coats-of-arms and the message 'Except the Lord Build the House,

Their Labour is but Lost that Build'. There is a carving of a Franciscan here, for once this was a pilgrims' hostel run by the monks. Sunlight and shade dappled this quiet corner, where Canterbury bells filled terracotta pots and roses scrambled up the old brick walls.

I turned down Pump Street to find the pedestrianized shopping centre of the town and the grandest of Guildhalls, built in 1721. It has not only both Charles I and Charles II in shining gold, robed and crowned, but Queen Anne too – not to mention a tremendous panoply of spears and halberds inside, along with portraits of civic worthies, and an assembly room resplendent with chandeliers. (The Tourist Information Centre is here.)

There is much more to Worcester than this, of course; but I had too little time to explore the City Museum of Natural History (it has Saturday morning sessions for children), Art Gallery or Fort Royal Park (the battle site), for example. I was sorry not to have had longer in Worcester, a town that repays unhurried wandering down arcades or narrow lanes of medieval origin, and among ancient houses or inns.

23

Across Fens to a Medieval Port

London – Cambridge – Ely – Downham Market – King's Lynn

It takes more than half an hour to get through the drearier parts of east London. After that, the route is a fast one, with the coach able to pick up speed as it flashes through a predominantly agricultural landscape, hurrying past occasional weatherboarded or whitewashed villages seen among the fields. The crops of rape (grown for the oil-rich seeds) were in their full blaze of colour, the sun streaming down on them: vast sheets of vivid yellow that were more dramatic even than daffodil fields. This is a gently rolling landscape in which church towers occasionally peep over the rounded hilltops, or sometimes an angler is glimpsed sitting patiently beside a lake where ducks are more actively engaged. Though the road runs straight, it undulates gently – sometimes running between embankments cut in the hills, sometimes emerging into woodlands or between fields.

The route onward is particularly interesting because coaches call at two historic cities and an old market town, at any of which it is worth breaking one's journey for a while. The first is Cambridge where there are not only the splendours of the colleges to see (exceptional among them, King's College chapel) and 'the backs', gardens beside the river Cam, but the outstanding art and archaeological collections at the Fitzwilliam Museum and the lovely Botanic Gardens – 40 acres, second only to Kew.

The graceful 14th-century lantern tower of Ely's cathedral dominates the Fens for miles around. Once Ely was 'eel island', surrounded by marshes at the time when Hereward the Wake held it against the Normans. If you have time, walk along the bank of the River Ouse – from the cathedral to Cherry Hill Park.

Downham Market is named for the central square which fills

with market stalls. Here I ate well in converted stables at the historic Crown Inn – the old oak-panelled bar houses mementoes of the famous 'Pathfinder' air squadron which was based nearby.

After Downham Market the architecture began to change: instead of flint or brick walls, more and more buildings were made of the rough, orangey-red carr stone peculiar to the north of Norfolk. This was a sign that King's Lynn was near, and within minutes we had arrived at the coach station – conveniently central, as usual, and right by the town museum (which is always a good thing to visit first in order to understand the natural and the man-made history of what one is going to see thereafter).

King's Lynn

The town began as a string of houses along the edge of the then winding River Ouse, conducting so prosperous a trade with northern Europe that Lynn became England's fourth greatest port for a while. The big river, which provided a main route into the Midlands, was straightened and widened in Victorian times, but its original course is still indicated by the winding line of the town's most historic thoroughfare, built up in stages and now known as Nelson Street, Queen Street and King Street.

Along here are to be found buildings that go back to the time of the Norman bishops who founded and controlled Lynn; and a walk from one end to the other (terminating in the big Tuesday Market Place) will cover much of what is most interesting in Lynn. To get from the coach station to the start of such a walk, one passes the old Greyfriars Tower – last remnant of a big monastery (retained as a landmark for seamen), surrounded by a little garden where I was tempted to linger. This was just one of many monasteries that flourished here. The tower marks the edge of the old town: everything eastward was built centuries later.

Nelson Street starts at the little creek known as Millfleet, frequented by a flock of over a hundred swans. From a seat by the waterside, one can see the backs of the old maltings (sensitively converted to flats), moored boats and the tall chimney of what was once a cattlefood mill – now used for budding steeplejacks to practise on. Nearby in Bridge Street is a fine 17th-century house once known as the Greenland Fishery Inn because it became the headquarters of the whaling fleet. Along Nelson Street itself is another of Lynn's treasures, Hampton Court. Through a wide arch with little heads is a cobbled court surrounded by a mixture of buildings: 15th-century shops at the front, the warehouse of a merchant on what was the river frontage. Hampton Court stands by the junction of four ancient lanes, and it is worth risking life and limb to stand in the middle of the roadway here to look down each in turn – very little changed since the Middle Ages. Some of the timbered houses, with their upper stories jetted over the road, have attractive herringbone brickwork.

A few yards down one of them, Priory Lane, I wandered through a great archway (only recently unblocked) to find myself in a peaceful court of cobbles and flowers with a well at the end, and ancient buildings around it – once a priory – that have been restored for use as homes: beautifully done, the scheme deservedly won a conservation award. Along Lynn's old streets, there are many such arches with gardens beyond; small alleyways; and decorative touches like the pelicans that are the town's symbol carved above doorways or cast in iron as weathervanes.

A fortress-like building further along is a Hanseatic warehouse (the Hansa was a 15th-century league of German merchants to whom the king had sold trading privileges: not surprisingly, English traders were hostile to them and they built accordingly). Part of it became St Margaret's House: although the fine house with Georgian façade is now offices, one is free to walk in and I paused briefly to sit among the sunny flowerbeds in its cobbled yard. There are millstones laid out here: once, Lynn did a busy trade importing these essentials of life before the Industrial Revolution. Next to it is the house where Fanny Burney grew up.

A flower-bordered path leads to the door of St Margaret's church. On a unique and colourful dial above, the phases of the moon and the times of high tides are recorded – the ingenious work of a 17th-century churchwarden – and tidemarks by the door indicate the importance of such information in the life of Lynn: as recently as January 1978 the town was inundated by a freak tide, with 4 feet of water flooding into the church.

St Margaret's is a church of very great splendour, built by monks in the centuries of Lynn's greatest prosperity. A little Norman work remains, but some of its most decorative features are from the 14th century – the fine carving of the screens, for example, and two of the church's most famous treasures, a pair of huge brasses (probably of Flemish workmanship) which are the biggest in Britain. Here lies the portrait of a former mayor of Lynn with his first and second wives at either side, and along the foot a frieze depicting a banquet of considerable splendour – it's worth kneeling to study all the tiny details: bearers of roast peacocks, musicians, even the goblets and knives on the table, and the fashionably pointed shoes of the diners. On another brass, an everyday story of country life is the theme: there is a post-mill and (an allusion to a folk tale) a man carrying corn to relieve his tired horse.

Nearly every century has left its own distinctive touch on the church. The pulpit with its marquetry panels is Georgian, so is the organ which was made to the design of Fanny Burney's father when he was organist here. The aluminium altar that stands before the chancel is uncompromisingly of our own time, set within a grey brick surround of unusual shape.

Lynn's church has problems (all too evident when I looked at the startling angle of the arches under the great tower). The banks of the Ouse were marshy, and repeatedly subsidence below and gales or flood-tides above have done their worst. One of the ways in which money is raised for repairs is by serving refreshments on market days, within the church itself.

Just outside the church is the Saturday Market Place with the distinctive 15th-century Town Hall built of stone and flint in chequerboard style (the Tourist Information Centre is here). When I visited it, changes were afoot but even in disarray it was a building worth exploring – the sun poured in through great windows with views of the church, stone-flagged floors and ancient oak doors were succeeded by Georgian assembly rooms of faded elegance, all gilt and portraits, and the now deserted formalities of the old court-room. In an undercroft adjoining this building the town's regalia is exhibited, including a famous gilt cup (pint-size) of 1325, elaborately decorated with courtly figures, called King John's Cup.

To continue the walk, along narrow Queen Street, was a hair-raising experience, for big lorries thundered along this stretch with little regard for pedestrians on the scant pavements. Under these conditions, I gave the 18th-century barley-sugar columns of Clifton House only a quick glance (although the medieval interior is open to visitors, and its watchtower too), and was glad to walk a few yards back and find a quieter refuge behind a carved oak door, in the courtyard garden of 15th-century Thoresby College (which now combines a youth hostel and flatlets for old people). The seats among the lawns and shrubs were welcome at this point. One can go out on the far side to stroll along the South Quay (paved with setts). The tide was out and I could see the great build-up of mud which is such a problem in the Ouse: an incoming tide takes only 3 hours, but the ebb is slow (9 hours) which means colossal quantities of silt are deposited. A cargo ship was loading grain, and there was a fine view out to The Wash. A little further along, craftsmen were at work on jewellery and pottery in an old granary (in King Staithe Lane).

Thoresby College

Back then to the streets. At Purfleet creek, where the classical little Custom House stands with a cupola on top and a grandiloquent statue of Charles II above the door, King Street takes over – rather wider and mostly of more recent date than Queen Street. Although the fronts are Georgian, I could see in the alleys between them the half-timbering and old barns which date the houses as being much earlier. Nos. 28–32 are of particular interest: very recently a huge Norman stone hall had been discovered hidden in the heart of a more recent structure. Only some considerable magnate could have had such a home in those days. Accretions have now been stripped away in order to give the house a new life as a heritage centre. Along here there are some of the very earliest brick buildings, too. Lynn, having no stone at hand, began early on to use clay for brick-making, a technique learnt from the Dutch with whom they traded (which is why some buildings in this region have gables in the Dutch style).

The further I walked, the more interesting the street became.

The town's museum of social history is here (a graceful building – the hall has fluted pillars and an oval fanlight above). It contains old kitchens, dolls and domestic trifles (a brass-rubbing centre, too); and next door is the hall of one of the 26 trade guilds which flourished in King's Lynn, now owned by the National Trust. It is the largest 15th-century guildhall in Britain. A complex of old, red-brick buildings houses an art gallery, a good restaurant with water-front view and terrace, and an intimate theatre, under the wood-pegged 15th-century rafters of which artistes like Janet Baker and Kathleen Ferrier could be heard much better, they say, than in the huge concert halls of London.

The Tuesday Market is the great set-piece of the town. Back in the 12th century, the citizens of Lynn (which was in those days Bishop's Lynn and not King's Lynn) got their first charter to hold a market, from the bishop. Such a charter meant a lot to a town for it then received fees from the stallholders.

The Tuesday Market, King's Lynn

Lynn's Tuesday Market grew bigger and bigger. Hence this enormous square, surrounded by its grandest buildings: magnates' houses of stone or brick, the Corn Exchange with a distinctly sexy corn-goddess on top, and the great coaching inns. But more than commerce took place here. Where the rows of parked cars are packed in, people died. Two children were hanged in 1708 for stealing. A witch was hanged, too – her heart, it was said, burst from her body and struck a nearby building: look closely on the north side and there on a red brick façade is an outline of a heart, on (the story goes) the very spot which the flying heart struck. And most gruesome of all was the death in 1531 of a maidservant who poisoned her mistress. For a short period, boiling was a legal form of execution in England for this crime, and thus, lingeringly, she died.

I turned away from the outwardly gay square with some feeling of relief, to make one last visit. This was to the church in the fishermen's quarter, which is dedicated to the fishermen's patron, St Nicholas. It is a beauty, not to be missed – with a soaring angel roof and a multitude of fine monuments, some of marble, some gilded and painted. During the summer festival, the Queen Mother often attends concerts here. The music starts as the dying sun pours in through the windows; daylight fades; and at the end the angels are illuminated.

Back in the Tuesday Market Place I had wondered at people who chose to eat their sandwiches on the steps of a bank, surrounded by cars. I wondered even more when, just a few minutes away, I found behind St Nicholas' church (where old and new fishermen's cottages huddle together) a small garden and seat, providing a tranquil spot in which to end a town walk.

24

Through Constable Country

Chelmsford – Woodbridge – Wickham Market –
Saxmundham – Southwold – Lowestoft

There had been one of those abrupt summer cloudbursts in which rain bounces high off the pavements and cascades along the overflowing gutters. But as we set off it stopped as suddenly as it had begun ten minutes earlier, and very clear light began to struggle through the gaps that were now widening between the grey clouds. We joined the main road along which so many coaches and lorries make their way from the east coast ports, the latter laden with great shipping containers from all over the world.

The road ran straight ahead, across a flat landscape. We crossed over the River Stour and thus into Suffolk, rather more hilly and with more trees than Essex. This is Constable country (signposts pointed to Flatford Mill), with occasional thatched cottages among the orchards and the corn.

The River Orwell and a canal were crossed, and soon we were in Ipswich (see page 101) – but with only fleeting glimpses of its historic buildings, half-timbered and pargetted, and of ancient church towers.

Once beyond the rambling suburbs of the town, it is no distance to Woodbridge: the coach accompanied the shining River Deben downstream, passed Notcutts attractively landscaped garden centre, and drew up in a narrow street of terraced cottages with Georgian and Victorian façades and demure porches against pink plaster walls (but some with jetted upper storeys suggesting a medieval structure behind). Woodbridge is described on page 104.

As we moved on through the town, there was a momentary view of the estuary, a colourful picture of boats swaying in the water beyond banks sprinkled with red poppies and purple mallows. Past pillared mansions we went, and inns with window boxes of geraniums, and colourwashed houses with fretted gables. There were sedate gardens seen over the tops of mellow brick walls, cheerful cottage gardens, and businesslike nursery gardens. The coach paused in the centre of Wickham Market, giving a few minutes in which to enjoy a scene of country shopping: the half-timbered greengrocery, the butcher's striped awning, white shutters and baskets of lobelia and geraniums outside another shop – and no chain stores, plate-glass or strident advertisements.

On once more, through fields of brown barley and dark green spinach, repeatedly crossing rivers or streams. Sometimes walls were made from flints but often the houses were of brick with pantiled roofs and shapely gables – the Dutch influence – or, typical of Suffolk, colourwashed and with well-proportioned sash windows. There was a watermill on one of the rivers, many barns (black-boarded walls and red roofs), and occasional mansions in parks set well back from the road.

The flint church of Saxmundham came into view across the fields before we passed through the town itself – typically East Anglian, with plenty of antique shops and inns among Georgian houses draped with wisteria or creepers.

The fields grew steadily larger as the leafy road wandered on, gently up and down, passing thatched and whitewashed cottages and lodges of flint or of rustic-work. One field was a blazing sheet of poppies; in another strawberries glimmered within the cushions of leaves. Then, past a heath of sand dunes and gorse, came one of the most spectacular sights of the journey: Blythburgh's great church with its huge clerestories running all the way below each side of the roof, so that one can see right through them both and to the blue sky on the other side.

The agricultural landscape changed to marsh, river, and then sea views. Beyond banks of bracken, we could see into Gwatkin Nature Reserve – a place of reeds, streams, butterflies and birds. Even the verges of this stretch of road were an unofficial nature reserve, thronged with wildflowers: their names are enough to evoke an English summer – clover, briar roses, cow parsley, vetch, honeysuckle, buttercups, elderflowers, thistles.

Southwold has not one village green but a dozen, and we passed some on our way in and out. There was a close full of old-fashioned roses, and more than a few glass porches crammed to bursting with pot plants. The wrought-iron signs and striped awnings of the shops, a Victorian lamp-post with dolphins and hanging flower baskets, and rambler roses on sun-baked walls, all contributed to the discreet gaiety of the town. Many houses by the sea have glass verandahs, with canvas chairs facing the morning sunshine.

Southwold

We left the sea behind to follow winding country lanes that took us among oaks, across rivers bright with yellow water-lilies and past gardens of pansies, lupins and delphiniums. Suddenly busy Lowestoft had arrived. We entered it via streets of shabby Victorian guest-houses and ticky-tacky shops. Ahead, cranes and ships' masts showed where the harbour lay, but our route wound through backstreets not along the seafront, to reach the coach station just behind the main (pedestrianized) shopping street of the town.

Lowestoft

Lowestoft, England's most easterly town, has a split personality. There is historic Lowestoft, of which – apart from the fishing quarter – only traces are left. Commercial Lowestoft, which dominates the centre, is a dehumanized mass of fish-freezing factories and fast one-way streets that are a nightmare to motorists and pedestrians alike. Seaside Lowestoft – the southern half – is a pleasant resort with miles of golden sands for a traditional holiday. To this list one can add inland Lowestoft, with Oulton Broad – a watery wilderness as popular as any of the Norfolk Broads. So you need to pick your way carefully in order to find the particular kind of Lowestoft that you want.

Fishing was and is at the heart of Lowestoft, so I chose to go first to the harbour (a short stroll back across the bascule bridge – where I had lunch out on the South Pier, with superb views whilst I ate: a good start). Through big windows, I could see several harbours frequented by kittiwakes; one is used by the Royal Norfolk and Suffolk Yacht Club, with every kind of craft from sportive catamarans to the homely fishing-boats of the longshoremen, lifeboat and pilots' boats; another is for the trawlers. Angling trips set out from here. A huge oil tanker passed by – complete with cranes and helicopter pad – on its way to the North Sea oil rigs (sometimes one can see the massive parts of new rigs being towed out, huge structures as big as factories). Beyond lay the colourful buildings of the various vice-consuls' offices, the Fishermen's Mission and the fish market. One has to book ahead (tel. 0502 65989) to be sure of a place in the very popular tours of this, to see fish being landed and filleted, the ice factory and the auctions; and to go on board one of the trawlers. Occasionally there is a chance to board a visiting warship, or to watch sea-rescue demonstrations. You can buy fish from one of the warehouses in Battery Green Road at the kiosks of the longshoremen; or, as I did, from the historic smokehouse in Raglan Street (a listed building) where herrings are kippered in the proper, traditional way over slow-smouldering piles of oak chips.

The whole story of Lowestoft fishing is told in exhibits at the Maritime Museum near the north end of the seafront (best reached by bus, with glimpses along the way of the steep passageways known as The Scores) where I was lucky to be shown round by one of Lowestoft's characters – ex-skipper Vernil Tuck. It needs time to pore over the miscellany of treasures here – everything from traditional shipwrights' tools to a scale model of a modern oil rig, and poignant bits of wreckage such as the name-board of a trawler – sunk by U-boats – which came ashore 60 years later. There's an array of lifeboat models – and the marble trophy (given by Madame Prunier of fish restaurant fame) which went annually to the skipper who landed most herrings in one night: it is no longer awarded, for the days when some 50,000 were to be netted at a go have long passed.

Outside, scarlet salvias blazed beside a smooth bowling-green overlooked by the old, white lighthouse on a bank above, and in the adjoining suntrap gardens preparations were in progress for an open-air concert. Here is a café, too, and the Sparrows' Nest – formerly the headquarters of the Naval Patrol Service, and now a museum full of mementoes from the time when heroism was a daily occurrence as the small patrol vessels went out to clear mines from the waters of the North Sea during the Second World War. Close by is pretty little Bellevue Park.

The beaches up at this end of Lowestoft are sandy, with dunes, and if you choose to walk further along you come to Gunton Cliffs, a good picnicking spot with paths wandering among the heather and other wildflowers – and, if you get up at dawn, a fine spot from which to see some of the most spectacular sunrises in England.

Most people prefer the sands to the south, however, where there are piers, hotels, bathing huts, traffic-free esplanade, gardens and all the usual amenities of a popular resort. Yet even though I was there on a hot, sunny day in June, I found the miles of golden beaches uncrowded. Plenty of cafés, of course, but you can eat even better (yet still at a modest price) if you head for the Buttery Bar of one of the grand hotels, the Victoria. Those visiting by coach for just a day by the sea would do best to pop onto a bus for the few minutes' ride to Kensington Gardens, which stand just above the centre of the south beach. The Gardens have a Japanese-style rock garden, aviary, lake and café. This south front is where the children's narrow-gauge railway is, and the Punch & Judy show. Anyone choosing this coastline for a taste of the traditional seaside is likely to get plenty of sun, and little rain – but a windbreak is a rather necessary precaution.

As to Lowestoft's other main attraction, there are three ways to reach Oulton Broad: either by taking a leisurely riverside walk to it from Eastern Way, behind the railway station, or by rail, or by bus (no. 683).

The $1\frac{1}{4}$-mile walk is an attractive one, passing through the green acres of Normanston Park which has a wildfowl reserve (and a café) before arriving at the lock which separates the salty Lake Lothing, which is not really a lake but part of the River Waveney, from the fresh waters of Oulton Broad – acres of opportunity for boating or water sports (including world-class powerboat racing). If you do not want the entertainments (including free swimming pool) of the north end, in Nicholas Everitt Park, press on a little farther – to Oulton Broad South, where Marsh Road and a footpath lead to quieter banks from which to watch the sailing-boats go by.

25

Pilgrimage to a Saxon Shrine

Lowestoft – Beccles – Bungay – Ixworth – Bury St Edmunds

This journey was the only one that involved me in a serious delay. The local company's coach (from Yarmouth) simply did not turn up! Apparently its driver, to make up for time lost earlier in his journey, decided to cut Lowestoft (see page 229) out of his route, so there I waited in vain. After much telephoning, a car belonging to the coach company was sent from Yarmouth to carry me to Bury – which I therefore reached two hours late.

The first part of the route is a straight, fast road (between fields, golf course and woods) to Beccles, a market town dominated by the pale grey, 100-foot, detached tower of its church, and by a half-dozen maltings standing in a cluster. Around its Market Square are little Georgian houses with dormers or pantiled roofs. The River Waveney (a pretty sight, with willows, ducks and boats) marks the border between Suffolk and Norfolk.

Beyond here, the marshy land is low-lying – its peaty soil drained by dykes which wildfowl frequent. Willows border the road. As we drove westward, there was a succession of streams, flint churches, crimson roses on whitewashed walls and fields of dozing cows or sugar beet separated by hedges with immense trees (oak and ash, mainly).

Around Bungay's central feature, an octagonal market house with pretty cupola, stalls were spread out. This is a town of mature brick or colourwashed houses, inns with eye-catching signs and decorative wrought iron.

We crossed river after river, and sped by fields of golden grain flecked with poppies or of knee-high grass, then of potatoes – stretching for miles, as far as the eye could see. The size of the fields (and the barns) became immense: at one point the scene was prairie-like, an entire plain filled with wheat.

The church towers along this route were varied – from simple round ones or small hexagons, to huge pinnacled edifices carefully designed from knapped flints contained within a framework of finely dressed white stone. Billingford has an impressive windmill, Scole the great Scole Inn of red brick dated 1655 and with Dutch-style gables, Palgrave is pretty with black-and-white houses, at Wortham thatchers were at work, while in Botesdale – a very long village – every house seemed to be a different colour (various pinks, terracottas and greens); some were extra colourful with wisteria too.

Between the villages, there were high hedges and verges to enjoy – summer's wildflowers major on pinks, reds and mauves by contrast with the white and yellow of spring. Long, luxuriant grass, set swaying by the speed of passing traffic, flashed silvery in the afternoon light.

Ixworth is possibly the prettiest village along this route: a place of leaded windows, hanging flower baskets, and shining brass doorknockers beneath the porches. Roofs were mossy; façades of brick, or oxblood-coloured stucco, or pargetted plaster – some half-hidden by Virginia creeper.

Another windmill, and yet another river (filled with yellow water-lilies), and so on through still lovely scenery – woodland and pastures, flint-and-thatch villages with carved and colourful name-boards, rows of limes or chestnuts – until we came to Bury itself. The road into the town centre passed a terrace of dark green cottages with a dozen steps up to each front door and then some half-timbered houses. To the left were the colossal stone walls of the abbey, supported by great buttresses. The coach station is behind the Market Square and right beside Bury's local museum, which is housed in ancient Moyses Hall, a good place to visit before exploring the town.

Bury St Edmunds

Moyses Hall was so-called after its first owner. Clearly Moyses prospered, for his house was large, built of stone and has survived the years well. In the Norman undercroft, there is now a museum of local life – from medieval stone coffins and crossbows to the penny-farthings and barrel-organs of not so long ago. When I called, a party of schoolchildren with quiz-sheets were more interested, though, in Bury's celebrated murderer and his victim, 'Maria Marten of the Red Barn', to whom a section is devoted; and in the gibbet on which in previous times executed bodies were hung to rot. Plastic badges of Corder, the murderer, and death-masks sell briskly at the souvenir stall – where you can also buy traditional clay pipes with motifs as varied as Fred Archer's head or skull-and-crossbones.

Outside is the Georgian Market Cross building (designed by Adam – now an art gallery), and a mixture of others, old and new. Urns and garlands are on one façade, decorative pargetting on another, which also has historic figures including St Edmund himself. Brutally slain and beheaded in 869 by marauding Vikings, the body of the youthful King Edmund was brought to the monastery here for burial – whereupon miraculous cures at his shrine began to be reported. When the Viking Knut (Canute) ultimately conquered much of England, he compensated the monks for the previous devastation; and later monarchs, doing homage at the shrine, added still further to their rights and riches – hence the increased splendour of the abbey by Norman times, and of the town which the monks then laid out (on a grid pattern) outside it. Wide Churchgate Street, for instance, was the processional way to the shrine. The town and abbey were protected by high walls on three sides and by the river on the fourth. The abbey became a cultural centre (its illuminated manuscripts and other treasures are scattered among the great museums of the world), while the town became rich from the sale of wool cloth and farm produce.

But the prospering citizens began to resent the monks' dictatorship, and the story of bloody deeds in the 13th and 14th centuries makes riveting reading: townsmen looted the abbey, monks slew the townsfolk while in church, there were mass hangings, an abbot was kidnapped and ransomed; the Black Death took a heavy toll, followed by Jack Straw's rebellion, a prior and monks were murdered and punitive fines exacted before the town and the abbey learned how to live in harmony.

I wandered among the ancient sidestreets (Cornhill, The Traverse, Guildhall Street) which had once seen riots more violent than at Toxteth. Now they are relatively quiet roads with shops where one can buy crafts or curios, and studios of silversmiths and glass engravers. The old Corn Exchange is here (you can watch the dealings on Wednesdays), 17th-century Cupola House, the tiny Nutshell pub (smallest in England?), and Georgian or older homes.

Wide Abbeygate Street is a good shopping centre with a fine vista: Ridleys, the grocers, have been here for generations, and my purchases were handed to me in a bag reproducing their advertisement for Christmas 1895 ('. . . toy bonbons, ornamental biscuits in elegant tins . . . confidential orders will receive special attention').

Bury St Edmunds abbey gateway

At the foot of the street is the wide square of Angel Hill, with the impressive abbey gateway opposite, built in 1347 to replace an earlier one destroyed by rioters: portcullis and arrow-slits show that the monks did not intend their new gateway to suffer the same fate. Around this square are a clock museum (in a Queen Anne house owned by the National Trust), the handsome Angel Hotel for good food (a coaching inn when Dickens described it in *Pickwick Papers*), and the 18th-century Athenaeum (its elegant Adam-style assembly rooms still used for various functions) with a charming passageway of pink and green cottages beside it.

So much for secular Bury – now I turned to what is left of the monastery which once made the town great. Today there is little but ruins, surrounded by acres of tranquil gardens: groves, stumps of ancient walls, paths leading down to one of Bury's rivers, the Lark (the other is called, charmingly, the Linnet), pets' corner, café and a rose garden enclosed within yew hedges which American visitors always seek out. It was given by an American author, one of many Americans based near here during the Second World War (his book, *Suffolk Summer*, can be bought at the Tourist Information Centre, which opens up in the abbey gardens every summer).

One often hears American voices in Bury. As a great many Puritans emigrated from Suffolk to America, their genealogically minded descendants head for the town because the county's record office is here. The presidential White House is built of bricks made at Woolpit near Bury. I sat on a metal bench made from an American 'Flying Fortress' to enjoy the scent of all those roses before exploring further, and to reflect on times past in this historic spot.

St Edmund's silver and gold shrine vanished long ago: it was destroyed in a 15th-century fire. Then the rebuilt abbey (which must have been very colourful for there are descriptions of its painted roof, hangings, stained glass and fourteen altars) was largely destroyed by Henry VIII, who looted most of its treasures too. The graves of several abbots survived – and the momentous site where, on a November day in 1214, Cardinal Langton and the barons gathered to swear at the high altar that they would force King John to agree to Magna Carta – as indeed – they did at Runnymede the following June. A stone was set there in 1847 which reads:

> Where the rude buttress totters to its fall,
> And ivy mantles o'er the crumbling wall . . .
> Still we read in deathless records how
> The high-soul'd priest confirm'd the barons' vow:
> And FREEDOM, unforgetful, still recites
> This second birthplace of our native RIGHTS.

There also survived the tremendous span of the abbey's west front – now pierced by sash and bay windows, for houses were built behind it – from which one can look across the green where Elisabeth Frink's 'St Edmund' stands, and directly through the other great Norman gate-tower to the processional route of Churchgate Street.

The church to the right of the green (St James's) is Tudor, extended in the 20th century after it was given cathedral status. The superb nave was the work of John Wastell who designed King's College Chapel, Cambridge. On entering, the church seems to be a sea of blue – a thousand needlepoint kneelers are propped up in the pews, each stitched with an emblem of the school or parish which provided it. This is altogether a colourful church – angels of blue, scarlet and gold soar on high and in the very lovely chapel of St Edmund children have made a long tapestry with scenes from his life.

Out into the sunlight once more, to walk past the overgrown tombstones and medieval charnel house for bones exhumed to accommodate later burials) in order to reach an older church, St Mary's, at the corner of the abbey grounds, and to look at its famous hammerbeam roof with a procession of dark oak angels bearing incense and candles towards the altar.

The body of Henry VIII's sister was re-interred here after he destroyed its original resting place, the abbey itself. The tombstone is plain – unlike that of a local worthy, John Barnet, who long before he died in 1467 had his own bony cadaver carved and sited near his pew. Above is a more cheerful ceiling with emblems associated with him, decorated with flecks of looking-glass and the pious hope 'Grace me govern, God me guide'. The scent of stocks and pinks hung in the air, and the organ was playing softly.

Later, the curfew bell would sound. A draper was lost in the woods one night but St Mary's bell guided him home, so he gave money for a regular curfew bell. Another benefactor, Jankyn Smith, is remembered with a service and an annual distribution of 'cakes and ale' at the Guildhall which he gave to the town.

From here it is only a short stroll to the Theatre Royal, one of the few Regency theatres still surviving (it belongs to the National Trust), and then easily back to the coach station; for the early town planning of the monks means that Bury was and still is a neat and compact town, ideal for anyone to explore on foot.

26

Robin Hood, Byron and D. H. Lawrence

A coaching weekend in Nottingham

Nottingham

I had come to Nottingham for a particular purpose, which makes this chapter different from the others.

In this city – as in many others like it – the big hotels cater mainly for businessmen who sleep there only on weekdays, leaving the hotels empty from Friday to Sunday. Increasingly, therefore, such cities are trying to attract tourists at the weekends – not only by offering 4-star accommodation at a 2-star price but including all sorts of sightseeing opportunities in the offer. And obviously it makes sense to set off for such a weekend by coach not car if, throughout one's stay, one is transported about by coach – with that, too, included in the price. (For this year's 'Away Break' rates and programme, telephone 06073 3695.)

There were about 30 people who had booked, including two children. Like me, many thought of Nottingham as simply an industrial city and were not too sure whether a stay there was going to be entirely a pleasure. It turned out to be a memorable weekend: a really first-rate programme, a generous pack of booklets, good food and service for a reasonable price. And, a happy bonus for me, the Stakis Victoria Hotel, where we were based, is close by the coach station.

On Friday evening, a drink and an illustrated talk brought everyone together before changing for a medieval banquet (anyone so inclined was lent appropriate costume) consisting of game soup, help-yourself spare-ribs in barbecue sauce, a whole poussin, syllabub and cheeses, with mead and mulled wine. Meantime, Friar

Tuck, assorted jesters and knights entertained the company. Even I, who had arrived late and cross, began to cheer up.

Next morning a coach with two lively young couriers took us to the castle perched 150 feet above the city (floodlit at night), past two of the most ancient inns in Britain (the Salutation and the Trip to Jerusalem) and a much-photographed statue of Robin Hood. The so-called castle, surrounded by pretty gardens with a bandstand and viewpoints at every turn, is in fact an Italianate mansion of the late 17th century which was the home of the Duke of Newcastle, replacing the medieval royal castle that used to stand here. An excellent guide took us round, naming the distant buildings and showing us Mortimer's hole, down which the more intrepid tourists can clamber. This is the 100-yard tunnel through which supporters of the boy-king Edward III entered to seize his widowed mother and her lover Mortimer who had been responsible for the particularly horrible murder of his father Edward II. The porous and very soft sandstone on which the castle stands, with former marshes around, is riddled with holes like a sponge: some enlarged as stores, one as a rifle range; the 'blood hole' is where infectious patients used to be isolated; in another, erring monks were imprisoned. Many Nottingham houses have huge cellars gouged from this easily worked stone, all at an unvarying 68°F. There were people living in rock dwellings right up to 1968.

Severns Building, Nottingham

The house is now an arts museum. We spent an hour and a half exploring just a few of its treasures – from kitchen gear of 1320 (pipkins, pitchers and – for breadmaking – pancheons) to the largest hoard of medieval gold ever found. For its sheer beauty, the collection of glass held many of us; and there is an exceptional collection of antique jewellery too, including an unforgettable pair of earrings, each with a decorated jasper urn captive inside a crystal bubble. Strangest of all: a 17th-century tortoiseshell casket containing twenty mourning slides – tiny mementoes, with initials and skeletons or other symbols of death, to be worn on a ribbon around the neck. On through galleries of silver, pottery, militaria and paintings we wandered, to end up with cups of coffee in the museum's attractive buttery, which has far views through arched windows, before walking downhill to the cobbled lane of old houses where the costume museum stands, with the Lace Centre in a half-timbered house close by.

Lace-making has been important in Nottingham for centuries; and this centre is the place to go for an appropriate souvenir (anything from a wall-hanging of lace down to a collar, frilly garters or handkerchief – or else buy a bobbin kit to make your own). In the museum there are period room-settings to show off costumes – the Georgian squire with port and pipe, crinolined Victorian ladies among their whatnots and davenports. Galleries of fal-lals are packed with fans, undies, handbags and buttons: the fans with microscopic embroidery on muslin, or made of fretworked horn, or with paintings on feathers; cotton drawers of 1900 succeeded by the pink silk crêpe of the 1930s. How many pricked fingers went into the making of schoolchildren's test pieces (meticulous darning and button-holing); and whose eyesight was strained while stitching by candlelight the vast tapestry map that shows all the villages of Nottinghamshire in 1632?

Only a few yards away, the old Brewhouse also has a story to tell. As well as relics from its brewing days exhibited in cellars gouged from the sandstone, it recreates the daily life of a century or more ago in a bedroom, two kitchens, and a chemist's shop with blue jars and green bottles, essences of frangipane and patchouli, pills (Zox's 'death to pain') and potions (Rooke's Solar Elixir). There is a leisure room with a strange cross-section of pastimes (half-forgotten children's games like diabolo and bandalore, a box of cockfighting spurs). One room is devoted to a history of shaving, another is full of Valentines. Mementoes of the Second World War are in yet another of those famous sandstone cellars below the house.

But I think everyone's favourite among this cluster of museums is the old School House, a few yards away. It recreates one of the first 'ragged schools' (set up before compulsory education, when the first task of any school was to provide adequate clothing), and is now filled with trifles salvaged from the past. As we lifted up each desk-lid in turn – ink-stained, and carved with the names of long-departed Terrys and Henrys and Hughs – we found inside every one a different display. There were examples of copper-plate handwriting, smudged exercise-books devoted to labours with vulgar fractions, and well-thumbed atlases with half the world coloured an imperial red.

It was time to embark in the coach again, to hurry along Mansfield Road (where many of Nottingham's smaller hotels are) and so out into the countryside for an excellent light lunch with aperitif and wine at Newstead Abbey, reached at the end of a long winding drive flanked by brilliantly colourful rhododendrons.

The Abbey ruins, and the house built onto them, are surrounded by a vast park with lake and waterfall (at each end of the lake is a mock fort, built by the fifth lord who conducted miniature naval battles on the water), a rose garden and a Japanese garden. Little remains of the abbey, destroyed on the orders of Henry VIII, except for the very wide and beautiful west front. The estate was bought by the Byron family who built their house around the former cloister, resulting in an unusual mixture of monastic and domestic architecture. The poet Byron loved the family home but, with debts mounting, was forced to sell it in 1817.

We entered through the former crypt where painted alabaster monuments are housed under the rib vaulting (Nottingham was once a centre for alabaster carving). In the former cloisters is a herb garden with fountain, and the medieval chapter house still stands, too – now a chapel, colourfully decorated with stencilled flowers and emblems. There is a small who-did-what exhibition of monastic life, detailing the roles of cellarer, infirmarer, precentor (librarian), sacrist (maintenance), kitchener, succentor (ceremonial); and the daily routine, from midnight mass right through to 9 pm each day.

We moved on, in time as well as space, to the heyday of the Byrons – with the poet's lordly fourposter (swagged and tasselled, gold and black) and elegant wallpapers transforming what had been rugged stone walls in monastic days. The most interesting room is the Byron gallery with some of the poet's clothes, exotic costumes, sports gear (although lame, he was skilled in fencing, shooting, swimming and boxing), memorabilia of the many women in his life, his manuscripts and his racy letters (even his handwriting is impetuous). Of Newstead Abbey itself, in the years when he could no longer afford its upkeep, he wrote:

> Through the cracks in these battlements loud the winds
>   whistle,
> For the hall of my fathers is gone to decay;
> And in yon once gay garden the hemlock and thistle
> Have choak'd up the rose, which late bloom'd in the way . . .

There was still more to see, such as the crimson salon with aquamarine ceiling and panels of birds and flowers, where concerts are held (Byron's own Hebrew Melodies are sometimes played on a piano of his time, or Christmas carols sung, for instance); and the great baronial hall with banners and minstrel's gallery. But we had to press on.

The route to Sherwood Forest was an attractive one: bluebells and broom blossomed in the wild, lilac and peonies in gardens. There were occasional glimpses of collieries' winding-gear beyond the trees. Walkers in orange anoraks pored over damp maps during a brief shower. Bowlers and cricket players were out in their white clothes undeterred by the rain; and a bride in white posed at the church door to be photographed with her groom. On the fringe of Sherwood Forest a fair was in full swing. Typical Saturday scenes.

We parked close to the Forest's interpretation centre and café (from which nature trails and guided walks set out) before scattering separately among the great oaks and yews of the forest. Most visitors headed for the 1,000-year-old Major Oak (within the hollow 36-foot trunk of which Robin Hood reputedly hid), after going through the labyrinth of the Robin Hood exhibition which tells in displays and ballads all the old legends of this favourite among folk heroes. Maid Marian is there of course ('a smurkynge wench . . . none of these coy dames') but so also is more substantial evidence about real life in the 1320s: the miller's work, village relationships, inside the castle, the use of the longbow. There is an audiovisual show, too, to explain the life of the 400-acre forest today: part of it is a Site of Special Scientific Interest with unusual insects, deer, and sixty species of birds (best spotted in April when the trees are not too leafy). Alas, since this visit vandals set the

Major Oak on fire, jeopardizing its survival. There was an hour-and-a-half for wandering before returning to the coach.

We went back to Nottingham via beautiful Clumber Park (National Trust) where drifts of bluebells could be seen in the woods beyond the avenues of limes, to return to the hotel for dinner. Most of us felt it had been a full day; but some still had enough energy left to see Danny La Rue at the theatre, others to explore a few of the innumerable pubs which are a feature of Nottingham, noted for the number of its breweries.

Next morning, we were joined by two honorary officers of the D. H. Lawrence Society, to point out as we travelled the villages, farms and churches which appear (under other names) in Lawrence's books. 'Nottingham, that dismal town . . .', he had written – but he loved the country around it. We saw, in the city, the college where he got his teaching diploma (an unprecedented achievement for a miner's son); went past the park where the annual Goose Fair is held, described in his story about the fair, and paused in the village of Cossall, described in his book *The Rainbow*. Here stands the home of Louise Burrows who was his fiancée for two years: the Burrows (whom he renamed Brangwyns), the church and the nearby marsh are all in the book. In the church we saw carvings made by Louise's father, listened to the organist playing (the church is affiliated to the Royal School of Church Music), and then strolled among the old cottages and lozenge-paned almshouses so well preserved that the village recently won a European conservation award. It would have been easy to spend several hours here, exploring the footpaths and canalside.

A little way on we had views of the spot where Lawrence parted for ever from Jessie Chambers (Miriam in *Sons and Lovers*), Greasley Church and the surrounding hayfields (described in *Love among the Haystacks*), Moorgreen Reservoir (the drowning in *Women in Love* was based on an actual incident here) and the farm where he stayed to recuperate when 19 and found so much happiness with the Chambers family. 'That is the country of my heart,' he wrote. 'The little red farm, where I got my first incentive to write. Jessie launched me like a princess launching a ship.'

We paused, too, outside Moorgreen Colliery (the 'mine among the cornfields' in *Sons and Lovers*), before visiting the miner's cottage, one of a terrace, where Lawrence lived from the age of 2 to 6. It has been furnished with items from the 1880s given by local people, many of whom remembered the Lawrence household. Gas lights burn, there is a rag rug on the tiled floor in front of the range and a tin bath hangs on the wall. The privy is still at the end of the garden. (The upper floor is a self-catering flat, available to rent for holidays: 051 653 8710.)

Lawrence's mother insisted on a move to a better house and we looked at this too, with its valley of 'one vast cockleshell' of green, where he lived until 18; at the Three Tuns (which he renamed the Moon and Stars in *Sons and Lovers* and which now has a D. H. Lawrence bar lined with memorabilia); at Greasley Board School which he attended; at his aunt's cottage (this he put into *The Widowing of Mrs Holroyd* – by now, we were all wishing we had brushed up our reading before we came!); and finally – after a light lunch – we stopped at his birthplace in Eastwood.

Here his mother had a small shop in the front parlour for Nottingham lace and babywear which she made. The window has again been filled with such things, including a tucked bonnet bought from her. There's an inkwell Lawrence made from a lump of coal, miner's kneepads and 'snap-tin' (for bread-and-dripping or bread-and-jam) and a photograph of Mrs Lawrence in her thirties looking as careworn as if she were 60. The house is a small Lawrence museum; and around the corner is a cluster of craft workshops of which Lawrence would surely have approved. We left Lawrence country for the last visit of the weekend: Wollaton Hall. This tremendous Elizabethan mansion now houses a museum – or, rather, two. In the outhouses is an industrial museum (the first lace-making machine, attacked by Luddites in 1808; and early telephones and typewriters – among much else); while in the stately rooms themselves is a huge natural history museum of considerable distinction. There are some bizarre combinations – a stuffed giraffe soaring above one's head is dwarfed by the height of the hammerbeam roof, embellished with grotesque heads, in the great hall where it stands. The stuffed badgers in their setts seem extraordinarily real – while the bees and ants *are* real, viewed through perspex domes or panels, as busy as Nottingham streets at the rush hour. The 800-acre grounds alone deserve a day's visit: gardens with statues and fountains, deer park, a lakeside nature trail, camellia house and varied events from flower shows to veteran car parades or international archery contests.

It had been a weekend packed with incident and variety. Exhausted but well pleased, we piled back into the coach to return to the Victoria Hotel for a substantial tea, with just enough time left for me to catch my homeward-bound coach. Of all the towns I had so far visited for this book, Nottingham had been the greatest surprise: the one at which I had expected least and found so much!

IMPROVING BUS SERVICES

How you can help: see page 215

27

Non-Stop to the West Country

London – Plymouth

The coach service to Plymouth used to take 6 hours, stopping on the way. But in 1981, the 'Rapide' service was introduced; and this clipped 2 hours off the long journey. So popular was this development that other Rapide services were introduced, now serving over 200 towns and cities.

Since there are no pauses along the way, Rapide coaches have some seats replaced by a cubicle containing flush w.c. and washbasin; and a uniformed hostess plies one with various hot and cold drinks, soup, sandwiches and other snacks. On two small screens overhead (one up front and one mid-way) a film is shown once the journey is under way: a rather old film, as a rule. On my trip, those who preferred silence were outvoted by those wanting the video turned on (some coaches have individual headphones); but as the windows were not curtained it was still possible to enjoy the view instead – which I preferred to watching a rather youthful Henry Fonda through the magenta thicket of two punk heads just in front of me. Certainly these diversions help to while away the boring bits of journeys which are inevitable when one starts out from central London and has all the suburbs to get through before the countryside starts. (Reading, letter-writing or a cassette player with lightweight headphones are alternatives – if that lost art, contemplation, is not enough.)

The route to the West Country is mostly along motorways: the M4 goes through Berkshire and Wiltshire to the Bristol Channel, and then the coach turns south along the M5 into Somerset to reach Devonshire's less busy roads.

Berkshire's landscape is sedate rather than spectacular. As we passed, rooks flew up from old trees burdened with ivy, pheasants pottered among the furrows of a newly ploughed field and, on a series of water-skiing lakes created from disused gravel-pits, coots swam busily about their affairs. This is an area where sandy soil (supporting pines, larches and silver birch) is succeeded by chalk, which yields up flints that go to make the characteristic walls of the county. Winter was only slowly giving way to spring: tender green shoots of wheat were thrusting up and daffodils grew wild on some banks, but still there was smoke drifting from many a cottage chimney.

In the distance rose the tower blocks of busy Swindon, slightly tinted by the sun's rays, but once they were out of sight the scene became wholly rural. We pressed on through green hills. More than once, we crossed the winding Avon, running clear and calm. Fields had dry-stone walls or hedges with hawthorn in full bloom, the bright yellow flowers of coltsfoot at their feet. Then the sea came into view, and the high cranes of Avonmouth, Bristol's seaport.

Again, the local architecture changed with the changing geology: church towers, high and battlemented, showed the red sandstone at its most striking. The scenery became more dramatic as the route rose up above the vast plain, with great cuttings hewn from rock to give the road an easy passage through the hills. Down steep and wooded hillsides we went, into Somerset, county of rich brown earth and willow-lined streams. In this part of it, once marshy, great fields have been reclaimed for cows to graze on, but all are still criss-crossed with drainage ditches. Often streams ran beside the road, clogged by reeds or clumps of bulrushes (more accurately, reedmace), no longer brown or velvety but with their seedheads burst wide open and looking like ragged mops. The trees were still bare enough to reveal great round clusters of mistletoe high up, but in the fields there were already buttercups and daisies.

Around Tiverton we passed cider orchards, soon to become a spectacle of pink blossoms; and then the flat landscape gave way to gently rounded hills through which the River Exe winds – wide enough for a small cargo ship to be making its way, as well as sailing-boats.

The coach swept across the heath with far-distant views and through the pines and birches of Exeter Forest. There were kingcups glowing at the brim of a pond, an old stone dovecote, cows patiently waiting to be milked and a medieval bridge before the rural tranquillity changed: a huge quarry of granite dominated one side of the road, clawed out of the hillside. But this was soon behind us, and there were still country scenes to enjoy – a donkey in an orchard, black-faced lambs, white farms with slate roofs, stone barns and stony beds to the many bubbling streams hereabouts, and in the background the wilderness of the moors – until at last the unappealing outskirts of Plymouth enveloped us.

Despite the speed of the coach (which regularly overtook others on the road) it had been a very smooth ride, the four hours hardly seeming so long.

Plymouth

Bretonside is the name of the street where the coaches stop, and this name explains in a word much of Plymouth's history. Facing Brittany and, beyond it, Spain, the town was vulnerable to attack from either of these countries. The Bretons so frequently set fire to houses behind the harbour that this area became known as 'the Breton side'. Right up to this century, Plymouth's history was therefore dominated by the need for sea defence against the French or the Spanish, which explains much of what one sees when walking around the older parts.

But it was from the air, and from a German enemy, that the most recent attacks came, devastating huge areas (which is why the heart of Plymouth consists only of modern buildings). Just north of the coach station the shell of a bombed 17th-century church has been retained as a memorial to that destruction.

To find what remains of historic Plymouth by the old harbour, I walked south – making a slight detour to visit the Merchant's House in St Andrew's Street first, because inside this fine half-timbered Tudor building is a well-mounted exhibition that explains how the town developed, from prehistoric times onwards. In the Middle Ages it was merely an outpost of Plympton (now just a suburb) where a great priory stood. Henry VIII improved Plymouth's fortifications and Charles II extended them still more. Now the action is farther afield – at the Devonport end of the town where from a great naval dockyard, many of the task force ships sailed to the Falklands in 1982.

There's a replica of Drake's drum in the Merchant's House ('If the Dons sight Devon, I'll quit the port of heaven, An' drum them up the Channel as we drummed them long ago'): the real drum is at his home, Buckland Abbey. The Civil War siege of Plymouth by the Royalists is re-enacted in a diorama of model soldiers; and I particularly enjoyed mementoes of the merchant himself, mayor of Plymouth in 1601, who owed his wealth and honours to the capture of Spanish treasure-ships – until he was reported to be 'unfit for his work, being old and corpulent'.

Nearby Southside Street is the oldest lane in the Barbican quarter ('barbican' means defence-works), lined with interesting shops and restaurants, historic inns, craftsmen's studios and old warehouses that were once stacked with casks of wine. The distinctive Plymouth gin is distilled here in ancient premises that incorporate a medieval hall once used by Huguenot refugees, and which can be visited. To each side are narrow cobbled opes – the local name for openings or alleyways between the high stone houses.

The granite quay of the Barbican overlooks a harbour busy with fishing-boats, and I bought plaice from a waterfront fish market which looks uncommonly like a Victorian railway station (not surprising since its designer was a railway engineer). Across the water is the big 'China House' where the first real china was made in England from fine white Cornish clay, lovely examples of which are displayed at the city museum. French prisoners of war were housed here during the Napoleonic Wars (some whiled away the years by making superb models of ships, or of working guillotines! – from meat-bones – and these too are now in the museum). There's a story here of a ghost that cries 'Au secours!' A little further along is a jetty covered with plaques recording many historic embarkations from this point. The most celebrated of all the migrants were, of course, the Pilgrim Fathers whose last sight of England in 1620 was from the *Mayflower* as she drew away from Plymouth. Over the *Mayflower* memorial fly the Union Jack flag and the Stars-and-Stripes, while a board on the house where the pilgrims stayed before embarking lists the names of those who sailed and their trades.

A narrow flight of steps opposite leads up to all that is left of Plymouth's earliest, medieval fortifications and thence to the famous Hoe (meaning 'headland').

The Hoe, too, is only a short walk from the coach station (via Hoegate Street) or from the Barbican (up steep Lambhay Hill). After the jostle in the narrow lanes of the Barbican, I found it a

The Barbican, Plymouth

relief to be up here where all is space and light – a tremendous expanse of feltlike lawns and flowerbeds with the great blue panorama of Plymouth Sound spread out before me, and sea breezes making the row of flags of all nations flutter gaily. This headland is deservedly world-famous. Often in the past it was the gathering place for citizens when an attack was expected, for archery-practice, or to watch executions. Now it is a promenade for holidaymakers picnicking on the lawns as they watch warships and sailing-boats in the Sound far below, strolling to look at the many memorials (to Drake and other Devon sea heroes) or climbing up inside Smeaton's red-and-white lighthouse of 1769, brought back here simply as a landmark when a new lighthouse replaced it on the lonely Eddystone rock 14 miles out to sea. Eddystone (meaning a rock round which the ocean currents eddy) is where the very first lighthouse out at sea was built in the 17th century. This one was destroyed, but Smeaton's – designed to the shape of an oak trunk, and made of interlocking granite blocks – was impregnable: storms split the rock but not the building. When a new lighthouse replaced it on another rock, it was brought here: a much-loved symbol of England, which used to be on our pennies until metrication changed them. Exhibits from both these early lighthouses are in the city museum.

At the Barbican end of the Hoe is the great, angular Citadel built by Charles II (and still garrisoned – you may see gun-training or other exercises going on) from the 60-foot ramparts of which I had even finer views of Eddystone, of Drake's Island, and of Rennie's mile-long granite breakwater completed in 1841, which is what turned stormy Plymouth Sound into a sheltered anchorage. It, and Drake's memorial, are floodlit in summer. (Other good sea viewpoints are the buffet-bar at the top of the Holiday Inn, and the top of the Mayflower Hotel. From the back of the Citadel, I enjoyed views over the city's rooftops to Dartmoor.) Below the Citadel is Plymouth's world-famous aquarium, belonging to the Marine Biological Association.

The other end of the Hoe stretches out in front of a terrace of stately stucco mansions, one of which belonged to Lord and Lady Astor when they were the city's lord mayor and MP respectively (this, and some of Nancy Astor's emeralds, were given to the city for use on ceremonial occasions). It is in this direction that some of the best hotels and guest-houses lie.

Drake's statue stands on the site of that famous game of bowls, and bowls are still played on the Hoe. It is also the place where all the world and his wife congregate to watch sea races and the air show; or the Lord Mayor's procession wending its way along the promenade each year.

Standing in the centre of the Hoe and looking inland, I saw a tremendous vista cutting a green swathe right through the modern heart of Plymouth to the rail station nearly a mile away – lawns, flowerbeds and fountains all the way. This imaginative use of space right in the middle of the busy city was made possible only because Plymouth was so dreadfully flattened by the bombing of the Second World War. Off Armada Way lie the principal shops, the Tourist Information Centre, the Guildhall with its stained-glass windows, and the high-rise Civic Centre, the rooftop of which provides yet another of Plymouth's spectacular viewpoints (there are often exhibitions in the Centre). Royal Parade crosses Armada Way: at its west end is a theatre which puts on plays of West End standard; to the east (in the direction of the coach station once more) is St Andrew's church with the Prysten (priests') House behind it. The parish was originally under the control of the big priory at Plympton and it is generally believed that the prior used this house on his visits, dispensing justice in its galleried court and using the ancient oak throne still on view. The old lattice-windowed house was well worth a visit, and in one room there was an exhibition of herbs (which one could buy). In another, a team of volunteers was hard at work on a 240-foot tapestry telling the history of Plymouth – they had been at it for years. And in a third was a great model of Plymouth in 1620, the layout of its fortifications quite different but the Barbican lanes much the same as now.

The medieval church had to be rebuilt after bombing, but some of its monuments survived. Catherine of Aragon worshipped here, so did the Pilgrim Fathers. Drake's wife was buried here, and the great east window is a memorial to Nancy Astor. I liked two modern touches: the kneelers, each embroidered with a different wildflower of Devon, and the sound of the carillon floating out over the city.

Annually the American ambassador or consul comes to this church, and to the 'Door of Unity' by which the Prysten House is entered, for a special service. It commemorates the honour paid by the English to an American naval commander killed in the 1813 war between the two nations, who is buried beside that door.

Plymouth's city museum (a few minutes' walk from the coach station) is exceptionally good – and varied. I spent a long time in the wildlife gallery where a typical rock-pool has been created with live gobies, hermit-crabs and brittle-stars; and was absorbed by the display of colourful limestones, each from a different local quarry, which I had been seeing on the façades of banks and other buildings in Plymouth. Upstairs is a silver replica of the 1698 Eddystone lighthouse, and a cutaway model of Smeaton's version – complete down to every bucket and bunk-bed. The Eddystone men were given medals exempting them from being press-ganged; the only one to survive the centuries is on display. Drake's silver-and-gold 'cup' is there: a globe supported by sea gods, commemorating his voyage round the world. There's a fine collection of Plymouth china; and another of Lely and Van Dyck portraits – including one of Philip III's son as a ruffed and bejewelled toddler in the 17th-century version of a pushchair. Altogether the museum is well worth a lingering visit.

28
Where Spring Comes Early

Plymouth – Liskeard – St Austell – Truro – Redruth – Penzance

The coach, once it was beyond the outskirts of Plymouth (see previous chapter), crossed the Devon-Cornwall boundary at one of the best viewpoints in the West Country – the long bridge over the River Tamar. This is side by side with Brunel's monumental achievement, the iron railway bridge on which he proudly had his name inscribed in huge letters (even though it is named after Prince Albert), together with the date when it was completed – 1859.

To allow naval ships to pass freely, the bridge had to be 100 feet above the river and cross it with a 300-foot span – but for reasons of economy, it is only wide enough to carry one rail-track. Travellers by train do not, of course, have a view of the bridge but one gets a splendid sight of it from the coach, and of its two 1,000-ton, curved trusses from which the track is suspended. When the first truss was floated out to be raised into position, a vast crowd watched this feat in a dramatic hush (Brunel insisted on silence) until, the tricky manoeuvre completed, a Royal Marines band burst into 'See the Conquering Hero Comes', accompanied by a storm of cheers. Later, a popular song celebrated the opening of the bridge with a chorus:

> From all parts of England you'll now have a chance
> To travel by steam right down to Penzance.

But Brunel the tireless did not live to make that journey across the bridge himself: worn out, he died that year aged only 53.

From high up on the modern road bridge, the sailing-boats and barges on the wide blue waters of the Tamar far below looked like toys. Then on once more through undistinguished suburbs until the countryside was reached, with glimpses of stony-bedded streams, occasional watermills and medieval stone bridges. Often on the horizon there appeared distant church towers standing four-square and pinnacled, distinctive landmarks typical of this part of Cornwall. These medieval granite towers have a fortress-like strength about them, but are lightened by the delicate touch of the little crocketed spires that adorn the top. Signposts point to villages (hidden in the folds of the hills) that have splendidly idiosyncratic names such as Doddycross and Merrymeet, Widegates and Catchfrench.

The coach ran fast and smooth along a stretch of dual carriageway with fine views, to pause in the pleasant town of Liskeard where even modest terraced houses have pillared doorways, and the central square is surrounded by early Victorian houses stuccoed or slate-hung, with handsome detailing of doorways and broad eaves. Its fine church is the second largest in Cornwall. 'Lis' is Cornish for capital, and the place was once the capital of a Cornish king.

Onward once more, and as the road curved this way and that it brought into view white farms sheltering between hills and a huge railway viaduct of eight colossal stone arches spanning a deep valley. When Brunel built the railway to Penzance, he had to construct more than three dozen such viaducts – in timber, replaced only in stone when the line was doubled in 1908 – which were so dizzying that many people refused to travel across them.

As we went further west, the winding route grew steadily more attractive, with wild daffodils and primroses by the thousand growing on the banks by the road. The trees were in bud, cottagers busy in their gardens, lambs cavorting in the fields. The stone hereabouts is reddish, like the soil, and the dry-stone walls built from it and then topped with green turf soon attract colonies of equally colourful wildflowers. Woodlands alternated with uninterrupted vistas ending in a blue haze of hills far away. I was travelling in April: tulips and tulip trees were in bloom, camellias and flowering cherries too – about a month earlier than in more northerly parts of England.

Beyond St Austell, we continued alternately to zoom down into valleys and strive up hills. Now the views were of moors and of a strange white lunar landscape beyond, created by the immense tips (or 'burrows') from the mining of china-clay, one of Cornwall's major industries. The tips rear up in strange shapes, some like the pyramids of Egypt, one like Cape Town's Table Mountain. The fine white clay is simply granite that water has decomposed. It was discovered in Cornwall in 1746 by William Cookworthy and now a million tons a year are exported: no country except China itself has such fine china-clay. But for every ton produced, five tons of waste are added to mountainous burrows.

Then, throughout the rest of the journey, there began to appear another of Cornwall's unique landscape features: the tall, abandoned chimneys of engine-houses, often ivy-covered and ruined, of the abandoned mines. From Roman times or before, Cornwall was mined for its tin and other minerals, fortunes being made or lost as new seams were opened or old ones ran out.

The road wound its way on through lush green fields and hedges with tall trees. The coach's passing blew off the gossamer seed-heads of dandelion-clocks. Occasionally there was (another very Cornish touch) a stone cross by the roadside, continuing a tradition that goes back to Celtic times. Through Trevellick (a picturesque street of cottages and small Georgian houses) we went, past a wide river bordered by reed-beds and then along a serpentine road which wound as much as the twinkling stream with which it kept company. The hilltop views were superb, once we had edged our way past a minibus of 'Cornish Tartan Majorettes' from America which, laden with all their gear, was making heavy work of the hills.

Soon the coach rumbled over the granite setts of Truro, to draw up by Lemon Quay (from which there is a good view, beyond the roofs, of the cathedral's three spires – built a century ago). The county town of Cornwall, Truro is thronged with people on market day (Wednesday). An inn and a street are named after the 18th-century Admiral Boscawen, known as 'Old Dreadnought', whose family seat was nearby.

The onward road continued over moors, still with those white china-clay tips in sight. 'Wheal Jane' and 'Wheal Busy' and 'Wheal Tehidy', said the signposts – wheal means mine. The ruined tin-mine chimneys were all about us now.

At last, a glimpse of blue sea to the right – it came and went in a tantalizing flash. We were entering an industrial part of Cornwall, with few fields or woods from here on.

Redruth is the 'capital' of the tin-mining area of Cornwall. One of its most striking buildings is the huge Wesleyan chapel built in 1826: Cornwall has been strongly Methodist ever since Wesley rode on horseback, over the rough moorland tracks of the 18th century, to make repeated missionary tours throughout the country, preaching in the open air and attracting a tremendous following.

Up on the high barren tor of Carn Brea (the Cornish words mean rocky hill), where granite boulders jut through the sparse heath, stand a castle and a monument which Sir John Betjeman likened to a bedroom candlestick and candle. They kept appearing and disappearing from view as the coach wound its way on. The castle is a sham 'gothick' folly, and the pillar is dedicated to a local benefactor, who died in 1835 and was buried in St Paul's Cathedral.

On the way to Camborne we passed other monuments to mining past and present – a particularly fine engine-house with flywheel (preserved by the National Trust), more of those ever-present chimneys, and the important School of Mines at South Crofty. Camborne itself, with its terraces of granite cottages for the miners (and yet another Wesleyan chapel of some grandeur), was the birthplace of Trevithick whose statue stands there, and after whom a local pub is named. He was the youthful inventor of the first railway engine which, in 1804, pre-dated Stephenson's by ten years though Stephenson got all the fame. Perhaps more significantly, Trevithick developed the beam-engines for which Cornwall became famous. By pumping water out of the many mines that would otherwise have remained unworkable, these engines completely transformed the scale of tin-mining in Cornwall at the beginning of the 19th century.

And so the last lap of the journey was reached. From the lofty windows of the coach, I could see over even south Cornwall's high hedges – green banks topped with bushes of golden gorse. Approaching Hayle and its estuary (hayle is Cornish for estuary) there are colossal towans in the distance – sand dunes higher than houses – and then (within an unlovely suburban sprawl) the coach ran alongside the river itself, where small boats were moored by stone jetties. Because the road twists itself round, the coach went twice under the same stone railway bridge here. The tide was out, so waders and gulls were busy feeding off the mudflats. Two swans sailed out on the steely-blue water in the distance. (See also page 141.)

After that it was a quick ride into Penzance, past houses alternating with fields (a fairground had taken over here, and 'Cockrell's Thrilling Musical Rides for All' was going merrily round). The road passes the heliport where nearby cows grazed unconcerned by the noisy comings and goings, and skirts the wide bay with the castle on St Michael's Mount dramatically dominating the scene; and so to Penzance, stopping right by the harbour.

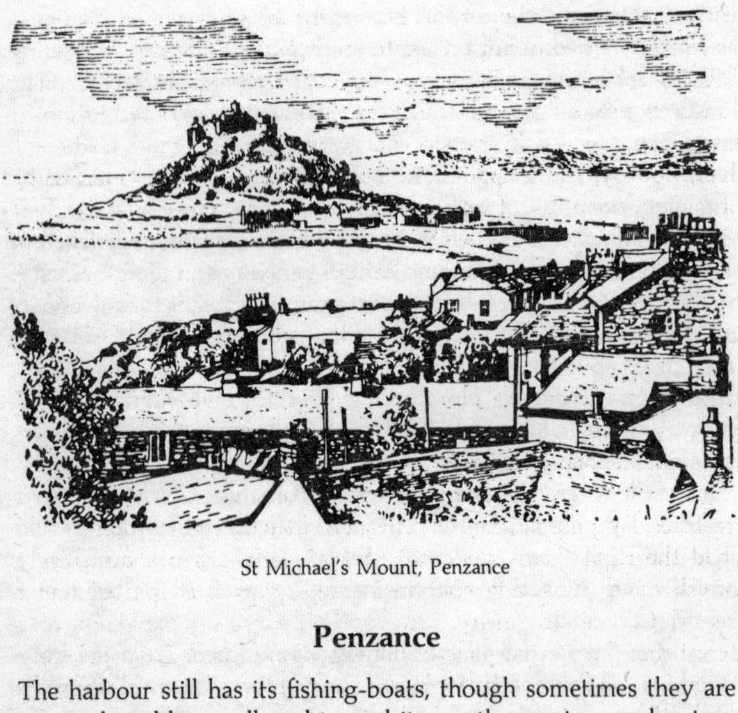

St Michael's Mount, Penzance

Penzance

The harbour still has its fishing-boats, though sometimes they are outnumbered by small yachts; and it sees the comings and goings of the sleek white ferry taking visitors across to the Scilly Isles. The lighthouse pier – with another great granite jetty – shelters the harbour waters from what can at times be a very wild sea beyond. Once there was so much trade that a dozen countries kept consuls in Penzance. Once, tens of thousands of migrants departed from this harbour to start a new life in Australia and America. Now its liveliest scenes are early in the year when loads of narcissi and daffodils from the Scilly Isles are unloaded here.

I walked along the quay, looking down into the dry dock where ships come for repair and at the huge red buoys brought in to the Trinity House depot for their regular overhaul. Out on Battery Rocks a sea-water bathing-pool has taken over the site where once guns pointed out to sea, and is overlooked by terraced gardens on the hillside. Penzance rises up steeply, and the only level walk is along the seafront. The early Victorian promenade extends westward nearly all the way to the next town – the busy little fishing-port of Newlyn (see page 148) – from which one can easily take a bus back. The beach here is pebbly – for safe, sheltered sands, one has to go in the other direction, towards Mount's Bay.

Facing the sea is the Barbican crafts centre which was previously old warehouses but has now been turned into a series of workshops where you can watch craftsmen at work and buy their wares – silver, pottery, leather and what-have-you. Below is an aquarium containing examples of all the local fish – flat turbot undulating their way into the sandy bed to lie there camouflaged; great eels in tunnels specially made for them in rocks (head protruding at one end, tail at the other); yellow seahorses; anemones very, very slowly going walkabout; and crawfish that seem all eyes and feelers. An excited family came in, bearing a more exotic find – a two-foot leathery turtle they had just discovered washed up from afar on the beach (mum had inadvertently sat on it), for which they hoped the aquarium would find a home.

At the far end of the quay is a narrow lane called Coinage Hall Street, recalling the heyday of Penzance when, in the 17th century, it had the right (like Camborne) to assay and coin tin from the Cornish mines. The lane continues steeply upwards into Chapel Street, lined with so many 17th- and 18th-century buildings of interest that there is a 6-page leaflet describing them. They include restaurants, bookshops, guest-houses and antique or crafts shops. Among them are a Georgian hotel (the Union) from the gallery of which the victory at the Battle of Trafalgar was first announced; the Nautical Museum, which not only has finds from historic wrecks but a full-size section (four decks) of an 18th-century man-o'-war; the 13th-century Turk's Head with log fires and a smuggler's tunnel leading from its cellar bar; the beamy 16th-century Admiral Benbow inn and restaurant, crammed with colourful figureheads and other marine salvage ; and the most curious of all, the Egyptian House – named for the bizarre decoration of the façade, which looks like a colourful stage-set for

Aïda. It was built in 1835 to house a geological museum, fell into decay, and was restored only ten years ago: the National Trust has a shop below and there are holiday flats above. Just off Chapel Street is the 'pen sans' (holy headland) that gave Penzance its name, where the parish church now stands on the site of an ancient chapel to which Chapel Street originally led. The present granite church, built in 1832, is a charming example of gothick architecture, and from its peaceful, leafy churchyard there are fine sea views to sit and enjoy. (For more about Penzance, see pages 143–6, 258–60.)

Also within short (though sometimes steep) walking distance of the coach station is a network of quiet roads with pretty houses, interspersed with small parks that were once the gardens of mansions. I found the small 'Town Trail' leaflet a great help in wending my way through the maze of Regency and early Victorian terraces in stucco or granite to discover the pretty villas of Regent Square, the Morrab Gardens and their graceful fountain, some fine Georgian houses, Penlee Park (which has tree ferns and other subtropical plants in its fifteen acres, and an excellent museum of local history and wildlife) and ultimately emerging on to busy Alverton Road where the Geological Museum stands: well worth a visit for it illuminates so much that is the essential Cornwall, its rocks and minerals. From here it is not far to get back to the harbour and coach station, via Market Jew Street ('jew' is Cornish for Tuesday) which is dominated by a statue of Sir Humphrey Davy, inventor of the miners' safety-lamp, standing on the site of the house where he began his experiments.

29

A Cathedral of Tragic Queens

London – Peterborough

This northward route is one of the few that is interesting even during the first hour spent getting out of London from Victoria. It does not go through industrial or down-at-heel suburbs as some do, but skirts Belgravia, Mayfair, St John's Wood and Hampstead.

The coach started its journey along Elizabeth Street – still flanked by elegant terraces with wrought-iron balconies and window-boxes of trailing plants. This is a street of little hotels (handy for non-Londoners who are using Victoria coach station); among them are small shops of quality and bistro-style restaurants. Then the coach joined the traffic inching its way past the Rifle Brigade memorial and up Grosvenor Place which has the high garden wall of Buckingham Palace on one side and prestigious buildings of Portland stone and polished granite on the other – embassies, the headquarters of British Steel and suchlike. It skirted the green island of Wellington Place with its memorials to the Duke of Wellington and other heroes of battle; in the middle is the Wellington Arch of 1823 (the figure on top, of Peace in a chariot, was added just before the First World War). It sped past the Ionic colonnade (1828) of Hyde Park Gate, with copies from the Parthenon frieze in the middle, and past Apsley House, designed by the brothers Adam and once the Duke of Wellington's home (now a museum to him). Travelling up through one side of Hyde Park, there are views of the Achilles memorial to the Duke (cast from captured French cannon) and other sculptures on the lawns to one side, and of Park Lane's elegant buildings beyond trees to the right – delicate bow-fronted Georgian houses (Disraeli lived in one) dwarfed by the most expensive of towering modern hotels. Around the Roman-style Marble Arch (intended, in 1828, to be the gate of

Buckingham Palace until it was found to be too narrow for state coaches) shrubs were coming into bloom and ducks paddled among the fountains: a serene contrast with this spot's bloody past, for here was Tyburn – until 1783, site of executions and religious martyrdoms. Cromwell's body was dug up and gibbetted here on the orders of Charles II.

In Portman Square I caught a quick glimpse of the Wedgwood-blue plaques with classical figures on the corner house built by Adam in 1773 (now the Heinz Gallery of the Royal Institute of British Architects) before we made our way up Gloucester Place – as in Elizabeth Street, most of the attractive houses of 1810 (decorative fanlights above colourful doors, pretty balconies, lamp brackets, blue plaques showing where Victorian authors lived) have become small hotels. We passed the site of the original Lord's Cricket Ground of 1787, now Dorset Square, before going along Park Road, which is lined by the backs of Nash's Regents Park mansions and the mosque with golden dome and minaret recently built for London's Arab community, to the present Lord's (to which the Dorset Square turf was removed in 1814, invisible behind a high brick wall opposite the classical church of St John's Wood and its flowery park.

Finchley Road, which begins with attractive early Victorian villas in their gardens, changed character as we went north – blocks of luxury flats being succeeded by a good shopping area, and then suburban houses veiled by lilac or laburnum.

After picking up more passengers outside Golders Green tube station, we moved off at gradually increasing speed and soon shed the northern heights of London to start the steady ride up the A1. Signposts stated simply 'To the North'. This, once known as the Great North Road, was originally a main stagecoach route, and along the way there are still some old posting inns to be seen – one is now named after the road's most notorious highwayman, Dick Turpin.

Gardens and fine views back to London's rooftops (a surprise to see how many trees survive among them) were soon succeeded by fields and woodland, streams and glimpses of lanes leading to white-washed villages and to cricket greens. A traffic hold-up provided a few moments to enjoy the scene: white Queen Anne's lace in abundant flower beneath poplars lining the road.

The further we went, the more agreeable the views became:

silver birches and rowans, nursery gardens, a splash of scarlet and blue on green (golfers making good use of the early sunshine), fields of new wheat or of seedlings, languid streams or rivers with colouful small craft, and many glasshouses. This side of England is heavily cultivated, for the dark brown soil is rich. The only problem is lack of rain, hence the many and varied water towers visible along the way.

The first thatched cottage of the journey came into sight – roof-ridges neatly scalloped, tidy 'eyebrows' sheltering the windows. After crossing the boundary of Cambridgeshire, the fields became noticeably larger – almost prairie-like in scale. In some, hundreds of acres of rape were in brilliant yellow bloom.

There were fewer trees now, except where lines of them marked the route of a wandering stream. Signposts now began to refer to this fen or that. The rich black earth is part of the Great Fen, nearly 700,000 acres that was largely bog until it was gradually drained from Saxon times onwards, mostly in the 17th century. Draining meant that wildfowlers and watermen would lose their livelihood. Cromwell became their spokesman (before the Civil War) and thus acquired the nickname, Lord of the Fens.

Away to the right, dozens of tall red chimneys rose up like a petrified forest: brickworks. From the clay soil in the vicinity are made many of England's bricks; and later I was struck by the great variety of colours used in the new buildings of Peterborough that are built from bricks made here.

We approached the city via, first, a new industrial zone where every factory looks like a colourful plastic box of enormous size, featureless and neat. Then came a very interesting development, the brand-new community of Orton. A garden suburb has recently been created, using those bricks to good effect – soft browns and ochres well combined with dark weatherboarding – with brick-paved shopping precincts, wide greens, and plenty of roadside planting though the trees were only saplings. Everything was on a human scale (no tower blocks) and Orton looked as if, when mature, it would be a very happy place in which to live.

And so to Peterborough itself, approaching it past a lake of swans, a river with boats and a lock, mansions among their cedars and lawns. Then suddenly, after a brief glimpse of the cathedral's towers, we arrived: drawing up to the surprise of a coach station that is right in the middle of Peterborough's newest achievement –

a huge and spectacular shopping centre, all glass and marble, fountains and coffee-shops, gliding escalators and sparkling lights.

Peterborough

I had expected all the bustle of a thriving industrial city, but much traffic is now routed away; so, once I was clear of the Queensgate shopping centre and its vicinity, I soon found myself in peaceful streets. I headed for Priestgate and the city's museum, which I hoped would give me some idea of Peterborough's origins. The street is lined with the sort of handsome houses that soon get snapped up by solicitors and estate agents for their offices. Two are associated with Squire Cooke: he lived in one (now the museum) after leaving his estranged wife in the other, next door (its curious tower and spire were added after part of the house became a Congregational church in 1864).

Upstairs in the museum I found Victorian rooms and old shops recreated, and lingered over the tins and packets in the grocer's, bearing long-forgotten brand names and slogans: Mazzawattee tea, Wills' Woodbines, Jiffy dyes, Servants' Friend black-lead, Bile Beans for Biliousness, Luton straw-hat stains, nightlights, and packets containing crystals and 'cat's whiskers' for wireless-sets.

The mysteries of archaeological digs and identification of strata are made clear in a careful reconstruction from a local site, inhabited by successive peoples for nearly a quarter of a million years; while another room is filled with exhibits from the local prisoner-of-war camp which, in 1797, held 7,000 French prisoners, some clad in distinctive yellow garments. Their rations are on a list here (not bad: 1 lb beef a day, 4 pints of beer, Gloucestershire cheese specified, and greens 'stripped of their outer leaves'). Some of the French got out of imprisonment by enlisting in the British forces; a number married Peterborough girls and their descendants bear French names to this day. Others earned money by making and selling crafts – not only the bone models I had seen in the museums of other towns which had a POW camp nearby but straw marquetry: delicate boxes and other trifles, their intricate patterns still gleaming. Only the cheapest of materials were available to the prisoners – hence such other crafts as paper flowers or carved wood. Of the Museum's many information sheets, I found the one about these prisoners the most interesting.

In 1856, the Crimean War and Florence Nightingale's efforts had made people conscious as never before of the need for proper hospitals, particularly to cope with (in Peterborough as in other cities) cholera and typhoid spread by sewage that contaminated the water supplies. The museum building became (until 1928) the town's hospital, and the rooms I was walking around had once been wards.

At the end of Priestgate is Bridge Street (with the Tourist Information Centre housed beyond the great portico of the Town Hall). This street was the original centre of the town, laid out by its Norman abbot in 1133. Turning right, I walked past restaurants and down to the bridge over the Nene. Here stands an old Custom House – from the cupola on top, a lantern guided ships in at night to unload on the riverside where now there are pretty gardens for picnicking while watching the pleasure-boats go by. The town's modern theatre stands on the embankment here, and theatregoers can stroll by the waterside during the intervals.

I retraced my way up Bridge Street, towards the cathedral's medieval gateway, the grooves of its former portcullis still visible. Across Cathedral Square stand the colourful buttermarket and Guildhall, built during the 17th century to provide an upstairs meeting-place supported on columns, in the cool shade of which farmers' wives used to sell their butter and eggs, right up to 1926. Under the clock are the royal arms of Charles II. Among Cathedral Square's many other interesting buildings is a mock-medieval shop (Hepworths) with statues of men famous in the history of Peterborough.

Just beyond the square lies the spacious old church of St John's (built in the reign of Henry IV – his antelope emblem is over the south porch). The sound of its bells two centuries ago guided to safety a traveller called Wyldbore who was lost in a fenland fog: ever since, a special bell-ringing which he endowed peals out each March.

Turning from Cathedral Square, it is pleasant to walk through the gateway and into the quiet cathedral precincts surrounded by centuries-old buildings. For over 1,300 years, this has been a holy place – beginning with a Saxon monastery of such wealth that Vikings came upriver to pillage it. A Norman abbot took over after 1066, so repressive in his rule over the local population that the revolt led by Hereward the Wake followed – the last stand to be made against the Norman conquerors. The wooden town went up in fire, but was rebuilt to prosper once more.

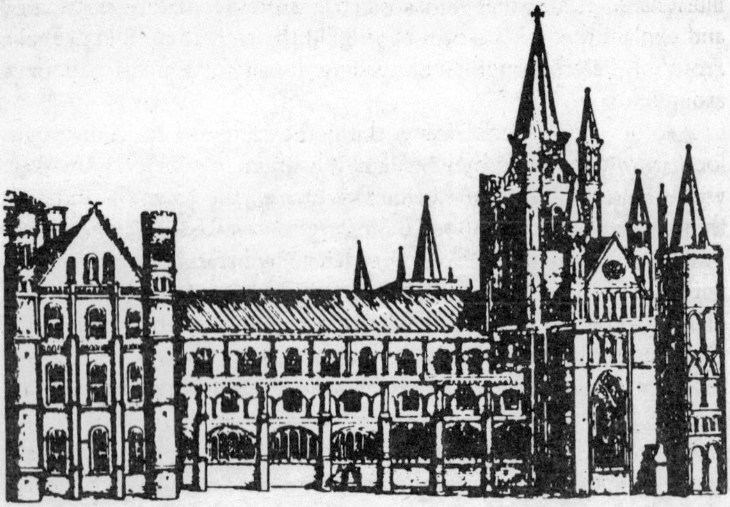

Peterborough Cathedral

The building of the cathedral started in 1118, with the Benedictine abbots' dominance over the area continuing until Henry VIII's dissolution of the monasteries in 1539. However, he let the cathedral survive, perhaps because Catherine of Aragon is buried there (though it did not remain unscathed, for Cromwell's troops desecrated and destroyed some of its finest monuments, its stained glass, and the tomb of Catherine, its position now marked by her Spanish and English banners overhead).

I stopped awhile to admire the great west front, added in 1237: each of its three immense gables houses the statue of a different saint – Peter, Paul and Andrew.

Inside all is space and clear light. One of the cathedral's great splendours is the painted wooden roof of 1220 (unique in England), immensely long and colourful. Press-button lighting and a mirror-trolley make it possible to study every detail of the saints and flowers that decorate it. Beyond lie the elaborately carved choir-stalls and a pale, luminous baldachino of Derbyshire alabaster over the altar: an illuminated focal point when darkness falls.

There are mysteries associated with both the famous features of Peterborough cathedral, the west front and the painted roof. Both depend upon certain optical illusions for their dramatic effect, illusions so subtle that it has taken a professor of optics to spot and explain them. It's worth buying, in the cathedral, 'The Leaning Front of Peterborough' and reading it carefully before looking around.

Another very special thing about the cathedral is its use of a local marble (quarried by a creek at Alwalton), distinctively marked with the fossils of oyster shells. The font is made from it, and also the sculpted tomb of Abbot Benedict.

Behind the altar, three centuries later, the building was extended with superb fan-vaulting probably created by the great craftsman of King's College chapel, Cambridge (and here concerts are held). Outside are quiet cloisters with lawn and well, in which to sit and reflect; above the porch is the treasury where historic silver is on display. And at the west end hangs this memorial above the tombstone of a gravedigger who died, aged 98, in 1594. (The two queens mentioned in it are Catherine of Aragon and Mary Queen of Scots, the latter brought here at night in a purple-and-black procession of candle-bearers, after her beheading at nearby Fotheringhay, but reinterred later in Westminster Abbey on the orders of her son James I.)

> You see old Scarlett's picture stand on hie
> But at your feet there doth his body lye.
> His gravestone doth his age and deathtime show,
> His office by these tokens may you know.
> Second to none for strength and sturdy limm
> A scarbabe mighty voice with visage grim
> Hee had interr'd two queenes within this place
> And this towne's householders in his live's space
> Twice over. But at length his own turne came.
> What hee for others did, for him the same
> Was done. No doubt his soul does live for aye
> In heaven though here his body clad in clay.

Light was fading. The sexton tolled the calling-bell for evensong, and the choirboys in scarlet-and-white filed into their places. Their young voices rose unaccompanied to fill the lofty chancel, followed by the surge of the organ which at its crescendo made the stones vibrate. Candlelight flickered on the medieval brass of the eagle lectern. At last, reluctantly, the final echo died away from those ancient pillared arches.

30

The Nelson Touch

London – Petersfield – Portsmouth

The coach swung out of Victoria Coach Station and headed towards Chelsea. Pimlico Road, lined with antique shops, leads to the Royal Hospital (not a hospital but the 17th-century home established for army veterans – the famous Chelsea Pensioners, still wearing traditional uniform), the National Army Museum and the Physic Garden, a historic botanical garden sheltering behind a high wall. Along Cheyne Walk, which faces the river, there are innumerable blue plaques to be spotted, commemorating famous past inhabitants of the pretty houses, their cottage gardens in colourful bloom – George Eliot was one. Carlyle and Thomas More are commemorated by statues along the way. The Thames bridges here are colourful fantasies of iron – Albert Bridge painted in lollipop pinks, greens and blues; Battersea Bridge in rich turquoise and red.

A cluster of houseboats, inhabited mainly by artists and actors, marks the end of this distinguished area: the next stage is along the less fashionable end of Kings Road where Chelsea turns into Fulham. More antique shops, restaurants and Wray's world-famous lighting emporium line the road. Quickly past Parsons Green (with a few pretty houses surviving the centuries), Hurlingham (polo) and the historic Fulham pottery to cross the river at Putney Bridge (an ancient church at either end), from which the Oxford and Cambridge boat race starts each year.

It's a slow crawl along Putney High Street and up the hill (Swinburne's house on the left – one of the many writers who inhabited the borough) to Putney Heath and then the unlovely Kingston Bypass. Esher Common is attractive (an expanse of gorse, birch and pine). Down a turning at Wisley is the Royal Horticultural Society's 300-acre estate, with attractive walks among the varied gardens there. Passing Guildford, I saw its great modern cathedral dominating the skyline.

From then on there was scenery to enjoy, particularly when the road climbed up into hills from which there were distant views. In a green field, a newborn calf was being nuzzled by its mother, its black coat still shining wet. Whitewashed cottages around a village green were succeeded by sandy heaths with pines and gorse. The road snaked up and up, until we were speeding along a hillside with (on one side of the road) treetops level with the coach and furry catkins brushing its sides. We wound around the Devil's Punch Bowl, looking down into its tree-filled depths patterned with sun and shade. This was one of the National Trust's earliest purchases, saving it from being bought as a building site. It owes its curious formation to a number of springs that washed away the sandy soil until the clay bottom was reached. A roadside stone commemorates the murder of a sailor returning to Portsmouth in Nelson's time.

On through Hindhead and Liphook – small towns of antique shops and restaurants, posh schools and mock-Tudor mansions, rhododendrons and holly thickets. The air of these heights is reputedly healthful, made fragrant by pines, which accounts for the number of nursing-homes along the way.

The road takes a downward turn into Hampshire and little Sheet where plump white ducks were dabbling in a sparkling stream. The coach paused awhile in Petersfield, outside Dragon House, its handsome Georgian porch and brass knocker typical of the town's architecture. Ahead lay great, sleeping humps – the South Downs. Once more we wound our way upward. The sandy heathlands of Surrey lay far behind and here all is chalk: a bright white cutting cloven from the green hillside let the road through. In the grassy fields were black-stockinged lambs, and gulls picking over ploughed soil were a sign that the sea could not be far away.

Quickly past Queen Elizabeth Country Park and a windmill glimpsed on the horizon, and soon the outskirts of Portsmouth came into view together with the shining water of a great natural harbour, small boats at their moorings and birds probing the mudflats. Ten minutes of ugly suburban sprawl followed, a whiff of hops blew in (Whitbread's brewery stands where once ale was brewed for Henry VIII's navy) and then the coach drew up right by the historic Royal Naval Dockyard, HMS *Victory* and the waterfront busy with tugs and ferries.

Portsmouth

One of the good things about visiting Portsmouth out of season is that, unlike some places, it keeps its most celebrated places of interest open all the year. Another is that many are close together, which means a lot can be seen in limited time.

HMS *Victory* is what brings most visitors to Portsmouth but she has a rival right next to her. *Mary Rose*. This amazing ship, resurrected after more than four centuries on the sea bed, was installed in 1982 with all the world's eyes on her: hundreds of television cameras and nearly a thousand journalists reporting the event.

Why the excitement? *Mary Rose* was the pride of Henry VIII's fleet, manned by a crew of hundreds. But calamity struck. While the king was watching his fleet sail out to prevent a French attack on Portsmouth, he saw the *Mary Rose* heel over, perhaps in a gust of wind, and, as her gunports were open, sink within minutes. The story of how one man's persistence led to the rediscovery, in 1967, of where she lay and how hundreds of volunteer divers worked on her excavation for twelve years is in itself dramatic; the actual raising of the ship was the grand culmination of much that had gone before. *Mary Rose* has proved to be a time-capsule, the mud having preserved every small feature of Tudor life as it was on that fatal afternoon in 1545, even down to the fingerprint of the ship's doctor in a jar of ointment and many pocket sundials – the Tudor version of wristwatches. These unique finds are now on show.

As to HMS *Victory*, she has a very different story to tell. Seeing all her gilded and immaculate splendour now, it is amazing to recall that, before the Battle of Trafalgar, she had just been an old hulk, mouldering away in the Medway estuary. Nelson spotted her, liked her lines, and got her refitted as his flagship – but even he could scarcely have guessed at the immortal reputation that was to be hers. He did not see the victory that was won at Trafalgar. The place below-decks where he died after a gunshot wound early in the battle is now preserved like a shrine. It was not, however, the story of that famous occasion which left most impression on me but the privations of the unnamed hundreds who served on board, the punishments and spartan shipboard life they endured.

Facing HMS *Victory* is the Royal Navy Museum, with more mementoes of Nelson as well as other naval exhibits.

Spit Bank Fort, Portsmouth

The Royal Naval Dockyard dates from Tudor times. But Portsmouth was the coast's greatest stronghold long before that. A short walk or a five-minute bus ride takes one much further back in time – to the tip of Portsmouth Point. I got off, however, at the start of the old High Street which leads down to the Point in order to enjoy walking along it and looking at its Georgian and earlier houses, old inns and Portsmouth Cathedral, parts of which are Norman.

The Point was where Portsmouth began. It is ringed with towers, batteries and bastions which one can walk in or on, some dating back to the time of Agincourt. There are quaint buildings along its main street and in its alleyways and courtyards; and behind it lies the Camber, the sheltered anchorage (now busy with commercial shipping) where once lay ships waiting to take Richard Coeur-de-Lion and his crusaders to the Crusades. And it was from near here that the very first settlers embarked for Australia: there is a striking modern memorial to them.

From a seat at the end of the Point I sat watching today's shipping going to and fro in the Solent on less hazardous missions, a breeze merrily flicking up small waves and setting the ships' flags dancing: ship-watching is not the least of Portsmouth's diversions.

And so to another bus (in summer, an open-topper) and another scene, for Portsmouth is a city of contrasts. East of the Point there used to be marshes but, once drained, the area became an ideal spot for a seaside resort on this most sunny of coasts where the bathing is safe, though the beach is pebbly. In the time of George IV, Thomas Owen saw the potential and began to build. It is to his acumen and good taste that Southsea owes its handsome streets of Regency and early Victorian houses, biggish hotels on the front and small ones behind. But what I most enjoyed about Southsea is its unique 'green belt' – lawns, commons and flower gardens running for miles along the shore, more than compensating for the lack of sands on which to sunbathe or picnic. Among the gardens are diversions for children – boat ponds, a model village and so forth – and there are two piers.

It was on this stretch of shore that Henry VIII built his watchdog, Southsea Castle. I made my way up to its ramparts and looked out, as he had done from this spot, to the waters where the *Mary Rose* sank and imagined the reactions of that choleric monarch: perhaps it was just as well for the commander that he went down with his ship!

The exhibitions inside the castle are excellent, making plain how Portsmouth and its fortifications developed over the centuries.

This is another good spot from which to watch all the big ships that throng the Solent on their way to Portsmouth or Southampton. Each day the nearby Tourist Information Centre puts up details of major vessels that are due to pass.

Still further east is Royal Marines' territory at Eastney (reached by buses). The public are allowed into the barracks to see their award-winning museum, overlooking lawns and seafront: another good picnicking spot. The Victorian building is palatial, its decorative ceilings and staircase brilliantly coloured and gilded: the museum would be worth a visit for this alone. As to the exhibits, I'm not sure what I found most absorbing – some ancient ships' biscuits, iron-hard and indestructible enough to have survived since 1820; or the vivid audiovisual recreation of the battle of Zeebrugge in 1918, with tiny models and realistic sound-effects.

Close by the barracks is another monument of the Victorian era, the century-old pumping station. Its purpose was utilitarian – the shifting of Portsmouth's sewage out to sea – but the Victorians were rightly proud of their achievement in bringing sanitation to teeming cities previously honeycombed with typhoid-laden cess-pits, and they built their pumping-stations with panache, like temples of engineering. When Mike Thomas was a schoolboy thirty years ago, he used to stand outside and watch through the windows the massive steel pistons gliding rhythmically up and down. But in 1954 they stopped: designed to pump 300,000 gallons an hour, the coal-fired steam engine could not cope when the expansion of modern Portsmouth resulted in millions of gallons, a task for diesel. The end of the story? Far from it, for the beam engine has recently been restored, the gleaming pistons pound away once more and in charge of one of the city's most popular exhibits when I visited was Mike Thomas.

Just beyond Eastney is a ferry to take passengers over to Hayling: it is at the terminus of the open-topped bus which runs along the Southsea shore. Waiting on the other side of the water is another open-topper to take you from there to the further side of the island, unless you prefer to walk along the beach. Unlike Southsea, the Hayling coastline is sandy: this is the place for children's bucket-and-spade activities when the tide is out.

In between amusement parks are quiet stretches of heath and sand, but the parts of Hayling I most enjoyed were to the east where byways lead to Chichester Harbour and wild spots frequented only by birds, fishermen and small sailing-boats. Buses wander up country lanes on this side of the island and it is a simple matter to hop off at one point, picnic basket and binoculars in hand, to find one's way to the waterfront and follow a footpath there, picking up another bus further along the route (a free bus map is very detailed and shows such byways and footpaths).

31
Medieval Splendours

Heathrow – Winchester – Andover – Amesbury – Salisbury

The first part of this journey, via modern Basingstoke, is soon over and the rest is much more enjoyable, particularly if one has time to stop at a fine cathedral city on the route – Winchester, for centuries the capital of Saxon and Norman England (which is why a statue of Alfred the Great dominates Broadway). The Norman cathedral is one of the longest in England (over 550 feet) and its interior far richer than Salisbury cathedral's, with elaborate carving in seven chapels, splendid royal tombs, colourful glass and murals. Its surrounding lawns are flanked by historic buildings; medieval city walls and gateways still stand; and many houses from the 14th to 18th centuries survive. Riverside paths and gardens are ideal for a picnic.

Winchester Cathedral

The next stretch of the journey took us into the attractive old town of Andover, where the coach drew up right by the clear, shallow river – every pebble and every strand of bright green waterweed reflecting the sun. The High Street was made particularly wide, to accommodate the market. An idea of its size is indicated by the fact that on 28 June 1887 Victoria's jubilee was celebrated with a dinner for 5,000 people, seated under decorations and illuminations. These details are recorded beneath dolphins on the blue-and-gold lamp-post which stands at the head of the street. Between it and the 1825 Guildhall behind is a circular concourse made of flints decoratively arranged – its date 1855, embedded in the middle. The citizens of Andover seem to have a passion for dates – they appear on many buildings, particularly the coaching inns: the Globe (its courtyard for coaches now used for antiques) dates from 1742, but the George from 1586. The doorway of the White Hart proclaims that Charles I stayed there several times during the Civil War. In a town like this it is always rewarding to look up, ignoring the 'special offer' placards and other razzmatazz of the shop-fronts, to see the fine upper stories and old roofs above.

We left Andover via a road of sedate Victorian mansions keeping a seemly distance in their grounds, to return to a landscape of fields and occasional woods. The route runs along the top of a ridge and so there were often magnificent views over the hedges at both sides, well seen through the wide windows of the high coach. We passed small wayside inns and the first thatched houses of the journey.

The coach purred steadily along (a dawdling van in front made speed impossible). The gently rolling hills, cows slowly fording a stream, the acres of tranquil green (which visiting Australians always envy so much!): all combined to make this a very relaxing stretch of the journey.

We crossed the boundary into Wiltshire and could see ahead the hills and clumps of trees which mark the beginning of Salisbury Plain. The onward road switchbacked up and down, and the views stretched even further to the distant horizons, a patchwork of fields (some brilliant with crops of yellow rape) with hills beyond.

A tinkling stream and old stone bridge marked the arrival of Amesbury (see pages 95–6): many flint walls, greens and Antrobus

House, a Georgian mansion which now houses a museum. Fields then became huge: bigger even than the airfield or the golf course that lie among them. This is the edge of Salisbury Plain.

Just after we crossed Salisbury's city boundary, we passed a sign pointing to Old Sarum on the right. Officially Salisbury is still known as New Sarum, the name given to it when Old Sarum, the original city, was abandoned and the new one begun (of which more later). The famous 500-foot spire of Salisbury Cathedral kept appearing and disappearing behind rooftops. We drove by a park, almshouses, dusty Georgian terraces and the library (housed behind the striking façade of what was once the city's market hall), and the half-timbered Chough Hotel. In the big Market Square, stall-holders were beginning to pack up their wares for the day. And then we had arrived. The coach stopped in the bus station, with a Tourist Information Centre conveniently adjoining it.

Salisbury

I sometimes have Australian visitors at my home who, accustomed to cities that are built in orderly style (space being no problem), say it's impossible to find their way around our higgledy-piggledy medieval towns, straggling down the hills on which castles were built or squeezed inside city walls, a honeycomb of courts and alleys. They should go to Salisbury where the streets are laid out as squarely as a chessboard – thanks to a 12th-century quarrel between church and king.

The original town was elsewhere, on the windy hill now known as Old Sarum (where ruins of the Norman castle and cathedral still stand, on a site occupied as far back as the Iron Age). The castle, originally built by Bishop Roger early in the 12th century, was soon afterwards annexed by King Stephen (who flung Roger into one of his dungeons to die). This led to such endless strife that eventually the clergy decided to move away from the hill and build a new cathedral elsewhere – in a fertile valley within a loop of the River Avon. Around this a new city quickly developed, an early example of town planning. The streets were laid out in a grid, and the squares thus formed were often named Chequer this and Chequer that – names still used today. So New Sarum (as the city is still officially called) is simple to explore.

Nearly a hundred medieval houses have survived, though to

identify them one may have to look above the frontage of a coffee-bar or souvenir shop to spot the telltale mullioned windows or jetted beams of the floor above. The best starting point is the great Market Square (near the bus station in Endless Street), with the architecture most conveniently seen on any day but Tuesday or Saturday when the whole area is seething with market stalls and crowds.

As I looked around the Square, a brewer's dray drawn by great shire horses was delivering kegs to one of the many old inns with latticed bay windows. The Square is surrounded by buildings of great variety, some half-timbered and some Georgian, painted or tile-hung, the skyline made pleasingly irregular by gables and dormers. Near the old Court House, with huge portico and walls of rusticated stone, are shops of quality. The most celebrated one is known as the House of John A'Port, at Three Lion Chequer. Although this is now a large (and varied) china shop, sightseers are welcome to explore its 15th-century rooms. Some of the upper ones have fine panelling or cornices added in the 17th century. Above a fireplace are carved Isaac being sacrificed and St Martha (patron saint of cooks). In a much older room, the ancient wattle-and-daub construction of the walls is exposed to view, together with the great hammerbeams of the roof and the clover-leaf outlet for smoke before chimneys were invented.

From an upper window, I could see the lanes that had gradually been built where once only market stalls lined up, in ranks of various specialities: Fish Row, Butcher Row, Oatmeal Row, Ox Row and Silver Street.

I walked via Fish Row to New Canal (the name refers to the channel which, in this as in other streets, once ran alongside the road to provide the citizens with water). Here I found the most unusual cinema in England – fake gothic outside but the real thing within. Its foyer has a sumptuous roof with angels and a stone fire-place painted in its original colours. This was once the home of a wealthy mayor, Halle, who started the china shop I had just visited and a 'dogge hall' (warehouse for pots and pans), among his other enterprises such as exporting wool and importing wine. Pugin had much to do with the restoration of his stone hall, adding a fancifully carved screen and stained-glass windows with Halle's coat-of-arms.

New Canal Street is where the horse-drawn carts from villages always parked, and still on market days the buses from outlying villages line up here – carriers of people, goods and the week's gossip.

A little further, beyond the 14th-century poultry cross and the half-timbered houses of Silver Street, I found an old watermill, flint-walled, beside its fast-flowing leat where swans and mallards dabble among the green weed. There were young on nests below walls draped in purple toadflax, unperturbed by shoppers hurrying over a small bridge where once a railway line went right into the nearby market hall (now the library). This was the market which features in Hardy's *Jude the Obscure*.

St Thomas's Church (near the mill) is in the book too. Here is another fine angel roof, part of it painted and gilded as it was when new; and a 15th-century 'doom' painting of heaven and hell, with Christ seated on two rainbows. I spotted a king and a bishop both being pushed into the jaws of hell – perhaps a comment by the populace on the unpopularity of both in a town so constantly riven by disputes between Crown and Church. There were finely carved tombstones of slate underfoot, a grand chapel with much woodcarving, stone angels playing musical instruments, a curious holder for the mayoral mace – both the lion and the unicorn being double-headed – and much more.

The 15th-century jacks beneath the clock were striking the hour as I turned away to walk towards the cathedral, wandering along the High Street – past old assembly rooms with cupola, bookshops, the National Trust's House of Steps, a pilgrims' hostel and finally the handsome gateway in the wall that firmly separated secular Salisbury from the cathedral and its precincts. The gate is still locked at night, as in the days when the bishops lived in a state of hostility with the citizenry, or in fear of catching the plagues that regularly decimated the city in the Middle Ages.

I had had only a taste of Salisbury's town life. There are many other streets to explore, with old inns and the meeting places of guilds, more churches, the modern playhouse, an arts centre (with brass-rubbing room), 14th-century almshouses, many waterside meadows or gardens, and the old town gaol underneath the Victorian clock-tower. Salisbury has, of course, its local museum (in the Close) with, among more celebrated items, a room containing the 'drains collection'. This unappealing description covers a multitude of objects retrieved when piped water was laid on and the filthy, typhoid-infested water-channels in the roads drained and filled in: unconsidered trifles from the daily life of nearly seven centuries.

Salisbury Cathedral's spire is high and its green close enormous: a picture familiar all the world over from countless chocolate-box and calendar reproductions of Constable's paintings of it. But not even this plethora of cheap reproductions can detract from the tremendous effect made by the famous scene as one walks slowly towards it.

The way to the cathedral lies past Wren's Matrons' College (almshouses) and Choristers' Green, surrounded by historic buildings where wisteria and magnolia drape themselves on mellow brick walls and the lead rainwater-heads declare their age (1701). Mompesson House belongs to the National Trust and is open to the public. The great Close, too, is surrounded by fine buildings, mostly medieval or Georgian; with, a modern touch, Elisabeth Frink's 'Walking Madonna' in bronze standing in the middle of the lawns.

After so much rambling, I was glad of a coffee in the cathedral's former 'plumbery' (workshop for the plumbers who looked after the lead roof). The café is manned by a rota of volunteers from neighbouring parishes, who bring in homemade food ('church mouse' lunches of soup and cheese were on offer) to eat at chunky tables made from the Close's fallen elms. The cathedral guides, too, are volunteers – they will take you up to the spire if you have a head for this, scrambling among the 14th-century internal scaffolding on which it is built.

Unlike many, this cathedral is all of one style inside, having been built in its entirety between 1220 and 1258. Recently its somewhat austere interior has been given a focal-point of blue (particularly vivid in early morning) by the 'Prisoners of Conscience' window over the altar – made in Chartres. You really need binoculars to identify in the complex abstract design all the familiar images of Christ's suffering, the identifiable portraits of some prisoners of conscience today, and symbols such as barbed wire and bars or the star of hope and the anchor of faith. Nearby is a 17th-century verse of George Herbert:

> A man that looks on glass
> On it may stay his eye;
> Or, if it pleaseth, through it pass
> And then the heaven espy.

As I entered, the 14th-century 'bishop's bell', the oldest working clock in the world, was striking, its visible mechanism attracting a group of spectators. I lingered at the many magnificent tombs in the cathedral (an early one of William Longespee, bastard brother of King John, is of special interest: dressed in chain mail, he lies with a long shield decorated with lions, the first known use of these as an emblem of English royalty); gazed up at the soaring Perpendicular arches that were added to strengthen the crossing when the 6,000-ton spire above was built in the 14th century; and at the marvel of the fan-vaulting in one of the chapels. Salisbury has the largest cloisters of any cathedral, with two immense cedars spreading their branches wide in the middle of them; and an octagonal chapter house with 13th-century figures from the Bible all round it. On a stone bench some medieval hand had incised the layout for a board game: a detail that William Golding (once a local teacher) noticed and used in his novel *The Spire*. He described how Jocelin, high up in the half-built tower, realized with horror that the wind was swaying it – because part of the board game scratched in a stone bench below seemed to move in and out of view as he gazed down.

The famous library, started in 1089, was closed when I was there but a few of its treasures were on display including one of the only three copies of Magna Carta to have survived for nearly eight centuries – all 3,500 words exquisitely written on a single parchment.

Despite its unique treasures, the interior of the cathedral is, to my mind, outshone by its exterior. The superb building is not hemmed in, like so many cathedrals, by houses crowding round it like chickens under a hen: the early bishops, when they designed their New Sarum, kept the plebs at a respectful distance outside the walled precincts. As a result, the great building stands in splendid isolation, a jewel lying on the green velvet of the surrounding lawns.

32

Moors and Mountains

A Tour of the North

Sheffield – Newcastle-upon-Tyne – Carlisle – Lancaster

My previous coach trips had been of only a few days each. Now I was off for much longer, to cover a 600-mile route with stops at four cities along the way. The distances of some journeys were greater than previously, yet even though I am a 6-footer with an arthriticky back, I did not find that hours in a coach were taxing.

The character of the places where I stayed was different from previous destinations: they were mainly industrial cities, some of them huge. For I had deliberately chosen, this time, to avoid such conventional magnets as York or Chester and to stay at places not ordinarily thought of as tourist centres. It seemed to me that no city which has its origins hundreds or even thousands of years ago could be lacking in character and interest, and so it proved. Further, each was totally different from the others.

Large cities can make a good change from seaside or country towns. In all weathers, they have certain things to offer which smaller places rarely provide in such abundance. For example, art galleries with exhibits of international fame. Theatres and concert halls that can afford top artistes and companies like the Royal Shakespeare or the Hallé Orchestra. Museums fit to compare with London's best (but not jammed with London's crowds), often free. Good public transport networks. Plenty of restaurants, speciality shops and entertainments. Large swimming pools, leisure centres and – a uniquely English institution – the finest of parks. They often have rivers and canals with boat trips; and a good selection of bus or coach tours. There is usually plenty to do on Sundays, and after dark, and out of season.

And another thing. Many big cities have a modern university.

And that means two things for the tourist: first, a campus likely to be open to visitors, providing a variety of amenities from parklands to avant-garde theatre, art exhibitions to sports centres; and secondly the possibility (outside term-time) of excellent, low-cost accommodation, either with meals or self-catering.

And yet, even in cities that are huge by any standard except that of London, a bus may take one out to coast or countryside within about half-an-hour at most.

There was a heatwave when I went: was my tour really a good idea, I wondered? Perhaps the millions heading for resorts were right after all. But I found that, with the help of street maps (particularly city 'trails'), it is easy to walk where no fast traffic goes, and to relax in the quiet, green oases which usually only the locals know.

The interesting parts of a city are often close together in one compact area; and, these days, the pedestrianization of many streets makes walking a pleasure. Cities that motorists regard as a nightmare (seen only from flyovers or not at all from underpasses) can look very different to a walker of byways and park footpaths. Traffic congestion and parking problems do not bother the rider on coach or bus.

As it turned out, no trip that I made in the course of writing this book proved more fascinating than this rather unusual one. It was more original, and hugely enjoyable. I returned home feeling fresh as a breeze.

Sheffield

At first, the coach followed the same interesting route (through London's Belgravia and Mayfair to Finchley Road) described on page 261; and thence past the huge shopping centre at Brent Cross and through a no-man's-land of flyovers and loop roads to join the busy M1. Youngsters lined the roadside, thumbing car lifts. Then abruptly we found ourselves among the green fields and wildflowers of Hertfordshire. The M1 itself is not an agreeable road (too many heavy lorries pounding along) until one gets further north. The first part of this trip is the route that I described on pp. 261–2. Wheatfields were the colour of cornflakes, the hedges were high and blowsy, and the verges brilliant with rose-bay willow herb, sometimes aptly called fireweed. There were sun-umbrellas outside inns, golfers trod the greens, and magpies swooped across the fields. But this cannot be called a really attractive route. The country is too flat and the road monotonously straight. Pylons stride across the landscape, and every so often factories or some distant city loom above the fields, or else a cluster of cooling towers, steaming away in unison like a coven of witches' cauldrons.

We were about half way when we entered Leicestershire, county of cheese and steeplechasing – and there, sure enough, were the herds of cows and the lush green grass needed for the former and the needle-sharp spires of the churches for the latter.

We crossed the River Trent, with pleasure-boats moored near a frothing weir (this is the boundary of Nottinghamshire) and passed a huge reservoir, its surface set ablaze by the low rays of the brassy evening sun. Derbyshire followed, with the dominating profile of Hardwick Hall (built by Bess of Hardwick, of whom more later) up on a small hill. From here on, with changing geology, farms were more often of stone than of brick. Collieries and coal-tips multiplied.

The sky was no longer all blue. Sombre clouds had gathered, but were dramatically illuminated beneath by streaks of incandescent orange, the sun's last fling before nightfall.

Ahead, the whole landscape gradually filled with the huge sprawl of Sheffield. We threaded our way in past some of the cutlery and tool factories on which the city's greatness was built, past colourful canal-boats and soot-blackened stone walls (a reminder of what the entire city looked like before the great clean-up of the 1960s), and came to a halt in the huge, untidy coach station: one of the four biggest interchange points in Britain. After a rather long and hot journey, I was glad of a shower, followed by a comfortable bed.

The next morning was a Sunday: ideal for some gentle sightseeing, as the noisy hustle of weekdays was stilled and one could walk and look about in peace. Plenty of Sheffield's 'sights' open their doors on Sundays, and my only problem was which to go and see. Like many cities, Sheffield has more of interest than some conventional tourist resorts.

Close by the central bus and coach station is a towpath from which to watch the canal-boats but, better still, I found the *May Queen* taking passengers on canal trips. She was waiting by the bank of a small garden tucked away at the end of a former wharf.

The old warehouses, with gaping panes, are slowly being restored. On the cobbles, a family of ducks waddled among families working on the maintenance of the many small craft that are based here. The *May Queen* followed the canal from Canal Basin, passing alongside steel foundries, tool manufacturers, stock yards and other industrial sites synonymous with Sheffield's industrial heritage. The journey ended, after a six-mile trip, at the impressive flight of eleven locks at Tinsley. Before long the canal may be busy again, with the help of an EEC grant – not just with the local barges (known as 'tom puddings') but with 700-tonne giants carrying coal and aggregates to the east coast, for export.

Within a few minutes by bus is Sheffield's latest pride, its Industrial Museum – formerly the generating station for electric trams. The old buildings are on a city-centre island in the middle of the dark waters of the River Don (not as polluted as it looks for there are reeds, ferns, rushes, and marsh flowers as well as ducks paddling under the sooty walls). The whole place has an impressive personality. Looming high above the granite setts, iron bollards and former gas-lamps is a colossal Dalek-like structure: one of the last Bessemer converters used for smelting steel. A kind of pressure-cooker, it stood over a furnace which was never allowed to go out for half a century. Cold and still the convertor now stands, while spiders spin their shining threads across its black angles. As to the museum itself, Sheffield would be worth a visit for this alone. Beautifully laid out, it is a temple to the great days of steel-making.

I began by studying the animated visual that explains how each different kind of steel is made. All round me were the clicks and whines of exhibits in motion – massive pieces of engineering, or tiny models. The canal's history from 1819 was graphically told, too. But Sheffield's connection with steel, coal and waterways goes back much further than this: in 1630, 28 cutlers already had their wheels grinding away, driven by the many streams that run down the valleys and into the Don: it was the availability of this waterpower that started the great cutlery industry going. By 1740, with more sophisticated techniques in use, Sheffield was making half of Europe's cutlery.

Silversmithing followed, and beautiful craft-made exhibits are on show. But – past the moving steam-hammer with simulated red-hot ingots, past the intact workshop of a penknife-maker (in use until 20 years ago), past a tiny peepshow of a hand-rolling mill in action, past such fanciful exhibits as Victorian ice-skates shaped like a heron – past all these, I found the most absorbing show of all: a 'street' of Little Mesters' workshops. The Little Mesters were the one-man businesses which used to be so typical of Sheffield, each man with his own craft specialism. And here some of them still were: one man forging, the next grinding and a third finishing. I talked with an old grinder as he worked on blades for farriery knives ordered by the Canadian Royal Mounties. One in four is left-handed, he told me – and that it was here that the original Bowie knife was made (for Colonel Bowie of Alamo fame). His next job would be chiropodists' scalpels. This is, in every sense, a 'working' museum. Its most spectacular working exhibit is a colossal engine of 12,000 h.p. which powered a rolling-mill for armourplate up to 1955 and then another for the heavy plate required in nuclear reactors and oil rigs, up to 1978.

Abbeydale, Sheffield

A short bus ride away, beyond the many acres of wooded hills near Beauchief Abbey, is Abbeydale – an industrial hamlet that, from hundreds long vanished, has been preserved for visitors to see. Here the smells of iron, wood and coal still linger, and the splashing sound of water led me to a large old workshop where great waterwheels still power huge grindstones and much else. Massive timbers groan, pistons swish gently up and down. They activate a Heath Robinson – but entirely practical – network of implements, from metal-cutters to the bellows at the forge. There is a further series of small workshops, each with its own forge and anvil. The first lead smelters settled here in Norman times. Beyond rooms used as a museum, the Dickensian clerks' office has been preserved too: high stools, guttered candles, leather ledgers with copper-plate handwriting.

Although it is this industrial history that makes Sheffield uniquely interesting it has a lively cultural side too – and superb scenery up in its enclosing hills (and beyond them, for the Peak District is only a bus-ride away). For example, within a few minutes' walk of the central bus and coach station are the Perpendicular cathedral and the Graves gallery (with a notable collection of European and oriental art). Just behind the cathedral is Paradise Square, an unspoilt Georgian square, where Wesley often preached.

Short bus-rides away, I found the particularly lovely Botanical Gardens on a hillside, with 18 acres of flowers, lawns and an elegant early Victorian conservatory; and, in the university quarter further north, another art collection, the Mappin Gallery (this one concentrates on 18th- to 20th-century British paintings: Turner, Constable, the pre-Raphaelites) and also the City Museum (which has good exhibits on local natural history, as well as a collection of Sheffield cutlery and plate).

Sheffield is a good city for bus-riding. Although some stretches of road are ugly, there is more than compensation in the spectacular views that regularly pop into sight, for high hills form a ring around the centre. Sheffield has a great many parks and woods up on those hillsides, too: they are not all exclusively covered by workers' stone cottages, chapels and breweries of Victorian vintage, nor by the high-rise blocks of our own time. (In fact, there is a circular walk of 10 miles which goes through park after park.)

I had time for only one other facet of Sheffield: the Mary Queen of Scots connection. To the south-east, on yet another of those hills, stands a lonely Tudor turret with a few ruined fortifications in the surrounding grass. Its windows are lozenge-paned, and on the roof above is a small cupola. Butterflies fluttered among the lavender bushes near the door, and all around (where once there was a deer park) stood a modern housing estate. This is Sheffield Manor where Mary was held prisoner for about a third of her life, in the charge of the Earl of Shrewsbury and his wife, the redoubtable Bess of Hardwick. Was Mary consoled by the views from here, by the fine plaster ceilings and heraldic fireplaces in this turret built specially for her? The windy site did not suit her: she suffered from rheumatism. Her story is told in a book by Keith

Cheetham on sale at the Tourist Information Centre in the Town Hall.

Newcastle-upon-Tyne

After the next coach had gone a mile or two, I glanced back for a clear view of Sheffield sheltering within its ring of hills. We wound our way at first through a largely industrial landscape; whenever a stretch of woodland survived, it soon gave way to dark satanic chimneys again, or coal-tips. But this did not last for long: one of the best stretches of the M1 followed, among rolling hills, woodlands, footpaths through bracken, and field after field of grain that was now brown as toast. We passed what must have been a deer farm, with dozens of young ones grazing in the paddock.

For once, I did not mind when occasionally cuttings through the hills cut us off from the superb views, for at this time of year the high embankments are crammed with wildflowers and as colourful as any herbaceous border: pink fireweed, in particular, and great drifts of yellow ragwort – but dozens of others too (purple thistles, huge daisies, sorrel, vetch, scabious and many more).

We turned into Leeds (see pages 16–18, 176–7), passing gasometers, featureless modern blocks and a canal with water splashing down its lock-gates. I had to change coaches here, with a half-hour wait in a small and sleazy coach station which has no attractions except for a graffiti-collector ('Humpty Dumpty was pushed' said one. Below another, too scatalogical to print here, was the comment 'Nice writing. A shame about the brain.'). But at the back of the coach station I discovered a pleasant retreat, York Place, where the sedate Georgian houses have basements now used for wine bars and bistros.

The outward route showed Leeds to better advantage, with a view along the main street (The Headrow) flanked by handsome civic buildings, followed by a green with Georgian houses, and then cricketers playing on a hilltop near the stump of an old windmill – but the inevitable high-rise blocks dominated. Soon, however, we were among a patchwork of fields, woods, hills and valleys again. The sunshine filtered through the trees as the road pursued its course, often with far views. We passed haymakers at work and neatly clipped sheep with black faces, and came to Wetherby (see page 16).

Then we joined a stream of traffic through a flat and monotonous landscape under a pallid sky. We crossed the River Tees and thus entered County Durham. Fine parks and houses of dignity stand on this side of Darlington (see pages 9–10), and we had a superb view of the church (its tall spire is exceptional) beyond the willow-fringed river which is crossed by a pretty, balustraded bridge: not the industrial aspect usually associated with this town. The next stretch of the A1 was more interesting – cows dozed among buttercups with the outline of the Pennine Hills beyond, blue and as if veiled in gauze.

The huge, resolute tower ahead of us could be only one thing: Durham's Norman cathedral (see pages 6–9). We had a good view downhill as we entered the city – of the river that curves nearly all round the rock whch cathedral and castle share, and a sharawaggi of rooftops. But in a minute the perspective was reversed, with the cathedral towering above us and the red brick houses, too, piled up on the steep slopes. From the bridge, there was a glimpse of the frothing weir.

Back, then, to the main road, passing the castellated turrets of Lumley Castle (now a hotel) before arriving at the smoking factory chimneys of Gateshead on the outskirts of Newcastle. Gateshead has the finest park in the north – with woods, rose gardens, lake and aviary – and the excellent Shipley Art Gallery. Not long ago, a vast Tintoretto was discovered mouldering in a vault of Newcastle Cathedral. Now restored, it hangs among other comparable art treasures here. The gallery houses a crafts centre too. The coach moved fast, leaving me with a medley of impressions (the several bridges over the Tyne, waterfront cranes downstream, the cathedral's exquisite 'lantern' tower, church ruins, the classical façades for which Newcastle is famous) before it came to a halt in the Gallowgate coach station.

Newcastle-upon-Tyne is a city of considerable architectural splendour; and with a history that starts when the Romans set up camp here. The city's walking-tour leaflet recommends a trail which starts near the coach station and goes downhill to the waterfront via Blackfriars. This former Dominican monastery for preaching friars now houses not only the Tourist Information Centre, craft workshops, an excellent café, a lawn with seats and an exhibition about the Dominicans but also a first-rate museum explaining Newcastle's origins, which doubled the interest of what I was about to see in the streets beyond.

After Henry VIII's dissolution of the monasteries, the buildings were used as meeting places for the city's trade guilds, and some of the rooms are still furnished accordingly. In one, I sat with other viewers around an oval table, pressed a button, and a vivid re-enactment took place of more than a million years of change on this site. The 'magic' map in front of us showed ice ages come and go, early settlements spring up, Roman roads, the building of the 'new castle' by the Normans, then the city walls, and the steady

'The Friars'

spread of industry and homes. The show over, I went to the next room which has a dozen miniature cross-sections of some notable Newcastle buildings – each from a different architectural period, and with actual samples of the materials used at that period. In a third room, an audiovisual show described the industries of Newcastle – but with no smooth-voiced commentator. Instead, the workers' own voices recalled everyday life in the shipyards, factories, breweries and railways.

In Blackfriars you could buy anything from leather clogs to a patchwork cot-quilt or a record of Geordie (that is, Newcastle) songs which are still sung in that great Northumbrian institution, the working men's clubs. I watched archaeologists excavating the monastery church. Blackfriars is half a day's entertainment in itself.

Streets wind steeply down from here, past remnants of the city walls, to Dean Street (where bistros, antique dealers and craft shops congregate) and a cobbled byway between the medieval cathedral (floodlit at night) and the Norman castle. The gatehouse of the latter houses a bagpipe museum: Northumbrian pipes differ from the Scottish variety, making a more civilized sound, Geordies claim – you can hear them played at the museum and judge for yourself.

Further still lies the historic waterfront, with Guildhall (it houses a 'flea market' on Saturdays), quays (Sunday markets), the medieval Cooperage, the Baltic Tavern for seafood meals (at a price), Trinity House (a museum of lighthouse and maritime safety history), a fine Custom House and views of Newcastle's many and varied bridges. Beyond Trinity House is a quiet corner for a pause or picnic, with grass between old walls. Footpaths and steps lead one upwards again, dodging the flyovers and fast one-ways that make Newcastle a nightmare for motorists, and with intriguing views at each turn.

Much of Newcastle's finest architecture is attributable to John Dobson who, in the 1820s, designed one noble building after another. Many still remain, giving the city its unique character: Grey Street, with monument at the top, is world-famous. The wide, formal roads are designed for vistas, and the classical late-Georgian buildings harmonize with one another. Despite some ruthless chopping up in our own time, Newcastle still has a handsome wholeness, best appreciated with feet on the ground rather than on accelerator and brake, and often unexpected views of it spring into sight when walking the alleys and passageways.

A little breathless, one arrives at the 17th-century almshouses now known as the Joicey Museum: a quiet retreat even though the traffic swirls around on flyways at roof-level. Each little bedroom is now a mini-museum with its own theme: one, for instance, houses Bewick's wood engravings and a reconstruction of his workbench; in another there is a diorama of old Newcastle and, at the press of a button, the great flood of 1771 is re-enacted (it swept away the original bridge, which had houses on it, like old London Bridge) and the catastrophic fire of 1854 – complete with the sound of crackling wood and screaming victims. Shooting game on the moors is very popular with the workers of Newcastle, so a tower room houses a celebrated collection of locally made guns (with audiovisual); and the armourer's workshop from Alnwick Castle is now here, complete down to the last rivet and even the furnace ash. In a series of furnished rooms (Stuart to the present day) children are encouraged to try on Cromwellian armour or use the 1900 telephone. Every mid-December, there is a queue to sample soup made from the recipe of a Victorian soup kitchen for the poor, while in summer there are brass-rubbing and war-gaming sessions. A small courtyard provides an opportunity to rest or picnic.

Great though Newcastle is, its green belt is quickly reached by bus (there can be few cities of this size where cows graze only ½ mile from the Civic Centre). Leazes Park is a vast area by the university (with flowers, tennis and a boating lake) but much more picturesque is Jesmond Dene in a valley with rocks and waterfall, near which many of the smaller hotels and the youth hostel are found. Artists hang out their work here on Sundays.

There was much more to see in the city, had I been able to stay longer. Right in the centre is a vast and very modern shopping centre, wrapped round Georgian Eldon Square (it even includes a Victorian market with Marks & Spencer's first 'penny bazaar'). I preferred the characterful old Handyside Arcade opposite this Centre. (Most of the city buses go out from the bus station in the Centre: the three other bus stations serve the environs to north, west and south. The Centre also incorporates a super Leisure Centre with all the usual indoor sports.) Only a matter of yards away is the Laing Art Gallery which houses British art of international importance – from the 18th century to today.

There are two more outstanding museums within a short bus-ride, or even walk: the Hancock, for natural history, and the Museum of Science and Engineering – second only to London's Science Museum. But one could go on and on – photographic museum, the *Turbinia* (the world's first turbine-driven ship), arts workshop, theatres, the gardens and statuary of the modern Civic Centre: like much else, these are all quickly accessible on foot, by bus or using the city's smart new underground railway (Metro) which even goes as far afield as the coast: a fascinating coast, incidentally, which I have described in my book *England by the Sea*.

The Metro provides one way to reach Jarrow (as an alternative to the buses) where the remains of Bede's monastery overlook the Tyne and its shipping. Like other museums in the county of Tyne & Wear, the Bede museum is exceptional. I started by learning the story of the monastery from an audiovisual with actors playing monks. Bede's monastery became a centre for producing the richest of illuminated manuscripts, now in museums worldwide, and the earliest stained glass. Excavated fragments of the monks' tools and few possessions, displayed in the museum, are more meaningful after seeing the pictures of these in use, and the tiny models of the monastery as it used to be. As I wandered round, the air filled with a recording of monks chanting (one of the exhibits is a letter from Bede recruiting a harpist). The ending of monastic life here was described in the Anglo-Saxon Chronicle, which speaks of flashes of light and fiery dragons in the sky presaging rapine, slaughter and 'the harrying of the heathen': in other words, Viking invasions.

In the café, one can eat Saxon-style bread and soups (using horn spoons); the excellent souvenir shop has Saxon replicas; and medicinal herbs of Bede's time are grown in the garden: pennyroyal, comfrey, feverfew, tansy and rue. Incidentally, this is the only museum I know which has a pretty sitting-room with sofas for weary visitors, alongside a room for modern art or crafts shows. Outside are remains of the monastery and its church into which are built chunks from a Roman temple, proving how ancient a holy site this is.

Carlisle

The elderly coach belonged to a Scottish bus company (its ultimate destination was Glasgow), and there were plenty of Scottish voices on board as we shook and rattled our way out of Newcastle by terraces of Victorian working cottages. The far Pennine hills could be glimpsed hazily between them.

For most of the route, we were running through 'the debatable lands' over which Scots and English had fought for centuries. The Roman wall, built to keep the Scots out, lay a few miles out of sight to the north of the route (except at one point, on Newcastle's outskirts, where vestiges of it can be seen in the grass verge).

The road ran straight at first, between meadows where hay was lying to dry in the scorching heat or where it still grew high, with wildflowers amongst it. Some huge fields were full of ripe barley, in others sheep or Highland cattle grazed. By the roadside, thistles and big harebells (the 'blue bells of Scotland') were another reminder that the border was not far off.

Sometimes there were deep tree-filled clefts where a stream ran down to join the River Tyne, or the underlying rock bared itself through the grass – the stone from which the local farms, the dry-stone walls and Hadrian's mighty wall itself were built.

Soon the grandeur of the scenery to come was already evident on the horizon. Some of the buildings in the pleasant old town of Corbridge are made from Roman stones: the great Roman fort nearby is well worth a visit.

We resumed the main road and, passing castellated Beaufront Castle up on its hillside, were soon at Hexham (see pages 4–5). Its largely Norman abbey is bigger than many cathedrals, dominating the attractive market square.

After that, we saw rather more of the River Tyne (with which the road runs roughly parallel), following it so closely that every shining boulder in its shallow bed could be seen. Larch and ash cast long shadows in the late sun, still strong enough to make colours blaze – the scarlet of the poppies, the pink of rose-bay willow herb.

In autumn, the hillsides are covered with purple heather; but even now they were colourful – a patchwork of greens and browns spreading down into the valleys between. There were occasional dark plantations of conifers, with birch trees providing a light touch at their edges.

The scenery became increasingly varied and beautiful as the road wound up and down. A weir, old bridge, and little houses by the waterside comprised the village of Haydon Bridge. Very typical of the area, the stone cottages (with stone or slate roofs) had white sash windows and a multitude of bright flowers outside.

As the miles passed, the geology changed: boulders in the river bed were mainly reddish now. At Bardon Mill a big circular kiln is still in use, no longer for firing chimneys but to make big strawberry-pots, sold in local shops. Occasionally, one spots a fortified farm with squat and castellated pele tower: another relic of border warfare (the cattle would be herded in below, the villagers would defend from above).

Up and down the road continued, vetch and clover by the wayside, pale-coated Charollais cattle grazing in the rich pastures between the copses, up on the hilltops bare moorland, and in the valleys trees and bracken.

Beyond Haltwhistle, where roses clambered on terraces of stone cottages, the road continued among fields that rose and fell, outstretched to the Scottish horizon. The verges were full of yarrow, lady's bedstraw and meadowsweet; green bracken grew high in the beech woods; and ferns sprouted from crevices in the dry-stone walls or the walls of great barns. It was evidently a good year for hay – barns were crammed with it, with haystacks alongside, and repeatedly we encountered tractor-drawn loads being borne along. The whole scene was one of abundance – even the cottage windowboxes could hardly be seen for the profusion of petunias and lobelia brimming over them. The barley fields were golden, the sheep (black-faced and curly-horned) looked plump. We passed a trout farm where bare-chested young men were busy with nets at the tanks.

At Brampton, the colour of the building stone began to change to a deep red. Brampton is an attractive place, with a green, cobbles in front of its moot hall and inns, and pleasantly varied houses around them – roofs varying in pitch, stucco in different colours. There was a short pause here before we continued by more sunlight-dappled streams, and verges with grasses so long that their heads bowed under the weight of ripening seeds. To the right of the road stood an old abbey by the river. But soon the road straightened out, hurled itself across the busy M6 and past a cattle market, and brought us into the suburbs of Carlisle. There were glimpses of Victorian Carlisle: terraces behind neat rows of lime trees, red sandstone churches, the classical lettering of street names carved into stonework, and – very typical of Carlisle – decorative brickwork (the arrangement of bricks known as Flemish bond creates a chequered effect). We turned right at the Citadel, rebuilt about 1810 to house law courts and council offices; had a view of Lowther Street's dignified banks and wrought iron; and came to a halt in the coach station.

The heart of old Carlisle is only a few steps from the coach station: the Market Square, which is the starting point of the walk recommended in Carisle's 'town trail' leaflet. I found it an excellent route, and a quiet one too.

In the centre of the Square is a colourful 17th-century market cross, from the steps of which Bonnie Prince Charlie – on the first stage of his abortive march south from Scotland in 1745 – proclaimed his father King. The lion on top guards the book of city bye-laws in its paws. Behind stands the elegant pink town hall, early Georgian, with a double staircase leading up to the Tourist Information Centre; and further back is the much older Guildhall with grotesque figures carved among the medieval half-timbering (there is a local history museum inside).

I turned down tiny St Cuthbert's Lane, which has small shops, to find myself in a quiet green with beech trees and a Georgian church on one side: it has a blue-and-white gallery inside, and a movable pulpit on a kind of railway. I walked past the immense tithe barn (its ancient roof timbers visible through windows that have been put in) to emerge on top of the Norman city walls. Here the walk looks down over roofs and treetops to one side (with a huge, early cotton-mill in the distance), and has good views of the cathedral above red sandstone walls on the other. The houses along here include the deanery, which incorporates a Norman pele tower – one of the fortified houses which were so necessary in the centuries when wars between Scots and English were endemic.

An alley led me to Abbey Street, largely Georgian, and 17th-century Tullie House, surrounded by a garden where ancient stones and a Roman catapult (replica) stand among the potentillas and wallflowers. Inside is a museum – very static and old-fashioned compared with those I had visited in Sheffield and Newcastle. Its Roman exhibits are the most interesting; sculpted tombstones of forgotten matrons and monuments to goddesses (a few Celtic gods too).

On the other side of Tullie House is Castle Street which leads down to the dramatically sited and very red Norman castle which

Carlisle Castle

withstood centuries of sieges and assaults – an exhibition tells its history. This was the first of many prisons for Mary Queen of Scots, though she did not have to endure gloomy dungeons where the sad graffiti of lesser prisoners can still be read. There are superb views from the ramparts and beyond lies parkland with riverside walks.

After retracing my footsteps, I turned into the cool shades of Long Lane (which has an interesting craft shop) as a short cut to Fisher Street. This is the place for browsing among antique, craft and bookshops, or others selling pikelets (scones) and pies, in Georgian or Victorian premises. The Dundas coffee bar combined snacks with a multiplicity of stalls selling anything from old postcards and books to Victorian babywear and pans; and twice a week the local Women's Institutes bring in their produce for sale nearby. There's an excellent covered market, too, with ham cured in Cumberland style, northern or Scottish specialities like black pudding and haggis, Cumberland rum butter and pats of butter impressed with cows' heads. Bargains, too, in earthenware or cheapjack fabrics – and two stalls for gourmets, one with nothing but cheeses, the other with every kind of coffee. The market is worth seeing for its architectural details as well.

Finally, Carlisle's greatest jewel – the medieval cathedral. After the heat of the day, I was glad to sit in the cool silence of the choir, the dark oak of the elaborately carved stalls contrasting with the brilliant colours elsewhere. The east window, in Decorated style, is enormous and dazzling, one of the finest in Europe; the coffered ceiling is blue with gold stars; great, coloured angels bear coats-of-arms aloft; and the cathedral was full of flowers that day. There is plenty of detail over which to linger – from the fossils in the pale stone slabs of the floor to the recently restored series of big paintings found on wood screens (15th-century picture-strips telling the stories of saints and apostles; now once more their colours are vivid). In a side chapel, the cathedral has a tremendous 16th-century Flemish altarpiece brought here, after restoration by the Victoria and Albert Museum, from a chapel near Penrith.

The cathedral needs an unhurried visit. There is the prior's room to see, too, in the pele tower (its ceiling timbers painted in the manner of some Scottish and Scandinavian mansions) and, a welcome end, a café in the undercroft of what was once the monks' refectory.

Lancaster

Carlisle is an excellent base from which to visit several of England's best touring regions – the Scottish borders, the Eden valley, the northern Pennines and, of course, the Lake District which was where I wanted to visit friends (by bus) before resuming my tour. (Because it was high summer, I found the lakeland towns and many roads seething with tourists: Carlisle's byways had been tranquil by comparison.) I returned to my coach tour at Keswick.

The coach left the town past houses built from slate blocks, overtook bronze-backed walkers, and climbed high. Dry-stone walls zigzagged up the sides of shapely hills where hay was waiting in bales or bracken spread a green cloak. People were lunching at wooden trestle tables outside low, whitewashed inns with roses round their doors, while cattle slept in the noonday sunshine. We climbed higher still, among thickets of birch or larch and rocks jutting through greensward, with views of the long rippling lake (Derwent Water). There were wayside chapels, old slate tombstones and telephone boxes painted grey because the customary red would strike a discordant note. Streams dashed down headlong through grooves which it had taken millennia to carve in the hard volcanic rock – contrasting a few minutes further with soft green sheep pastures that were as billowy as an eiderdown.

The pass descended then, to a wide green valley with farms sheltering in knots of trees. There were more slate-block houses at Grasmere (a flowery, neat place with the Wordsworth museum at Dove Cottage), a hump-backed bridge, children clambering on rocky outcrops and a pause at a slate shelter for coach or bus passengers (the starting point for guided walks up the fells). We squeezed between craft shops, Sarah Nelson's 'original gingerbread' bakery, and cottages that are now guest-houses. Beyond, the waters of the mere sparkled and shone bright blue.

The coach passed from sunshine to shade in glens where bracken and last year's rusty leaves patterned the ground beneath the trees. Another blue lake (Rydal Water) came into view, reed-fringed, with the hills on the far side descending to the edge, clad with green bracken. I saw water-lilies, a stream, cheerful red-and-white sun umbrellas outside an inn and then Rydal Hall up on the hillside. More streams – picnickers – cows – sun, shade, and sun again: the summery scenes flashed by.

Ambleside, another busy little town, has the Lake District Historical Centre, and Victorian hotels where visitors still take tea at white cast-iron tables in grounds that overlook the lake (Windermere): this one dotted with white sails, small motor-boats, a pleasure launch and bathers around its shores.

Windermere town next (see also page 172), via meadows of wildflowers: its streets flanked by grey stone houses with decorative fretwork at their gables. Beyond we followed roads with burdock and vetch by the wayside and geese in a field, up to great heights from which to look across a multitude of small fields and copses in the wide valley to the hills beyond. The coach gave me a fine view over the tops of walls, to huge barns or into gardens abundant with flowers.

The descent into Kendal was steep. Here the rough-textured building-stone changed to the palest of greys. In Kendal's shady bus station, there was a reshuffle of passengers. The coach that had started half-empty was now more than full and, a second one being on its way to relieve the pressure, people bound for London were put onto the latter for a fast journey all the way. The rest of us spread ourselves out once again.

The journey improved all the time. We went over an old stone bridge that crosses the wide and shallow river where ducklings and terns floated and children paddled, then passed a church beautifully sited among lawns and trees on the far bank, and a series of shallow waterfalls. After that the coach continued on a relatively flat course, stopping for a few minutes outside Levens Hall, its famous topiary just visible over high stone walls. The gate pillars were topped by immense stone pineapples. Pink lupins and golden rod grew outside the farmhouse opposite, its windows lattice-paned and its roof mossy.

The landscape from here onwards was gentler than among the rugged mountains of the Lake District, trees arched overhead and black-faced sheep grazed on the lush green grass.

Morecambe Bay came into sight – the tide was out, exposing the vast Sahara-like expanse of golden but treacherous sands. At Milnthorpe there were houses with little flights of steps up to their doors (the lower level having once been used to house cattle) and arches built high for wagons to pass through. Then came Beetham with a river, pretty church and the Wheatsheaf Inn. We were at the Lancashire border, close to Leighton Hall (where eagles fly free), Carnforth, and Hest Bank of the golden sands where fishermen had left nets staked out to catch plaice or fluke and children were out shrimping.

Within minutes, we had reached Morecambe's lengthy promenade strung with fairy-lights, overlooking miles of sands, bathers and small sailing-boats at anchor. Morecambe runs into Lancaster which announces its presence only when one suddenly sees the parish church, castle, monument and high steeple of the Catholic church – all towering simultaneously above the urban skyline.

As the coach crossed the bridge over the wide River Lune, there was a fleeting glimpse of the classical façades which give Lancaster its distinctive style, and then we halted in the coach station.

Lancaster's name describes its early origins – a Roman camp (*castra*) guarding the Lune. The waterway having been the lifeblood of the city until recently, it makes sense to go first to the old quay at the end of Damside Street, which is where the coaches stop.

St George's Quay, once humming with activity, is quiet now: silting prevents the big ships from coming upriver any longer as once they did to unload barrels and bales for the old warehouses that stand here, some with their wooden hoists still intact. The handsome Custom House, with sandstone portico and pillars, is now a maritime museum.

The 18th century was the heyday of the port, hence the multitude of fine Georgian houses in Lancaster, built of creamy sandstone; and this quay would often have been piled high with mahogany from the West Indies, needed to make furniture for them (of which more later). The Lancaster merchants were involved in slave trading too. Now all is quiet, but in one preserved building I found The Smokehouse where one can buy (or order by post) delicacies smoked in the traditional way, over oak chips – Lune salmon, eel or quails – and potted Morecambe shrimps, venison, wild duck and much more.

A shady footpath called Vicarage Lane leads steeply up from the quay to the hill on which priory church and castle dominate the town. St Mary's, which stands on the site of a Norman monastery, is a mainly 15th-century building. Inside I found finely carved medieval choir stalls, now backed with panels of modern tapestry; battle-torn military banners hanging in one aisle; and red-and-white posies at the ends of the pews. Slate tombstones pave the floor. As at many bigger churches now, there is an adjoining café, in which the church's silver is on display. Standing outside, I looked down over the rooftops towards Morecambe Bay in one direction; in the other, there was a panorama of assorted belfries, cupola, clock-tower and the great Ashton monument on its hilltop towering over all. Tiny alleys zigzagged downhill among the houses.

Alongside the church is the Norman castle – built on this hilltop for the same reason as Roman fortifications earlier on, to defend the crossing over the Lune. The Elizabethan turret above the ancient keep was designed to hold a beacon at the time when a Spanish invasion was feared. For centuries the castle has housed a large prison (but parts are open to view – including some rather creepy dungeons and the adjoining Regency shire hall), and also a court where celebrated trials have been held – George Fox faced prosecution here for his Quaker preaching in the churchyard, witches were condemned to death, and more recently the whole area was cordoned off while the 'Mr Asia' drugs trial took place. The great John of Gaunt gatehouse, named after the famous second Duke of Lancaster, is still equipped with a portcullis: the gate was built by Henry V; later his statue was placed on it. To this day, it is the monarch who is Duke of Lancaster. Around the gateway are grouped Georgian houses with pretty fanlights, and cobblestones in patterns. The stone bollards were hot from the blazing sunshine, and the smell of new-mown grass scented the warm air.

A partly cobbled way descends to Church Street; passing (on Castle Hill) a cottage housing a small museum of social history, and the Judges' Lodgings (on an embankment at the head of the street). This Jacobean house, the oldest in Lancaster because Royalists burnt so many others during the Civil Wars, no longer accommodates the visiting judges but contains a museum with an outstanding collection of dolls, and another of the fine furniture designed by Lancaster's celebrated cabinet-maker, Richard Gillow, in the 18th century. Church Street and surrounding roads have Georgian houses in the cellars of which Roman finds have been dug up. Several are now antique shops or restaurants; one, where Bonnie Prince Charlie stayed on his march south in 1745, is the Conservative Club – beside its fine doorway, I spotted the old iron snuffer in which were dowsed the torches used at night before street lighting came in.

I turned down little Sun Street to see the Music (or Muses) Room, a gem of a building, the original purpose of which is a mystery – it is an unusually elegant house to find in a cobbled byway. Corinthian pilasters decorate its narrow three-storied façade; and inside you can see remarkable plasterwork (the top floor can be rented as a holiday flat from the Landmark Trust which carried out the restoration of the building a few years ago).

City Museum, Lancaster

A passage leads to Market Street, now pedestrianized for shoppers and attractively laid out with paving, trees and bollards. Here is the City Museum in a Georgian building (once the town hall) that has scallop-shell decoration over its doorways and an assortment of exhibits – Cromwell's iron money-chest, a regimental museum, ship models, more Gillow furniture and clog-makers' tools (you can still buy in the city traditional Lancashire clogs – wood soles, laced leather uppers). There are quiz sheets to keep children busy; and free guided walks start from here.

Little passageways (Bashful Alley and Old Sir Simon's Arcade are two) lead off the street – some to the Market Hall where stalls sell local foods – Mr Burgess stocks the best Lancashire cheese, white and crumbly.

A little further is Lancaster's pride – Dalton Square, late Georgian – where flowerbeds and seats surround a particularly striking statue of Queen Victoria with a parade of Victorian celebrities around her feet, facing the grandiose Town Hall. (The Tourist Information Centre is in this square.)

It is not far to walk from here to Penny Street Bridge, over the Lancaster Canal, from which one can take a trip on the *Lancaster Packet*, a colourful narrowboat, with dinners served on board. There is a waterfront restaurant here, too. Or, more energetically, the canal can be walked – the towpath to the north goes through an area of old mills and other scenes of industrial archaeology, reaching Rennie Mackintosh's aqueduct (about 2 miles away) which carries the canal high over the river. The southward towpath is more rural, going past the village of Galgate (from which a bus can be taken back to Lancaster).

I had often seen from afar (it is impossible not to!) the colossal monument on a hill east of the city – a huge copper-domed memorial built by a local magnate (Lord Ashton) in memory of his wife. His wealth derived from manufacturing linoleum (the waterfront mill now produces vinyl) and in 1909 he spent what would now amount to millions of pounds on this incredible 'folly' tower, three stories of Corinthian pillars supporting a dome fit for a cathedral: the most sumptuous of useless buildings. A bus takes one to the gate of the surrounding park (previously quarries) but it is a stiff walk from there to the summit – worth it for the views, however. Shady paths twine among rocks and flowering shrubs and then one reaches the open sun-drenched summit, from which I could see the mountains of the Lake District westward across the blue sea of Morecambe Bay. Behind the monument is an orangery, and there is a little sunken garden with a pool. (What a place from which to watch the sunset!)

In 5½ hours, using the fast Rapide coach service, I was home in London. At the beginning of the year I had used buses but never a coach service before. Now I had completed some 3,000 miles of coach travel and was a convert to its pleasures.

Regional Tourist Boards

Cumbria
Ashleigh, Holly Road,
Windermere LA23 2AQ.
(09662 4444)

East Anglia
(Cambridgeshire, Essex,
Norfolk, Suffolk).
Toppesfield Hall, Hadleigh,
Suffolk, IP7 5DN
(0473 822922)

East Midlands
(Derbyshire, Leicestershire,
Lincolnshire, Northamptonshire,
Nottinghamshire).
Exchequergate, Lincoln LN2 1PZ.
(0522 31521)

Heart of England
(Gloucestershire, Hereford and
Worcester, Shropshire, Staffordshire,
Warwickshire, West Midlands).
2-4 Trinity Street,
Worcester WR1 2PW.
(0905 613132)

London
26 Grosvenor Gardens,
London SW1W 0DU.
(01–730 3450)

Northumbria
(Cleveland, Durham,
Northumberland, Tyne & Wear).
Aykley Heads, Durham, DH1 5UX
(0385 46905)

North West
(Cheshire, Greater Manchester,
Lancashire, Merseyside, High Peak
District of Derbyshire).
The Last Drop Village,
Bromley Cross, Bolton BL7 9PZ.
(0204 591511)

South East England
(East Sussex, Kent, Surrey,
West Sussex).
1 Warwick Park,
Tunbridge Wells,
Kent TN2 5TA.
(0892 40766)

Southern
(Eastern Dorset, Northern Dorset,
Hampshire and the Isle of Wight).
Town Hall Centre, Leigh Road,
Eastleigh.
Hampshire SO5 4DE.
(0703 616027)

Thames and Chilterns
(Bedfordshire, Berkshire,
Buckinghamshire, Hertfordshire,
Oxfordshire).
8 The Market Place,
Abingdon OX14 3UD.
(0235 227711)

West Country
(Avon, Cornwall, Devon, Somerset,
Western Dorset, Wiltshire and
the Isles of Scilly).
Trinity Court, Southernhay East,
Exeter EX1 1QS.
(0392 76351)

Yorkshire and Humberside
(North, South and West Yorkshire
and Humberside).
312 Tadcaster Road, York YO2 2HF.
York (0904 707961)

County Transport Co-ordinating Officers

Telephone numbers

Avon 0272 290777
Bedfordshire 0234 228638
Berkshire 0734 875444
Buckinghamshire 0296 5000
Cambridgeshire 0223 317740
Cheshire 0244 59474
Cleveland 0642 248155
Cornwall 0872 74282
Cumbria 0228 23456
Derbyshire 0629 3411
Devon 0392 273244
Dorset 0202 22151
Durham 0385 64411
East Sussex 0273 475400
Essex 0245 352232
Gloucestershire 0452 21444
Hampshire 0962 54411
Hereford & Worcester 0905 353366
Hertfordshiere 0992 555220
Humberside 0482 867131
Isle of Wight 0983 524031
Kent 0622 671411
Lancashire 0772 264607
Leicestershire 0533 871313
Lincolnshire 0522 29931
Norfolk 0603 611122
Northamptonshire 0604 256711
Northumberland 0670 514343
North Yorkshire 0609 3123
Nottinghamshire 0602 824824
Oxfordshire 0865 815600
Shropshire 0743 253031
Somerset 0823 73451
Staffordshire 0785 3121
Suffolk 0473 55801
Surrey 01–541 9365
Warwickshire 0926 493431
West Sussex 0243 777556
Wiltshire 02214 3641

Metropolitan Areas

Greater Manchester 061–273 3322
London 01–227 3703
Merseyside 051–227 5181
South Yorkshire 0742 78688
Tyne & Wear 0632 610431
West Midlands 021–622 5151
West Yorkshire 0924 378234

Youth Hostels

There are hostels at many of the places indexed overleaf. Here are their telephone numbers for bookings.

Ambleside 05394 32304
Aysgarth 09693 266
Brighton 0273 556196
Cambridge 0223 354601
Canterbury 0227 462911
Carlisle 0228 23934
Castleton 0433 20235
Cheltenham
(Cleeve Hill) 024267 2065
Colchester 0206 867982
Coniston 05394 41323
Dover 0304 201314
Ely 0353 3623
Epping 01–508 5161
Grasmere 09665 316
Hawes 09697 368
Hindhead 042873 4285
Isle of Wight
(Sandown) 0983 402651
Keld 0748 86259
Kendal 0539 24066
Keswick 07687 72484
Kettlewell 075676 232
King's Lynn 0553 772461
Land's End 0736 788437
Linton 0756 752400
Newcastle-upon-Tyne
091–281 2570
Oxford 0865 62997
Penzance 0736 62666
Plymouth 0752 562189
Portsmouth 0705 375661
St Albans 0727 51854
Salisbury 0722 27572
Shrewsbury 0743 60179
Southampton 0703 790895
Stratford-upon-Avon 0709 297093
Winchester 0962 53723
Windermere 05394 32304
Windsor 0763 861710

Index of Towns and Villages Visited

With telephone numbers of their Tourist Information Centres

VOUCHERS FOR HALF-PRICE TRAVEL

See over for INSTRUCTIONS FOR USE

CAMBRIDGE

50% off a ticket to or from Heathrow or Gatwick worth up to £4.50.

CHESHIRE

50% off a 'Lynx Day Wanderer' ticket for a day's bus travel worth about £4 (or, family ticket, £8).

ESSEX and adjacent counties

50% off an 'Explorer' ticket, worth about £3.50, for a day's bus travel.

GLOUCESTERSHIRE

50% off an 'Explorer' ticket worth about £2.50, for a day's bus travel around Cheltenham and Gloucester.

HAMPSHIRE

50% off an 'Explorer' ticket, worth £2.50, for a day's bus travel.

VALID ONLY IN 1988

Cut out and present to driver of any **Premier** coach.

Cut out and present to driver of any **Crosville** bus or **Town Lynx** coach.

Cut out and present at any office of **Eastern National** or **National Travelworld** in Essex.

Cut out and present at any office or to any bus driver of the **Cheltenham & Gloucester Omnibus Co.**

Cut out and present to driver of any **People's Provincial** bus.

VOUCHERS FOR HALF-PRICE TRAVEL

See over for INSTRUCTIONS FOR USE

HAMPSHIRE/SURREY

50% off a 'Traveller' ticket (or a 'Super Traveller', which includes trips to London) for a day's bus travel. Worth about £2.50 (or £5); or £5.50 (or £12) for family ticket. The ticket entitles you to reduced admission at a number of tourist attractions.

HANTS/SUSSEX (between Portsmouth and Eastbourne)

Reduction to £2 for 'Explorer' tickets (usable for a day's unlimited bus travel) which normally cost £3.50 (adult), £2.50 (OAP) or £2.50 (child up to 15). (Under-5's travel free).

HUMBERSIDE (north) and SCARBOROUGH area

50% off an 'Explorer' ticket for a day's bus travel worth about £3.

HUMBERSIDE (south)

50% off a 'Day-Rider' worth up to £2 for a day's travel in the area of Grimsby and Cleethorpes or off any other bus ticket.

ISLE OF WIGHT

50% off a pair of 'Day-Rover' tickets together worth about £8, for a day's bus travel.

VALID ONLY IN 1988

Cut out and present to driver of any **Alder Valley South** bus.

Cut out and post with £2 per ticket (up to a maximum of 5) to **Southdown Motor Services,** Walwers Lane, Lewes, Sussex and specify whether adult, OAP or child tickets are wanted.

Cut out and present at any office of **Scarborough & District** or **East Yorkshire Motor Services.**

Cut out and present to any bus-driver of the **Grimsby Cleethorpes Transport Co.**

Cut out and present to any office of **Southern Vectis Omnibus Co.**

VOUCHERS FOR HALF-PRICE TRAVEL

See over for INSTRUCTIONS FOR USE

KENT (north and west)

50% off an 'Explorer' ticket for a day's bus travel worth £3.60.

LANCASHIRE

50% off a 'John O'Gaunt' ticket worth about £2.25, for a day's bus travel around Morecambe, Blackpool and Lancaster.

LEICESTERSHIRE and STAFFORDSHIRE (east)

50% off a 'Gold Foxsaver' ticket for one (or two) week's unlimited travel, worth about £12 (or £23).

Counties around LONDON

50% off a 'Golden Rover' ticket for a day's bus travel worth about £4.

NORTHAMPTONSHIRE, BEDFORDSHIRE and adjacent counties

50% off an 'Explorer' ticket, worth about £3.50, for a day's bus travel.

VALID ONLY IN 1988

Cut out and present at any office of **Maidstone & District Motor Services.**

Cut out and present to any bus driver of **Lancaster City Transport.**

Cut out and present, with a passport-size photograph of yourself, at the **Midland Fox** travel centre, Gravel Street, Leicester.

Cut out and post with £2 to Commercial Manager, **London Country Bus (south west)**, Lesbourne Road, Reigate, Surrey, stating intended date of use.

Cut out and present at any travel shop of **United Counties** buses.

VOUCHERS FOR HALF-PRICE TRAVEL

See over for INSTRUCTIONS FOR USE

NORTHUMBERLAND

50% off an 'Explorer' ticket for a day's bus travel worth about £1.50.

NOTTINGHAMSHIRE

50% off a Gash bus ticket, worth up to £1.60, in the Newark/ Nottingham area.

OXFORDSHIRE and adjacent counties

50% off a 'Compass' ticket, worth about £3, for a day's bus travel

OXFORDSHIRE and adjacent counties

50% off a 'Londoner' ticket, worth £6, for a day's bus or coach travel in this area or for the Citylink coach to London.

SHROPSHIRE/WORCESTERSHIRE

50% off any ordinary **Go Whittle** bus ticket, worth up to £2.60.

VALID ONLY IN 1988

Cut out and present at any office of **Northumbria Motor Services.**

Cut out and present to driver of any **Gash** bus.

Cut out and present to driver of **Oxford Motor Services** bus. Not valid on the X70; 190/200 to London; 290/291 (except for Oxford/High Wycombe); and 390/490 (except for Oxford/Henley).

Cut out and present to driver of **Oxford Motor Services** bus or coach. Not valid on the X70.

Cut out and present at Kidderminster or Ludlow office of **Go Whittle** buses.

VOUCHERS FOR HALF-PRICE TRAVEL

See over for INSTRUCTIONS FOR USE

STAFFORDSHIRE

50% off any day or weekend coach excursion from Cheadle (destinations throughout England), worth about £2.50 to £40.

STAFFORDSHIRE

50% off any week-long coach tour in England, starting from Cheadle, provided another full-price ticket is also bought, worth about £100 to £150.

SUSSEX

50% off an adult 'Explorer' ticket, worth £2.95, for a day's bus travel around the Hastings area.

TYNE & WEAR

50% off any Armstrong Galley coach excursion from Newcastle-upon-Tyne, worth about £3.20 to £11.75.

WARWICKSHIRE

50% off an 'Explorer' ticket, worth about £2.80, for a day's bus travel in and around Warwickshire.

VALID ONLY IN 1988

Cut out and present at Cheadle office of **P. Stoddard & Sons.**

Cut out and present at Cheadle office of **P. Stoddard & Sons.**

Cut out and present at any office of **Hastings & District Transport.**

Cut out and present at Newcastle-upon-Tyne office of **Armstrong Galley.**

Cut out and present at any office of **Midland Red South.**

VOUCHERS FOR HALF-PRICE TRAVEL

See over for INSTRUCTIONS FOR USE

YORKSHIRE

50% off a pair of tickets for a guided half-day coach excursion from York to the Dales worth about £10.

YORKSHIRE (west and north)

50% off a 3-day to 13-day Key Card ticket for bus travel, worth £7.50 to £18 (with discounts on various goods and services in the area).

VALID ONLY IN 1988

Cut out and present at **Yorktour** office in York.

Cut out and present at any office of **West Yorkshire Road Cars.**